THE RESCUE SEASON

The Heroic Story of Parajumpers
on the Edge of the World

BOB DRURY

Simon & Schuster
New York London Toronto
Sydney Singapore

SIMON & SCHUSTER
Rockefeller Center
1230 Avenue of the Americas, New York, NY 10020

Designed by Amy Hill
Frontispiece photograph copyright © 2001 by Martin Kimble
Map photographs copyright © 2000 by Brian Okonek, Alaska-Denali Guiding, Inc.
Manufactured in the United States of America

10   9   8   7   6   5   4   3   2   1

Library of Congress Cataloging-in-Publication Data
Drury, Bob.
The rescue season : the heroic story of parajumpers on the edge
of the world / Bob Drury.
p.   cm.
1. Alaska. Air National Guard. Rescue Squadron, 210th—History.
2. United States. Air Force—Search and rescue operations—Alaska.
3. Special forces (Military science)—United States. 4. Unites States.
Air Force—Parachute troops. I. Title.
UG854.A4 D78 2001
363.34'81'09798—dc21   00-045006
ISBN 0-684-86479-7

The author gratefully acknowledges permission from the
following source to reprint material in its control:
From The Collected Poems of W. B. Yeats, Revised Second Edition,
edited by Richard J. Finneran (New York: Scribner, 1996).
Reprinted with permission of A. P. Watt Ltd. on behalf
of Michael B. Yeats.

For Liam-Antoine

CONTENTS

SEARCH AND RESCUE MISSIONS

ALASKA RANGE

May 1999

Site of Malcolm Daly's 200-foot fall, 2,500 feet above the glacier

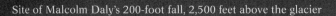

Tokositna Glacier
(7,500 ft.)

Archdeacon's Tower (19,500 ft.)

Denali Pass (18,200 ft.)

Start of Steve Ball's fall

End of his fall

Camp at 17,200 ft.

Mike Wayt's Korean rescue gully

Top of fixed line at 16,200 ft.

Camp at 14,200 ft.

Denali (20,320 ft.), seen from the Northeast Fork to the summit

Thunder Mountain (10,500 ft.)

PREFACE

I had never heard of the pararescue arm of the United States Special Operations Command until I met my first team of parajumpers in January 1995. They were posted to a top-secret Special Ops base the Pentagon maintains on the heel of Italy's boot, and I was on assignment to cover the hell that was soon to break loose in the Balkans, a biscuit's throw across the Adriatic. Frankly, I wasn't impressed. Next to the comic book–hero physical dimensions of the Navy SEALS, and the wizened, hard-eyed look of the Army's Green Berets, the Air Force's parajumpers—or PJs, as they are called—were a motley crew who looked as if they'd been rode hard and put away wet. In a subsequent magazine story about the new face of global conflict, I wrote about the testosterone of the SEALS and the battle-readiness of the Green Berets, with barely a mention of the PJs.

Upon my return from Sarajevo, however, I was braced about the Pararescue Corps by my friend Colonel David Hackworth (ret.), a veteran of three wars and a bestselling military affairs writer. Over drinks in a Seattle restaurant Hack regaled me with heroic tales of PJ search-and-rescue missions, from the swampy deltas of Vietnam to the dusty streets of Mogadishu. He described in vivid detail the perils of "The Pipeline," an eighteen-month training regimen along whose successive stops PJs are taught to climb mountains, rappel from helicopters, dive beneath oceans, survive in arid deserts, and free-fall from airplanes at recklessly high altitudes. Their mission is focused: locate wounded airmen, minister to their wounds, and bring them home. In a memorable phrase, Hack described the pararescue "career field" as the "unknown tip of the military's rescue spear." Then he suggested I see for myself just what it takes to become a parajumper, starting with the Air Force's grueling ten-week Pararescue/Combat Control Selection and Indoctrination

Course at Lackland Air Base outside of San Antonio, Texas—a course from which each PJ candidate must graduate before even entering The Pipeline.

Which is how in April 1999 I came to be standing over the former Navy SEAL Steve Wolf as he slithered on his belly through a mudhole crawling with West Texas fire ants while one Air Force drill instructor was digging the heel of his combat boot into the seam between Wolf's shoulder blades and another screamed maternal-related obscenities from a bullhorn a few inches from his ear. This particular exercise capped an eighteen-hour day that included enough physical training to drop an Olympic decathlete, and hours of "water work" that would drown a shark.

Steve Wolf had entered "Indoc" three weeks earlier with eighty-eight fellow recruits, culled from each branch of the services as well as civilian life. Wolf's classmates included a former Army Ranger, two ex-Marines, a championship kick boxer, and, paradoxically, a fresh-faced skinny Air Force Academy graduate. Twenty-six of the eighty-eight were still standing on the evening Wolf crawled through that mudhole. In seven weeks, only twelve would graduate. Wolf was their valedictorian. Indoc is a grueling gamut of physical and mental tests specifically designed to weed out about 90 percent of all candidates. "The whole idea is to teach problem solving and teamwork while they're physically exhausted," explained Senior Master Sergeant Rod Alne, the head training instructor at Lackland.

One night toward the end of the course, I managed to catch up with the twenty-six-year-old Wolf as he dragged his broken body back to his bunk at the close of another eighteen-hour day. We traded Bosnia stories—Wolf had been stationed in Sarajevo as a SEAL—and compared the PJ Indoc school with BUD/S, the Navy's six-month Basic Underwater Demolition/SEAL Indoctrination course. To him, the Air Force school was physically and mentally more rigorous. Then, making conversation, I asked him where he hoped to be posted after The Pipeline. Air Force parajumpers patrol the globe, and given both Wolf's background and zeal, I expected to hear him wish for a posting near a war zone with an opportunity for flash action. Turkey, perhaps, somewhere in the Mideast, maybe South Korea. I even mentioned something about the Iraqi no-fly perimeters being a hot "real-world" ticket.

Wolf looked at me as if I had two heads. "Are you kidding me?" he said. "I'm going to Alaska. Let me tell you something: pararescue doesn't get any more real-world than that."

I beat Steve Wolf to Alaska. And he was right.

The Rescue Season

Nor law, nor duty bade me fight,
Nor public men, nor cheering crowds,
A lonely impulse of delight
Drove to this tumult in the clouds

> —W. B. YEATS, "AN IRISH AIRMAN
> FORESEES HIS DEATH"

Denali

If you cannot understand that there is something in
a man which responds to the challenge of this
mountain and goes out to meet it, that the struggle is
the struggle of life itself upward and forever upward,
then you won't see why we go. What we get from
this adventure is just sheer joy. If you have to ask
the question, you won't understand the answer.

—GEORGE LEIGH MALLORY

Major Pete Katinszky banks his HC-130 Hercules in a swooping figure eight over the serrated peak of Mount McKinley and, eight hundred feet below, the ice-crusted pinnacle of the Denali massif surges through the vaporous cloud cover like a hulking ghost ship. Though it is nearing 11 P.M. on a frigid May evening, the summer arctic sun brazenly refuses to set and sits like an orange beach ball on the white-capped southern skyline. Katinszky squints against the reflection of the uncertain glim, throttles back, and maneuvers with a falcon's grace over McKinley's south summit just as his co-pilot, Major Terry Stiff, barks into the headset.

"Got 'em! Two o'clock. Both down."

Stiff's husky voice rises an octave. "No, just one. Jesus, other one's moving. Waving, I think. Down in the saddle. Below that rock chimney."

Katinszky shoots him the thumbs-up as Stiff crooks a finger toward the two stranded climbers huddling in the lee of the jagged granite spire at 19,500 feet.

Katinszky says, Roger that. Archdeacon's Tower.

The Herc and its crew have been circling McKinley for nearly six hours, five sets of binoculars sweeping the mountain's cloud-shrouded

tors and terraces, and Katinszky would have laid odds that the two Brits were long dead by now. But now he plots the grid coordinates that will give him an instrument-free "line of sight" elevation on the Archdeacon's Tower and levels off at 22,000 feet.

The wind-scoured obelisk is named after the Episcopal archdeacon and alpine explorer Hudson Stuck, whose 1913 expedition was the first to summit Mount McKinley, the majestic granite colossus at 20,320 feet the highest peak on the North American continent—known to Alaskans and climbers alike by its Indian name, Denali. Though Stuck's status in the pantheon of Alaskan mountaineering is legendary, he is also remembered as an itinerant preacher who punctuated his proselytizing sermons with thumping tunes from the portable organ he toted through the territory nearly a century ago. It crosses Katinszky's mind that the moaning winds high on McKinley often emit the same unresolved menace as the Archdeacon's ominous chords. He shakes the thought and marks the Englishmen's location on his console's computerized topo map. Then, over VHF frequency 122.7 he radios the mountain rangers assembling a rescue team on the ground. "Park Service, this is Rescue 2106. We have a visual on the package."

On his next pass Katinszky veers so close to the mountain he feels as if he can reach out his port window and touch the frothy lenticular cap, an ash-colored cloud—oblong-shaped, as flat as a Basque beret—suspended over the summit like a flying saucer. The cloud's streaming margins are shot through with primary colors and its forward edge, the result of a racing arctic high slamming into Denali's north face, boils over the mountain's southern flanks like steam overflowing a witch's cauldron. Driven by fifty-knot winds, the bill of the cap clings tight to the mountainside, diverted around a protruding ridge like a river divided by a huge boulder. Beneath it rages a storm of hurricane proportions.

"That's a roger 2106. Key your CB mike for us please, 2106. We cannot establish radio contact with the climbers."

Katinszky recognizes Daryl Miller's voice. Miller, the National Park Service's chief high-altitude ranger on Denali, is coordinating the rescue from base camp at 7,200 feet. For nearly a decade Daryl has worked hand in hand with Katinszky and the other flight crews and parajumpers from the Alaska Air National Guard's 210th Rescue Squadron. Fished with them. Climbed with them. Saved lives with them. Daryl is considered one of their own, an unofficial member of the corps who, through some cosmic mishap, happens to work for the Park Service. For his part the former Marine and two-tour Vietnam veteran has never seen a tighter group of men than the parajumpers of the 210th. Get in a fight with one, he's warned people, and you may as well hit them all.

Daryl tells Katinszky that he guesses the stranded English climbers' CB radio is dying. He's heard no "Mayday," but earlier in the evening the local bush pilot Jay Hudson, acting as a scout, probed for holes in the cloud cover in his turbo-charged Cessna 206 and picked up a series of rapid break squelches on one of his passes. Daryl and Katinszky both know that when the cadmium batteries in a handheld citizen's band radio run down or freeze up, they often retain just enough juice to create a break squelch when the mike is keyed. At the time, the ranger held out hope it was the Brits signaling a Mayday. It meant at least one of them was still alive.

At the first faint rumble of the aircraft Antony Hollingshead takes a deep breath and struggles just to rise to his knees. He is hypoxic, dehydrated, and with each movement, his dislocated right shoulder shoots high-voltage sparks of pain to his cerebral cortex. When he finally spots the plane, it takes him several minutes to get to his feet and give a short, uncoordinated wave with a "good" hand so swollen it feels as cumbrous as a canned ham. Then the wind blows him flat on his face. The thirty-four-year-old Hollingshead wonders what his co-workers back in the executive offices of the British Rail Corporation would think if they could see him now. Helpless. Chilled to the bone. In more agony than he ever thought possible. He lifts his head and layers of black, dead tissue slough off his frostbitten nose.

At least somebody knows we're up here, he says to his mate, Nigel Vardy. At least they know we need help.

Vardy is lying on his back in the hard snow and ice. He does not respond to his partner's encouragement. He is fairly certain he is going to die, and that the last thing he will see on this earth is the storm-battered pinnacle of the great American mountain whose summit he could not attain. Vardy's hands and feet are frozen solid, and each of his short, choppy breaths produces a gurgling sound deep in his chest, like water in a teapot beginning to agitate and flow before breaking into a boil.

Nigel suspects he is suffering from severe acute mountain sickness, a combination of high-altitude pulmonary edema and high-altitude cerebral edema. His lungs are gradually filling with fluid, and the pressure inside his skull is literally compressing his brain down into his spinal column. He knows that once contracted, death from AMS is but hours away. The only cure is a rapid descent to lower altitude. Nigel groans and wonders how it will feel to drown on dry land.

Hollingshead stares at his friend splayed across the névé and winces. Nigel has lost his woolen Tajik mountain hat, and his face looks like a hard winter breaking up. His left eye is frozen shut, and the eyelid has swelled to the size of a tangerine. Two Band-Aid–sized strips of decaying black flesh, like a football player's lampblack, run across the crest of his cheekbones. A thin stream of bloody spittle leaks from the corner of his mouth. Hollingshead is fairly certain the thirty-year-old Vardy also is snow-blind in his one good eye.

You've got to hang on, Nigel, he says, his voice as hoarse as a raven's. They're coming soon. They know we're up here now.

Nigel Vardy groans, but says nothing.

Up in the Herc, Pete Katinszky's communications officer pounds the key on CB channel 19 on the com deck for the next twenty minutes. There is no reply.

Negative audio, Katinszky radios the rescue party. We'll keep vectoring up here. Tell us what you need.

As Katinszky signs off, co-pilot Terry Stiff warily eyes the lowering lenticular cap. No way they can get a ground party up there with this cloud cover. And no way the Park Service's Lama flies through that weather, either. He turns to Katinszky with a hard look.

If they're coming down tonight, he says, they're walking.

The National Park Service's SA-315B Lama rescue helicopter was designed and built by the French company Aérospatiale Industries specifically to perform high-alpine rescues. Most rotor-driven aircraft, including those commissioned by the United States Armed Forces (with the notable exception of the Army's powerful CH-47 Chinook), are limited to a

15,000-foot flight ceiling and proscribed from landing, much less hovering, in the thin air above 10,000 feet. But the Lama's architects proudly advertise that their aircraft—essentially a giant turbine engine with a tiny Plexiglas bubble constructed around it—holds the world's helicopter elevation record of 40,820 feet. They do not broadcast the footnote that the French test pilot who took his Lama to that elevation flamed out the engine and was lucky to auto-rotate the dead machine back down to the ground.

The Lama, renamed the Cheetah by the Indian Air Force, has been landed at 23,000 feet in the Himalayas (where the latitude's thicker atmosphere kept its rotors buoyed), and once, in good weather, the National Park Service's contract pilot, Jim Hood, touched his skids down for a few brief seconds on the south summit of Denali. The Lama is a fine, squatty machine, credited with saving sixty-three lives since the Park Service began contracting it out for the climbing season in 1991.

One year ago, in May 1998, Hood successfully plucked two British climbers from close to 19,000 feet on Denali's West Rib. He took them together in a tandem shorthaul and deposited them safely outside the Park Service medical tent at 14,200 feet. That record still stands as the highest helicopter rescue in the world. But the extraction took place in perfect conditions, with no wind or weather to speak of.

Now, just after 11 P.M., Hood lands in base camp and calls Daryl aside. He's surveyed the route, he says, and there is no way he can put his helicopter down in the wind and thin air. "I'll never have enough power to get off the ground again." He thinks he can hold a hover at nineteen-five for twenty, perhaps thirty seconds, but that's the best he can do. Nearing midnight, Pete Katinszky keys the Herc's intercom and informs his flight crew that Daryl's checked in, and the Lama is going for it. "They're fueling up at seventy-two hundred right now. They'd like us to help find some holes in the clouds." Katinszky's four crewmates glance at one another in bewildered disbelief. Neither Jim Hood nor any other pilot has ever attempted a rescue that crazy. In the arctic latitudes of the Alaska Range, an extraction from 19,500 feet is verging on suicide.

With his wild black hair and Pancho Villa mustache, Jim Hood might be mistaken for a Grateful Dead roadie, but the pilot is one of the top sticks in the high-mountain rescue business. He figures on three solo runs up the mountain, each hover lasting no more than an instant. On the first he will drop to the British climbers a survival backpack containing radios, a thermal sleeping bag, a WhisperLite stove, a thermos of hot chocolate, and two screamer suits. Then back down to base camp to refuel while (hopefully) one of the climbers fits himself into the suit—in essence a zippered, nylon body bag with a harness sewn into it. The harness is attached by two carabiners to a wide, metal God ring at the end of a 100-foot double-looped rope that is, in turn, secured to the chassis of the Lama. Once hooked in, an evacuee takes a literal walk in space for the wild ride known as a shorthaul. The contraption is called the screamer suit because of the shrieks made by whoever is dangling at the end of the line.

The strategy is to shorthaul the first Brit down to base camp fifteen circuitous miles to the south, top off the Lama's 50-gallon tank with jet fuel, and repeat the process for the second climber. Hood feels less than comfortable attaching both men to his single line; relay camp is snowed in, and he will have to haul them over 12,000 feet, a twenty-minute journey, down to base camp.

To make matters dicier, up on Denali Pass, above 18,000 feet, the winds are gusting to 65 knots. "Picking a path through those clouds will be a fuckin' bear," Hood tells Daryl. In these storm conditions, he says, there is no way his 2,600-pound machine can chance the weight of both men.

There it is." There is the remnant of a Kentucky twang buried deep in the voice of Pete Katinszky's flight engineer. The F.E. has spotted the powerful little Lama from his position at the C-130's aft porthole. The angled sunlight throws the saw-toothed battlements of the Alaska Range into a stark chiaroscuro of snowy white cornices and shadowed ravines. The Lama, its yellow tail-boom light flashing against the chalky flanks of the awesome mountain, looks like a firefly buzzing a giant polar bear.

The Herc's flight crew watch wordlessly as Hood picks a zigzag flight line through the layers of clouds that are now dumping snow all over the mountain. The Lama clears the candy-colored tents of 14,200-foot relay camp, huddled in the lee of a sheer ice cliff known as The Headwall. It leaves a wispy, gray contrail over the ice caves of 17,200-high camp, buried beneath two feet of snow. The wind buffets the tiny machine, but finally Hood holds his hover over the stranded climbers at nineteen-five. He remains just long enough to drop the backpack containing the emergency gear, radios, and screamer suits.

Katinszky's crew cheer as Hood nails the drop, depositing the pack not ten yards from the disabled Brits. An insta⸱ ⸱t later he scoots back down the mountain as if running for his life.

While Hood refuels, Katinszky and his Herc crew squint through the scudding clouds, watching one of the stranded climbers crab-walk toward the pack. He has difficulty opening it. "Fingers most likely frozen," Terry Stiff figures, but the Brit finally has the thermos cupped in his hands and begins to force-feed his fallen partner sips of hot chocolate. Then the Englishman unpacks the radio and the Herc crew eavesdrop through their headsets as Daryl walks him through the checklist—the only one that really matters is making damn sure to secure the carabiners to the God ring at the end of the Lama's shorthaul line. Confidently, almost haughtily, as if ordering a Pyms in a Kensington club, the Brit says his name is Antony, and adds that it is imperative that he send his injured friend Nigel down first.

Now the Herc's flight crew watch as the one named Antony splays the black nylon screamer suit across the snow and begins cramming his partner's limp figure into it as if stuffing a sausage. It takes Antony several minutes to pull the zipper closed with his frostbitten hands. By the time he has completed the task, the Lama is back over him. Despite the howling gale, Hood manages to maneuver the shorthaul line directly over Nigel's prone body. Wobbling like a drunk, Antony lunges for the wavering God ring, and as if in slow motion, he clasps it and clips Nigel in. Then the Lama vanishes into the Rembrandt gloom, trailing a vacuum-packed body the size of a flyspeck.

One down, one to go. Twenty minutes pass, enough time for Antony to sheathe himself into the second screamer suit and for the Lama to refuel. No one on the orbiting Herc utters a word. The silence over the aircraft's intercom, usually as chaotic as drive-time A.M. radio, is disconcerting. Now the Lama is back—bucking, shuddering, fighting the wind, but it isn't moving off. The Brit has the rope in his hands, but something is wrong. The hookup is taking too long.

"He can't hold that hover up there." Daryl over the radio. Prodding Antony. Trying, without success, to mask the tension in his voice.

"Sorry, mate. Having a spot of trouble attaching your carabiners." Over the CB the Herc crew listen to the sound of metal scraping against metal. "I think they're frozen. I'll have to hook in with mine."

"No! No!" is Daryl's reply. The Brit is addled by hypoxia, what climbers call mountain madness. At this altitude a hypoxic patient can barely perform the simple tasks of lacing a boot or lighting a stove match, much less clamp a freezing metal carabiner onto a rope flailing like an unmanned fire hose one hundred feet below the belly of a windswept helicopter.

"No, Antony," Daryl says again. "Use ours. Your mind is playing tricks on you. Ours are fine. It's probably yours that are frozen."

Now Jim Hood from the Lama. "Hook in somebody's, please. I can't hold this aircraft much longer."

From the Herc's cockpit the helicopter appears to be losing altitude. This may be an optical illusion. So close to the peak, Katinszky is flying under Federal Aviation Administration–mandated VFR (visual flight rules), and the human brain, confounded by the huge dimensions of the mountain, prompts the eye to make it appear smaller and closer than it actually is. Katinszky is aware of this, but rechecks his instruments to be sure. The Lama has been in its hover for over a minute, twice as long as anyone expected it to maintain at that altitude.

"Gotta go now!" Hood's voice is incongruously calm. "Right now!"

"Take off." The English accent. "I'm in."

The Lama banks as if tumbling off the edge of the world. Then it straightens and disappears. Two hundred feet beneath the helicopter, dissolving into the gathering scud, Antony Hollingshead spins in the wind like an Olympic figure skater. The intercom remains silent as Pete Katinszky banks his plane for one final pass. Finally the pilot speaks.

"Man, it's gotta be hard for that helo pilot to walk with balls that big."

As volunteers carry Antony Hollingshead into a medevac aircraft in the rutted landing strip at 7,200 feet he strains for Daryl Miller's attention. "Thank you for all your help," the Brit says. His voice is a metallic rasp. "Thank everyone involved." The mountain ranger tells him he'll be fine, and begins to walk away. But Hollingshead's blistered, black fingers scrape at Daryl's jacket, and the ranger turns back.

The rescued climber's face contorts into an eerie grimace. "You do know that there's one more of us up there."

Daryl nods. Yes, he says, he knows.

ONE

Alaska Envy

It is my duty to save lives and to aid the
injured. I will be prepared at all times to
perform this duty quickly and efficiently,
placing it before personal desires and comforts.
These things I do, that others may live.

—THE PARARESCUEMAN'S CODE

The origins of Alaskan rescue contain the simplicity and obscurity of the frontier itself. The high north's harsh winters are more than metaphor, and each community's values are forged by their dark, brutal nature. This insidious essence seeps into the soul, and from downtown Anchorage to the smallest Inupiaq village the dual perils of isolation and loneliness are acknowledged realities. A professional rescuer in Alaska faces a complex web of small judgments and compromises that, like a spider's threads, are woven in unexpected combinations. A flat summer sea can turn into a cauldron within minutes. An alpine storm will strand a climber mere yards from his tent.

Or, as U.S. Air Force Master Sergeant Mike Wayt now considers on this Friday morning, May 21, some British idiot traversing one of Denali's fickle flanks will wander away from his climbing partners and never be heard from again.

As a member of the Alaska Air Guard's 210th Pararescue Team, Mike Wayt does not have to be involved in a rescue to feel his stomach churn each time one of his crewmates heads out from headquarters, especially when the rescue involves battling Denali. In reflective moments, the men of the 210th often think of themselves as a sort of modern-day equivalent of Mallory's Arthurian knights, a collective embodiment of the warrior spirit at its best and brightest, contributing to the quality of their fellow human beings in time of peace. These knights consider Denali their fiercest dragon—unique, immense, deceiving, and never less than potentially fatal even to those who know it best. Last night, for instance, the thirty-odd members of Wayt's pararescue team each felt as if he was a member of Pete Katinszky's crew as the pilot vectored the mountain searching for Antony Hollingshead and Nigel Vardy. They monitored the military rescue frequencies or called into headquarters for hourly updates. And when they heard the news that the mountain ranger Daryl Miller and the Lama pilot Jim Hood had finally recovered the Brits, a silent cheer rose from every member of the squadron no matter where he was.

Now, this morning, the sky above Mike Wayt is feathered with high-filling cirrus as he follows the contrail of another C-130 heading back into the Alaska Range in search of the third British climber, an auto mechanic from Staffordshire named Steve Ball. Mike has been on the horn to The Section, as the parajumpers refer to their Anchorage headquarters, and knows his teammate and friend Technical Sergeant Mark Glatt is a member of the Herc's crew. He hopes Glatt will be the first to spot the Brit.

Mike looks across his backyard to the north, across the coastal flats, where pearl gray clouds, billowing and ominous, are frosting the ripsaw crests of the Chugach Range. Although it is nearly June, a season of twenty-hour days and bruised-colored nights, spring snow in the Chugach is far from unusual. Mike turns to his thirteen-year-old daughter and smiles. Stephanie Wayt stands indolently, hands on hips, pondering the storm battering the lofty minarets five miles away. A limp volleyball net lies in the wet grass at her feet.

No worries, Steph, Mike says in what he hopes is his most reassuring tone. The mountains will trap those clouds.

Like most children of the arctic, Stephanie is something of an expert at tracking the path of a squall from its birth far out over the Aleutian Islands to the moment it begins tacking up the Gulf of Alaska like a dark, menacing pirate fleet. She can usually guess from the height of the vaulting cumulonimbi—the towering Qs—which storms will ricochet off the mountain chain and bounce back into the spruce-covered foothills that sheathe the Wayt's neighborhood, and which ones will wring themselves out on the corrugated peaks. As she and her dad gaze solemnly across the watershed that holds the city of Anchorage, a crenellated sugar bowl carved by the confluence of the Knik and Matanuska Glaciers some 10,000 years ago, Stephanie knows intuitively that this storm will play itself out in the Chugach. Still, she loves her father, so she smiles brightly and mimes an exaggerated gesture of relief before turning to plant the poles for the volleyball net.

Mike holds a steady gaze on his daughter. No longer his gangly colt, all arms and legs and clomping feet, she is already nearly as tall as her mother, and shafts of sunlight reflect off her long buttermilk hair. In this trick of light and shadows Mike sees instead of a little girl a young woman with the bearing of an arctic wolf. In contrast to her father, with his lank black hair and arched Asian cheekbones, Stephanie is graced with her mother's pert nose, and the merest trace of her Japanese grandmother's delicate, almond-shaped eyes. She carries herself in a manner Mike, the only Japanese-American parajumper in the U.S. Air Force, would deem regal

Mike keeps his eyes upon her as he sidles toward his backyard barbecue grill, unable to shake the feeling that his pararescue team is in for a long couple of days.

Mike Wayt likes to joke that he was born with a silver rip cord in his mouth. His father, Chief Master Sergeant Ron Wayt, led a nomadic existence as an Air Force aerial photographer who flew spy missions over Russia, snapping pictures of Soviet nuclear silos from the backseat of an F-104, and his three sons were reared on air bases up and down the Pacific Coast. As perennial outsiders, the Wayt brothers were acutely aware of the arcane, often baffling prejudices toward Japanese in the wake of World War II, as well as the unforeseen manner in which these prejudices can complicate life. All three learned to fistfight at an early age.

Mike was the youngest, and something of a jock. He was also smart enough to anticipate the limited career opportunities for a 140-pound Japanese-American tailback. Surprising no one who knew him, he enlisted in the Air Force immediately after graduating from high school. Mike's character, after all, had been hammered on the anvil of military tradition, and as early as basic training his drill instructors had pegged him as a lifer. He adapted smoothly to the daily grind and rigors of ser-vice life. What he loved best about it was being outside. For as long as Mike could remember, he was enthralled by the outdoors.

When Mike wasn't playing sports, he'd spent much of his youth tra-versing the woods. Depending on where his father was stationed, there'd be boar hunts in northern California, or salmon fishing down on Alaska's Kenai Peninsula. If nothing else, there was always a mountain that needed climbing. As a student his favorite courses had been the field trips he took with the Young Adult Conservation Corps, and after basic training he applied for a position as a field instructor at the Air Force's survival school at Fairchild Air Base in Washington State.

He augmented his survival training by passing the three-week para-chute course at Army jump school at North Carolina's Fort Bragg, and within two years he'd qualified as both a survival instructor and para-chute instructor at Fairchild. Then, after four years of "walking with my dick in the dirt" through the high passes of the Cascades, he'd accepted an invitation from a superior officer to switch "career fields" and enroll in the pararescueman's indoctrination course down in San Antonio, Texas.

Mike knew a little about the PJs. A few had passed through survival school up at Fairchild, and he'd eyeballed them good. Hell, he figured, whatever it is they do, if they can do it, so can I. He wasn't too solid on the specifics. But once he set his mind to it, Mike Wayt thought he could do anything. After The Pipeline, though, Mike gained more respect for those PJs he'd seen pass through Fairchild.

Most Air Force pararescuemen, like Navy SEALs and the Army's Green Berets, are a branch of the U.S. Special Operations Command. They are not unaccustomed to risking their lives for complete strangers, and are distinguished in the Special Ops community as the tip of the mil-itary's rescue spear. Because of their low public profile, they are fre-quently referred to in the corridors of the Pentagon as "the Special Forces you've never heard of."

In contrast to the SEALs and Green Berets, who number in the thou-sands, there are no more than four hundred PJs scattered around the world. A volunteer force of both active-duty airmen and the Air Force's reserve component, the Air National Guard, the parajumping career field culls members from civilian life as well as every branch of the U.S. Armed Services. Mike Wayt's thirty-odd teammates in the 210th's

Pararescue Squadron include an erstwhile gold miner and a forest fire-fighter, a former Army Ranger, and two veteran Marines (including one with two hitches in Force Recon, the Marines' Special Forces unit). The most recent arrival is Staff Sergeant Steve Wolf, newly separated from eight years in the SEALs, who can now trade fish stories with the one-time Navy long-distance rescue swimmer, the former commercial fisher-man, and the unit's team leader, Garth Lenz, who ran surf boats and cutters for eight years in the Coast Guard.

Following enlistment, pararescue candidates undergo the Air Force's standard six-week boot camp at Lackland Air Base. This, to the Air Force's supreme annoyance, is considered by fighting men to be the least strenuous of the four armed service's boot camps. But upon graduation, potential PJ recruits are put through ten weeks of a torturous Selection Course, or Indoc. No Army grunt, Navy sailor, or Marine degrades Indoc. So demanding are the physical and mental rigors of the Selection Course that it is not uncommon for a class of ninety-odd candidates to graduate fewer than a dozen. These few survivors then enter The Pipeline, eighteen months of even more grueling physical and medical training designed to push them beyond normal human limits.

Civilian rescues notwithstanding, a PJ's raison d'être is the recovery of downed American military aircrews. Since there is no telling when or where a U.S. military airplane or helicopter will crash or be shot down, parajumpers are a standard military "operational contingency" wherever the U.S. Air Force flies. Their training consists of courses at Army Com-bat Divers School in Key West, Florida; Army Airborne School at Fort Benning, Georgia; Navy Underwater Egress Training in Pensacola, Florida; Air Force Basic Survival School in Washington State; Army Freefall Parachutist School on the Yuma, Arizona, proving grounds; the Special Operations Combat Medic Course at North Carolina's Fort Bragg; and, finally, twenty weeks of fine-tuning at pararescue Specialist Recovery Course on New Mexico's Kirtland Air Base, known to PJs as The Schoolhouse. Successive stops along this Pipeline train and equip them to run on search-and-rescue missions in every environment. There are no officers in the parajumping career field, as pararescuemen are technically slotted as flight crew members under the command of their assigned aircraft's pilot. When grounded, a PJ team leader reports directly to a squadron commander, usually a colonel. Often, the PJ team leader is older and has more experience than his commanding officer, and senior officers move around him with a wary respect. Since the Pentagon counts them as front-line units, there are no pararescuewomen.

In the past ten years PJs have run combat rescues into Panama, Kuwait, Kurdistan, and, most recently, they recovered U.S. pilots shot down during the wars in Bosnia and Kosovo. They stand on global alert each time a NASA space mission is launched, poised to retrieve any astronaut—or "Spam in a can"—who has the misfortune to ditch or crash. This tradition dates from 1966, when three Okinawa-based PJs parachuted into the South Pacific in scuba gear in order to keep Neil Armstrong and David Scott afloat after their *Gemini 8* space capsule aborted in midflight and splashed down hours before Navy recovery ships could reach it. In 1989 a squad of PJs from the California Air Guard volunteered to crawl into the mangled ruins of a collapsed freeway overpass to rescue forty-two civilians buried by the San Francisco earthquake. And when *Air Force One* is flying, parajumpers pull continuous alert, prompting the axiom that when the White House dials 911, a PJ answers the phone.

Unlike the weekend warrior label sometimes pinned on America's traditional National Guard units—fat guys with bad wigs playing at war once a month—the Air Force classifies virtually all of the Alaska Air Guard's parajumpers as "full-time reservists." This seeming oxymoron means that rescue is their only occupation, and they chance their lives for a government salary of about $35,000 a year. What distinguishes the parajumpers of the Alaska Air Guard from their global brethren, however, is their arctic alpine experience and their almost daily involvement in civilian rescues.

Though the Anchorage-based PJs are one of three Air Guard pararescue squadrons stationed permanently on U.S. soil, vast, chaotic Alaska, at nearly one-fifth the size of the Lower 48, offers the ideal training ground for a unit of daredevil paramedics. Alaska sprawls across 21 degrees of latitude and 43 degrees of longitude, and superimposed on the contiguous United States, its southeast tip would reach the coast of Georgia and the Aleutian chain would extend past Los Angeles into the Pacific. Its bulging Bering seacoast actually extends into the Eastern Hemisphere, giving the state the northern-, western-, and easternmost points in the United States.

Captain-Commander Vitus Bering, the ambitious Dane who sailed under the flag of Russia's Peter the Great, was so overwhelmed by Alaska's immensity that he christened the boundless sheet of space *Bol'shaya Zemlya* (The Great Land). The diverse terrain, climate, and ecosystems of this virtual subcontinent are so extreme that when Secretary of State William Seward arranged its purchase from the Russians in 1867 for $7.2 million, or roughly two cents an acre, he predicted the territory would eventually be admitted to the union as several states. (That notion hasn't changed much in a century and a half; the joke on the North Slope is that Alaska should be cut in half just to piss off the Texans, who would then be living in the third-largest state.)

In addition to its thirty parajumpers, the 210th Rescue Squadron is a 105-man outfit that consists of four Hercs and their flight crews and six MH-60G Pavehawk helicopters and their flight crews. Their sophisticated backup staff includes a life-support section—a kind of high-tech maintenance crew that oversee everything from helicopter engines to radio upkeep—a weather shop, and a small intel unit. Although the squadron's PJs are predominantly full-time reservists, the remainder of the 210th is a fifty-fifty mix of full-timers and traditional part-timers.

The Alaskan PJs are part of a tight-knit, global pararescue community where courage is demonstrated, not displayed. There are five U.S.-based active-duty pararescue teams stationed on air bases in Florida, Georgia, North Carolina, Nevada, and Washington State. Overseas, the Air Force maintains a PJ presence in England, Italy, Turkey, Japan, Korea, Iceland, and Morocco. The career field is so small that most PJs, no matter their home port, have at one time or another served with their colleagues from the mainland and abroad—training together, jumping together, climbing together, and occasionally posting bond together. Moreover, every year a procession of pararescuemen from "outside" pull temporary duty, or TDY, with the Anchorage team in order to hone their mountain-climbing skills.

Unlike the 210th, however, the two other Air Guard teams in the Lower 48—Westhampton, New York's 102nd Rescue Squadron and the 129th Rescue Squadron attached to California's Moffott Naval Air Base—rarely receive the kind of emergency calls that lead the local newscasts or produce seventy-two-point Railroad Gothic newspaper headlines. (The disappearance of John F. Kennedy Jr.'s Piper Saratoga off the waters of Martha's Vineyard in July 1999, and the 102nd's subsequent HC-130 grid-search flights constitute the rare exception.) For this reason, the 210th's "action quotient" evokes friendly jealousy among most stateside parajumpers. Only this morning, as Mike Wayt's teammate Mark Glatt geared up in preparation for the search for the lost British climber, he'd been intercepted by an active-duty Okinawa-based parajumper posted to Alaska on TDY. Technical Sergeant Mike McBee, training with the 210th to hone his glacier skills, had been "in-country" only a couple of days before he began begging Glatt to secure him a slot on a Denali rescue mission.

Like all parajumpers, McBee is eager to shed his training exercises and go "real world." Since his arrival in Anchorage he has succumbed to what "outside" PJs refer to as Alaska envy, a condition similar to what the French call the Stendhal syndrome, the state of being struck dizzy by a beautiful work of art. Recovery operations in the high north do, in fact, present a sort of whimsical reverie of rescue: lost hunters wandering an endless tundra beneath the ghostly green northern lights; hikers stranded in flash arctic snow squalls on glaciers the size of Rhode Island; sailors, fishermen, and kayakers adrift in leaky or disabled craft along 33,904 miles of shoreline, twice the length of the lower 48.

And stranded climbers reeling in the thin air of the state's thirty-nine mountain ranges.

Mark Glatt peers through the starboard porthole of a C-130 Hercules "flying doughnuts" over the Denali massif. It is the height of the climbing season, and through his binoculars Glatt can vaguely make out an indented track, tamped in the snow like a toboggan run, curling out of the clouds and across the mountain's West Buttress.

Yesterday, beneath crystalline skies, the sloping trail up the long, rocky shoulder to Denali's summit was aswarm with hopefuls staggering single file across the knife-edge ridge—they'd reminded Glatt of the sepia-toned photographs of the gold-fevered sourdoughs of a century before, who formed conga lines into the interior. But the country's earliest indigenous peoples had presciently named their sacred mountain "The Weathermaker." Overnight, Denali has been socked in by storms.

Glatt sees no movement. He turns toward the port window and

resumes scanning the rocky tors for the missing British climber lost somewhere down in that soup.

The stout, pop-eyed Mark Glatt is one of those perplexing human question marks often found on the fringes of civilization. He has a brow as broad as a dolphin's, heavy eyelids, and a touch of figginess to his jowls. His manner is gentle and engaging, almost academic, though his studied, professorial mien is offset by a pair of piercing eyes the color of turquoise. The guys on the team ride Mark about being the squad's Poindexter, the know-it-all who can't stub his toe without expounding on conditions in the footwear industry. But this thirst for knowledge, both fundamental and esoteric, is what his teammates first noticed about Mark Glatt.

If such a thing exists, Glatt is the typical PJ. He grew up in a small town in the Appalachian foothills where his father was a general con-tractor who taught him the basics of welding, carpentry, plumbing, and electrical wiring, with a little explosive demolition work thrown in. His paternal grandfather, one of the inventors of the carbon resistors devel-oped for military radios during World War II, also influenced an inquisi-tive young Mark. And he refers to his mother as "the most curious person I've ever met," and credits her with his love of science. It was she who taught Mark that wonder was the heaviest element on the periodic table, for even a tiny fleck of it stops time.

Glatt enlisted in the Air Force after high school—"I was too wild for college; no sense wasting my parents' money"—and spent nearly five years as a munitions systems specialist, or "ammo troop," bouncing between Alaska and the Netherlands. In 1985 he separated from Anchorage's Elmendorf Air Base and decided to remain in the north. He tried on several lives, working his longest stretch as a newspaper printing press operator in Anchorage. Then his curiosity led him to a job as a gold miner along the Brooks Range. It sounded glamorous, but he discovered soon enough that it is hard, dirty work. Still, it was while gold mining that Glatt met his future wife, Melanie, a forest firefighter studying to become a geologist. In 1989, Mark read a small item in the local paper about the pararescue unit being formed by the Alaska Air Guard, and he reenlisted on the day the Berlin wall fell. "Working as a PJ just happens to be a collection of everything I enjoy," he's marveled to Melanie more than once. "I get to do a job that isn't, you know, really like a job at all."

Glatt can wax eloquently on subjects as diffuse as the annual productivity of placer gold miners to the disagreements over the tectonic formation of southern Alaska among geologists to the nature-versus-nurture theories of rearing newborn infants (he just had his first). When a flummoxed teammate needs to know the precise location of a patient's ruptured spleen, or the odds of a volcano erupting at any particular moment down in the state's southern ring of fire, or how to tell fool's gold from the real deal, the question is invariably directed to Mark Glatt.

Oddly enough, given the physical requirements of his profession, Glatt's appearance would attract no undo attention, say, standing in line to buy groceries at the local Quickie Mart. He is, in fact, in danger of being mustered out of the squadron because of his inability to make weight. No one on the team speaks of it much, but every PJ knows too well that because of the battering the job inflicts, a parajumper's career is short-lived. At thirty-eight years old Mark Glatt is fast approaching his sell date—that crossroads where even the most willing spirit cannot compensate for deteriorating joints and reflexes, not to mention a spare tire around the middle. "Mark might have a little bit of a problem keeping the weight off," one sympathetic teammate says. "But nobody on the team works harder at it in the gym than he does. He climbs a mountain like a billy goat, and let me tell you, there's no one you'd rather team up with to prosecute a mission."

After eight years with the 210th, there isn't a parajumper who wouldn't entrust his life to Mark. Of course, they'd never say that to his face. Instead, they insult him and anyone he's ever been related to, call him every name they can think of, tell him the only reason he even made it on the squad in the first place was because he was some lucky sumbitch. That way, Mark knows that his partners truly trust and respect him. This is the way it always plays out on the front lines of any war— even a war against nature and terrain—for a parajumper realizes that during every minute of a mission, his partner's life is in his hands. If you don't cuss his mother, he's going to think you don't like him. And as Mike Wayt explained, "You don't want your partner not liking you— especially when you're fuckin' around in Alaska."

After forty minutes Glatt lowers his scopes. There is no sign of life on Denali, and he turns and strolls through the fuselage of the C-130. Nearly 98 feet long, with a wingspan of 132 feet and standing 38 feet off the ground, the Herc is not a cargo jet so much as a flying club car. Its primary military tasks are to ferry and air-drop personnel and equipment, render long-range helicopter escort and midflight refueling, and, like today, provide an airborne communications, or com, platform during search-and-rescue missions. The C-130, or King Bird, is the Pentagon's all-purpose plow horse, a nearly indestructible combination of freighter, assault transport, and ambulance. It can remain aloft for eighteen hours, fly 2,300 miles without refueling, land on a rough dirt airstrip to evacuate wounded soldiers, and fly unscathed through a hurricane on the way home. The four boxy Hercs of the Alaska Air Guard's 210th Rescue Squadron have been shorn of all extraneous appendages such as gunlocks and antennas.

Now Glatt squeezes past the reserve 1,800-gallon fuel tank, as big as a water truck, and approaches the crew's loadmaster. He jerks his chin toward the mountain. "Anybody caught down in that is in for a world of suck."

Despite years of alpine experience and a fair knowledge of weather science, like many who come late in life to the high north, Mark Glatt has never quite grown used to the meteorological anomaly that allows Denali to be swathed in storm clouds while, just a few miles away, the faces of Mounts Foraker and Hunter—the second- and third-highest peaks in the Alaska Range—are bathed in soft, slanted orange sunlight, as if lit from within.

Rising 110 miles northwest of Anchorage, the 14,573-foot Mount Hunter sits nine miles due south of Denali and nine miles northeast of 17,400-foot Mount Foraker. Viewed from the rolling Matanuska flatlands, the three form a spiky barrier, like the spine of a stegosaur, rending the south central Alaskan skyline. The Koyukon people, a subset of the Athabascans who followed the ice-free corridors of the Yukon River valley southeast after crossing the Bering Land Bridge 12,000 years ago, named the mountains Deenaalee, Sultana, and Begguya—"The Great One," "The Great One's Wife," and "The Great One's Child." Believing the peaks to be the home of irritable gods, the Indians conferred mystical powers on all three, and gave each a wide berth.

In 1896 the Princeton graduate and gold prospector William Dickey, using a telescope-mounted theodolite, measured and renamed the tallest mountain in honor of the Republican presidential candidate, William

McKinley, a champion of the gold standard. The name never sat well with Alaskans, as evidenced by Archdeacon Hudson Stuck's appeal in his 1914 memoir, *The Ascent of Denali:* "Forefront in this book, because forefront in the author's heart and desire, must stand a plea for the restoration to the greatest mountain in North America of its immemorial native name."

It took nearly fourscore years, but in 1975 the state of Alaska's Geographic Names Board officially changed the peak's name back to Denali. The Federal Board of Geographic Names, however—lobbied vigorously by politicians from McKinley's home state of Ohio—refused to comply. It does not matter. Everyone in Alaska refers to the monolith as Denali.

Glatt turns back to the starboard porthole and absentmindedly raises his binoculars again. He spots a thunderhead building over Hunter's gnarled peak, like the blue fug of a good panatella hitting a wall and piling up on itself. His eyes pass quickly over the sheer west face of the Hunter massif, a cantilevered shoulder known locally as Thunder Mountain.

Glatt knows firsthand the havoc a storm in these mountains can wreak. Tornado-force winds. Temperatures—not wind chill, temperatures—diving to triple digits below zero. Blinding, days-long whiteouts. A mountain strips man of his basic human needs: food, water, shelter, and warmth. From mid-April through early July—the climbing season—the 210th's thirty-man PJ team runs continual search-and-rescue patrols on Denali in support of the Park Service's high-altitude rangers. Glatt has recovered his share of sick and stranded alpinists, and was once caught at 17,200 feet in a week-long blizzard that sloughed the earlobes off a tentmate. He begins to recount the story, but the loadmaster sticks a chaw of Redman tobacco under his lower lip, shrugs, and bounds the four steps up into the Rescue Bird's cockpit.

To all but the deluded or psychotic, the climbing season in the Alaska Range is roughly restricted to the last week or so of April, all of May and June, and—if it has been an inordinately cold spring—the first few days of July. On average, 1,200 men and women will attempt to summit Denali during that period. As a rule, half will succeed, 100 will need medical attention, and 12 will require major rescues.

After Independence Day, south-central Alaska's twenty hours of sunlight have pocked the mountain glaciers with mini-thermokarst lakes of standing water, sodden snowbridges collapse at the first footfall, and crevasses yawn wide enough to swallow a mule train. Conversely, prior to mid-April, temperatures and storm conditions are too prohibitive to all but the most experienced mountaineers, although there are invariably individuals driven to try. Most meet the same fate as Naomi Uemura.

Uemura, virtually unknown outside his native Japan, was a throwback to the era of Sir Francis Drake and Ferdinand Magellan—a man of physically small stature with an outsized thirst for adventure. Standing only five feet four, Uemura was a giant in climbing lore, as well as a prosperous writer of children's adventure books. He had walked the 1,700-mile length of Japan; sailed the 3,782-mile Amazon River in a one-man raft; mushed a dogsled alone nearly 8,000 miles on a year-long trek from Greenland to Alaska, and became the first person to reach the highest point on five continents, four of them solo ascents. He bowed only to convention on Mount Everest, where he was a member of a Sherpa-guided climbing party that attained the summit in 1971. (Though even on Everest, Uemura enhanced his samurai lore when, mere steps from the pinnacle, he wearily motioned to a countryman to pass ahead, thus granting Teruo Matsuura the honor of becoming the first Japanese to stand atop the highest point on earth.)

In January 1984, Uemura attempted to become only the fourth climber, and the first soloist, to summit Denali in winter. Lashing two 17-foot bamboo poles to his waist to prevent him from disappearing into crevasses, laden with foodstores consisting only of raw caribou meat, seal oil, and whale blubber, he clawed through strafing winds and darkening snowblast and in the process became a true Eskimo, an Athabascan Indian term meaning "raw meat eater."

On February 12, Uemura's forty-third birthday, he radioed two countrymen overflying Denali with the bush pilot Lowell Thomas Jr. that he had reached the summit and would descend through the storm to a snow cave at 18,000 feet. He made plans to rendezvous with his supply plane in two days. Uemura never made it.

Gale-force winds raked the peak throughout the next week, driving the temperatures down to ninety below. When Thomas and a small squadron of bush pilots finally took off on February 16, one spotted a moving speck he believed to be Uemura waving from a snow cave near an ice-crusted terrace at 16,400 feet. The Japanese was pinned down by the storm, and the pilot didn't dare chance a glacier landing. On February 20 the snarly weather broke, and by daybreak two more bush pilots were circling the massif. They overflew Uemura's likely descent route, but found no tracks in the fresh snow. On a windswept ridge at 13,000 feet they spotted his snowshoes where he had stowed them during his ascent. Over the next three weeks, rescue parties, including a hastily assembled Japanese climbing team from Uemura's Meiji University Alpine Club, scoured the mountain for clues. They uncovered several freshly dug snow caves containing Uemura's gear and provisions, but his body was never discovered. In his official report, National Park Service ranger Bob Gerhard concluded, "I suspect he just ran out of steam and got covered over."

Now, as Technical Sergeant Mark Glatt circles the mountain in the back of the Herc, he holds out about the same hope for Steve Ball.

TWO
Mayday

Because I could not stop for Death,
He kindly stopped for me.

                —EMILY DICKINSON

The forty-three-year-old Steve Ball was last seen twelve hours earlier by his climbing partners near the Archdeacon's Tower at 19,500 feet. Antony Hollingshead and Nigel Vardy had been too sick and battered to descend, and Ball made the gallant, if ill-conceived, decision to go alone for help. Now the search for Ball is concentrated between the tower and Denali Pass, an hourglass-shaped depression at 18,600 feet between the mountain's north and south summits. Denali Pass channels the gales that scream out of the Siberian arctic and hammer the massif, drawing freezing air through the defile as a venturi sucks fuel through the flow stream of a carburetor. There is no place to hide on Denali Pass, it is total exposure, and Ball, from all reports, is without food, water, or shelter.

The airmen seeking any trace of Ball have picked up the basics of the Englishman's plight at the 210th Squadron's morning briefing. Twice daily, at 8 A.M. and 4:30 P.M., the PJs and the Herc and helo flight crews pulling alert convene in a small conference room at Kulis Air Base, the 210th's home port in Anchorage, to receive the day's FCIF, or flight crew information file. This is a detailed rundown on everything from weather forecasts to the location of training exercises. The 210th has been operating on a "short alert status"—that is, flight crews and PJs up and running within forty-five minutes—since two Spanish climbers were airlifted to the city's Providence Hospital several nights earlier.

The Spaniards were part of a three-man team turned back 200 feet from Denali's summit by howling gales. On the downclimb their sweeper, the last man on the line, had lost his footing and dragged his partners 500 feet down a steep ice gully at 18,350 feet known as The Autobahn, a 45-degree slope with a long history as a man-killer. Most climbers, like the Spanish, encounter it exhausted on their way down the mountain. But the Spaniards were lucky. One was merely shaken up, and the others escaped with only broken ankles, cracked ribs, and snapped wrists as emblems of their efforts.

Then, two nights ago, on May 19, an Italian photographer named Franco Toso had peeled off a cliff when he paused in a serac field at 15,000 feet on the West Rib route to take a photograph of his partner, the high-mountain skier Mauro Rumez. In yet another example of incredible good fortune, Toso's 100-foot tumble carried him into the center of a small field of soft snow, where he was able to dig in his ice axe and self-arrest. An American climbing team witnessed the accident and, along with Rumez, clambered to Toso's aid. They fitted him into a screamer suit that was dropped by the Lama, and he, too, was airlifted to Providence Hospital, where he was treated for contusions to his chest wall, a broken leg, and acute mountain sickness.

Finally, last night, the Lama pilot Jim Hood shorthauled Vardy and Hollingshead. Mark Glatt learned at the briefing that the three British climbers had spent seventeen days breaking trail up Denali's rugged West Rib route. The West Rib is a difficult, grade four climb (out of a possible six) and a rather more technical ascent than the heavily trafficked West Butt, which accounts for about 80 percent of summit attempts and is, for the most part, rated a grade two. It was the first trip to Denali for all three Englishmen, and they had prepared for it over the previous nine months by scaling the Matterhorn and Africa's Mount Kilimanjaro, traversing a string of vaulting mountains in southern Tajikistan, and practicing on the slag rock spires of western Wales.

They knew enough to climb the West Rib expedition style—that is, carrying gear high, caching it, and descending a thousand feet or so each night to sleep low. Expedition climbers employ this kind of leapfrog ascent in order to acclimate gradually to elevation. The Brits were well aware of the Denali nostrum to climb twice and summit once. At about the time the Italian photographer Toso was plummeting through the serac field, Ball, Hollingshead, and Vardy broke camp at 15,900 feet. They'd decided to take advantage of the good weather and make a mad dash for the summit 4,400 feet above them. Carrying little water and overconfident about their acclimatization—thereby breaking perhaps the two most fundamental rules of self-preservation at high altitude—at 8 A.M. the three started up through the wind-scoured rocks and two prominent couloirs that distinguish the West Rib ascent.

Denali's high-altitude rangers admit that one of the things they fear most on their mountain is, incongruously, good weather. As Daryl Miller often preaches, "Good weather accelerates the problems on the mountains when it goes bad—and it always goes bad." What he means is that climbers are lulled into a false sense of security, and reaching the summit becomes more important than their judgment to stay alive. Denali is a gauntlet, Daryl advises all climbers—the most humbling mountain in the world.

Nearly twelve hours after breaking camp the Englishmen had advanced no higher than 18,800 feet. Around 7:30 P.M. they ran into Alaskan mountaineer Jack Tackle on his way down to 14,200-foot relay camp after an acclimatization dash up the west face. The veteran American climber was immediately concerned and stopped to tell the Brits that they were too far right in the couloir, thereby making a steeper ascent than necessary. He also noted with alarm that none of them carried overnight gear or a stove, and that Steve Ball had lost a glove. The British party brushed aside Tackle's subtle admonitions about traveling so light and ignored his warning that though the weather seemed tranquil, a major storm had just drawn a deep breath on the north face and was about to strafe their side of the mountain. Tackle tarried a half hour with the climbers, pointing out the West Rib's easiest ascent line, before bidding them good luck and resuming his descent.

Two hours later, back in relay camp, Tackle trained his binoculars on the cloud-obscured West Rib and tried to pick up the three climbers. His stomach sank when he saw that the Englishmen had barely progressed more than a few rope lengths in the time it took him to downclimb over 5,000 feet. Looking beyond the Brits, Tackle also spotted the lenticular cap foaming over the mountain. He headed straight for the camp's medical tent and warned Park Service ranger Kevin Moore that the three men would soon be in serious trouble.

By around midnight Wednesday the Englishmen had fought through the storm to within a hundred yards of the south summit before being blown back by a furious windstorm. By then they were all exhausted, dehydrated, and suffering from severe hypothermia and frostbite on their hands, feet, and faces. Vardy was already showing clear signs of acute mountain sickness.

"We'd done the hard bit, the plod, and we were sure we were in good enough physical shape to make it to the summit in one long push," was how Hollingshead recalled it to the flight engineer from the 210th who debriefed him at Providence Hospital's emergency room. Nearby, several doctors debated how many fingers and toes the British Rail executive was likely to lose. "We miscalculated," he added feebly.

To say the least, thought the F.E.

Hollingshead continued. As their expedition struggled back down following the aborted summit attempt, Nigel strayed from the trail and fell several times. The wind was so strong it didn't blow the snow so much as fling it like grapeshot. A walking zombie, Vardy would just disappear into the whiteout until one of his partners felt a tug on the rope line and realized he was gone. Finally, during one foray to steer him back on track, Hollingshead stumbled and dislocated his shoulder. Ball, in the best shape of the three, didn't feel he and Hollingshead had the strength to continue shepherding Vardy, so they clawed out an ice cave in the corner of a small crevasse and passed several hours praying for a break in the weather.

Throughout the ordeal they rationed the few glucose tablets and candy bar–sized protein packs they'd carried and cursed themselves for not bringing a stove to melt snow. The little water they'd brought was now useless, frozen in its plastic bottles, and a climber suffering from dehydration who tries to hydrate by eating frozen snow only worsens his condition. The energy lost melting snow in your mouth outstrips the benefits of the water. Eating snow also lowers the body's core temperature.

As if conditions weren't severe enough, their radio was dying. When Ball tried to contact park rangers at various mountain camps, all he received were garbled messages. They couldn't tell if anyone had heard their Maydays. (The word is an Anglicization of the French *venez m'aider*, "come and help me," and gets directly to the point.) "We didn't know if anyone even knew what kind of trouble we were in," Hollingshead told the flight engineer.

Trapped in their cave, Ball fell into a shivering fit. His body convulsed, and his teeth chattered so much his friends thought they would break and fall out of his mouth. Despite his throbbing shoulder, Hollingshead spent hours cuddling Ball in his arms. By 4:30 A.M. Ball felt some of his strength and willpower return. The climbers dug out of the ice and debated rappelling back down the West Rib. Given Vardy's deteriorating condition, however, Ball and Hollingshead decided their only hope of survival was a descent down the less technical, if more time-consuming, West Buttress. It was a Hobson's choice at any rate, for they'd hiked only a few hundred feet before Nigel fell again. That's when Steve Ball determined neither Antony nor Nigel had the strength to go on.

"So Steve said he'd go for help," Hollingshead said from his hospital bed. "He said good-bye . . ." and here Hollingshead held up a frozen, black hand, anticipating the F. E.'s next thought. "And, no, none of us thought it was for the last time."

In an adjoining gurney the withered Nigel Vardy looked as if he'd been rode hard and put away wet. Clusters of purple blisters, the size of small plums, encrusted his feet from shin to toe, and more frostbite had completely blackened his fingertips, nose, and cheeks. Barely coherent, he repeatedly pleaded with several doctors, "for just a peek at me feet to see what I'm going to lose."

Between ramblings, Vardy, at one point, did appear cognizant of the situation. He turned to his mate and whispered a question with a dry, hacking voice.

"Steve still out there?"

Antony Hollingshead nodded yes.

Hollingshead's narration runs through Mark Glatt's mind as he scans the frozen wasteland below. The Herc is in constant radio contact with two other Park Service rescue parties also traversing Denali in search of Steve Ball. The first, which includes two PJs, Technical Sergeant Marty Kimble and Senior Master Sergeant Carl Brooks, set out from relay camp at 14,200 feet, where Kimble reports temperatures of 38 degrees below with ten-foot visibility. He says just hitting the piss-hole across camp is like trying to cross whitewater in winter.

Kimble and Brooks have been stationed at relay camp since the climbing season officially commenced nearly a month ago. Every April a patrol of PJs and Park Service high-altitude rangers "open" camp at fourteen-two. Two Army Chinooks sling-load three months' worth of supplies up the hill—ropes, oxygen, litters, dried food, white gas, cooking stoves—including a portable, plastic honeycomb medical tent and a steel-frame, half-dome weather port with a wooden floor. In early July, at the end of the season, all gear and garbage are packed up and sling-loaded back down. The only structures that remain year-round are a radio antenna mast and the two outdoor, plywood shitters set over twenty-foot-deep holes. Inevitably these have to be redug the following season.

Below Kimble and Brooks in relay camp, a second ground party is grinding its way up from base camp at 7,200 feet, on the southeast fork of the mighty Kahiltna Glacier. This team includes two more PJs, Technical Sergeants John Loomis and Lynn Grabill, who are scheduled to begin their rotation on the mountain in relief of Kimble and Brooks.

The climb from base camp to relay camp is usually a three-day hike, and Glatt guesses Loomis and Grabill are probably rounding Windy Corner at 13,200 feet about now, perhaps iglooing up as they run head-on into the same mountain storm. He also wonders, somewhat guiltily, if his two teammates have discovered the ten-pound scuba weights he and another PJ, Technical Sergeant Greg Hopkins, hid in the bottom of their rucks. Ten pounds at 10,000 feet can feel more like fifty, and Glatt is feeling more than a little remorse over the prank. But Loomis, for one, can handle the stunt. One of the more battle-tested members of the team, he has summited Denali twice, fighting through hellacious storms on each occasion. His motto, he's told Mark, is "Unless you're sane there's nothing to it."

Two years earlier, following the midnight crash of a twin-engined Air deHavilland Caribou, Loomis was part of a three-man PJ team that performed a harrowing night drop through a "honking" winter storm onto Sparrevohn Mountain at the southern tip of the Alaska Range. The Caribou's pilot and co-pilot had been deadheading from Aniak on Alaska's west coast to the Kenai Peninsula when both its engines flamed out. The pilot sent a frenzied Mayday as he tried to shoot an approach into a nearby abandoned airstrip. Attempting a controlled crash, the throttle just above stall, he came up a mile short, smashing into the side of Sparrevohn instead.

By the time the Herc carrying Loomis, Technical Sergeant John Paff, and Senior Master Sergeant Mike Drummond overflew the wreckage, the Caribou's co-pilot was dead and the injured pilot was trapped inside the twisted fuselage, frantically signaling an S-O-S with a small flashlight. The three PJs parachuted into forty-knot winds onto an alpine pass, traversed to the crash site, cut the pilot out of the plane, and pulled him to safety up a 1,000-foot slope.

Glatt believes that the sinewy, irreverent John Loomis is the kind of soldier who might have served as a tunnel rat in Vietnam had he been born thirty years earlier. Loomis is notorious for sashaying around The Section in sweatpants so tight it is easy to discern what religion he isn't, and with his ubiquitous chaw and walrus mustache he looks like a throwback to the Rough Riders. Right now, though, Glatt is somehow comforted by the fact that he is somewhere on Denali, not charging up San Juan Hill. Finally, on the off chance that one of the patrols finds Steve Ball alive, a Pavehawk is en route from Kulis to Denali base camp. Its five-man flight crew includes two more PJs, Master Sergeant Steve Daigle and Staff Sergeant Karl Grugel, both licensed paramedics. Given conditions below, Glatt figures a coroner would be more appropriate.

After nine years on the job, Mark Glatt has stopped wondering when foreign climbers will come to grips with the perils of Denali. It isn't the fact that they have to be rescued that bothers him. He is, after all, in the business, and every business needs customers. What galls him is the hubris with which they confront the mountain. Most foreigners who challenge the Alaska Range are veterans of expeditions to the higher elevations of the Himalayas, or, like the three Brits, at least the more technical routes up the European Alps. As such, they approach the nontechnical course up the West Buttress with the dreadnought pretensions reserved for a stroll up a chilly sand dune. Glatt guesses that if it weren't for the recent explosion in mountaineering, notably the myriad expeditions to summit the highest peak on each continent—the fabled "Seven Sisters"—most foreigners would not even deign to run the West Butt. Yet give him a dollar for every Korean or German who sneered at the route only to end up limbless, or noseless, or, indeed, lifeless, and he'll foot the bill for the damndest party The Section has ever seen.

To be fair, Glatt knows, the Europeans and Asians don't have a monopoly on idiocy. Alaskans have a native word for outsiders: cheechako. It means "tenderfoot," or "greenhorn," and Americans from the Lower 48 have proven that they can arrive just as naive and unprepared for Denali's black moods as anyone else. Still, though foreigners represent only 35 percent of all climbers who have attempted to summit the peak since the Park Service began keeping statistics in 1932, they account for 59 percent of the 91 climbers killed. Since Glatt joined the 210th in 1992—the year avalanches and falls wiped out a four-man team of Canadians on the Messner Col, three Koreans on The Orient Express, and two Italians on the Cassin Ridge—the percentage of foreign fatalities has spiked precipitously.

At least the Asians, Glatt figures, have an excuse. The majority of their expeditions are government-sponsored, and deciding who will partake in them for the glory of the homeland is a highly charged political process. Thus these climbers carry a special national responsibility to summit: success is mandatory, failure leads to loss of face. But this mindset inspires foolhardy decisions. One Alaskan rescue axiom, proved more times than the Pythagorean theorem, has it that if a foreigner can get into trouble on Denali, he will. Subsequently, anyone who works around the mountain understands too well the macabre origin of nicknames for couloirs and ravines like The Autobahn and The Orient Express. Of late, there has even been a sub-rosa movement to rechristen The Autobahn Fleet Street, in homage to the number of Englishmen who have sailed off its trackless cliffs. One British climbing party actually showed up earlier in the season vowing to climb Hunter, Foraker, and Denali in the span of three weeks. As the average Denali summit expedition takes twenty-one days, someone remarked that this plan was similar to trying to fuck every hooker in Manhattan over the course of a weekend. The climbers never even made it past Denali's high camp before being smacked hard by the weather, packing up, and going home.

"If this guy Ball's trapped up near Denali Pass, he's hosed," Glatt again tells the loadmaster as he climbs down from the Herc's cockpit. "There's no place to hide. He's gotta somehow get down to high camp at seventeen-two."

Glatt's crewmate spits a stream of tobacco juice into an empty Coke can and nods. It is one thing to be a member of the 210th's flight crew out searching for these knuckleheads, he thinks. At least we don't have to leave the plane. It is quite another actually to volunteer, like Glatt, to venture out in such weather.

It has been three years since Mark Glatt plunged willingly from a Pave-hawk into what some marine scientists consider the most treacherous waters in the world. It was a cold night in early June, and Glatt was pulling alert with Master Sergeant Brent Widenhouse when the call from Alaska's Rescue Coordination Center lit up PJ headquarters. The RCC—a partnership between the state's Air Force and Army National Guards, Coast Guard, Civil Air Patrol, state troopers, and local community emergency service agencies—is the piston that drives the state's rescue engine. A sort of rescue clearinghouse run from a basement bunker on Fort Richardson near Anchorage, it employs a round-the-clock staff that monitors every military and civilian emergency radio frequency, as well as satellite beacon hits from aircraft ELTs (emergency locator transmitters), boat EPIRBs (electronic personnel international radio beacons), and hand-carried PLBs (personal locator beacons).

The RCC dispatcher informed the parajumpers that three fishermen were adrift in a disabled Zodiac boat out on Cook Inlet southwest of Anchorage. Glatt and Widenhouse learned that the fishing party, which included two off-duty Army reservists, had been setting salmon nets near the mouth of Turnagain Arm when their engine gave out and they'd sent up flares, which had been spotted and reported to the RCC by a commercial airliner on approach to Anchorage International Airport. Out of habit, the two PJs first checked the tide tables. Cook Inlet's maximum diurnal tide range in spring is almost thirty-nine feet, the second largest in North America, after Nova Scotia's Bay of Fundy, and, according to the charts, high tide would soon be sweeping the three fishermen toward Turnagain Arm.

Remembers Glatt, "Turnagain Arm is not the place you want to be when the tide's washing in."

On May 30, 1778, the English explorer Captain James Cook, sailing under orders from a British Admiralty consumed with discovering the

Northwest Passage, piloted the three-masted *Resolution* up the inlet that now bears his name. Oddly enough, from a distance the skyscraping coastal mountains and quiet, deep bays of the Alaskan panhandle appeared to be volcanic islands, similar to those Cook had just surveyed in the South Pacific. Upon reaching the stout peninsula where present-day Anchorage now rises, Cook ordered longboat parties to explore the two riverine corridors that flank either side of the headland, hoping they held the entrance to the passage. Commanding the expedition up Knik Arm, running northeast, was his navigator, Lieutenant William Bligh, who eleven years later would be cast adrift by the mutineers on HMS *Bounty* (and whose name commemorates Bligh Reef, the shoals upon which the supertanker *Exxon Valdez* grounded in March 1989, pouring 11 million gallons of North Slope crude into Prince William Sound). Meanwhile, Cook's second in command, Lieutenant James King, led a second party of two longboats down Turnagain Arm.

When neither tidal estuary proved to be the illusory Northwest Passage, Cook collected and sailed from the northern waters disappointed. However, in the arm that flowed southeast he *had* discovered the second-largest tidal bore in the world, "bore" deriving from the Middle English word for "wave." Cook christened it Turnagain Arm—unaware of the similarity to its Tanaina Indian name, "Back Water."

Rough seas are not uncommon in Alaska. The state derives its name from the Aleut word *agunalaksh,* meaning "the shores where the sea breaks its back." But Turnagain Arm is something else altogether. The large tide of Cook Inlet is funneled as if through a nozzle as it enters the narrow, shallow strait—known locally as a skookum chuck—of Turnagain Arm. It usually takes the shape of a series of five to fifteen undulating swells averaging between two to three feet in height, with one or more frequently breaking all the way across the mile-wide channel. Depending on the phase of the moon and the earth's location in its elliptical orbit about the sun, the tide can at times be barely visible, or—as when Cook saw it—the surf can pound in on spectacular six-foot breakers with the force of hard, snapping jabs. Beluga whales can sometimes be spotted riding these breakers like thick, black longboards. Conversely, when the tide retreats, it exposes quicksand-like mudflats that trap any man or beast that tries to ford them. There they remain, mired in thigh-deep glacial silt, until they are broken in half by the wall of foaming water that roars back in at speeds reaching ten knots. It is a horrible way to die.

As Mark Glatt and Brent Widenhouse scrambled from Kulis, Turnagain's high tide was due in soon. An hour after liftoff their Pavehawk hovered a hundred feet over the disabled Zodiac. Black swells approaching six feet recalled not only Captain Cook's log, but also, to Glatt's mind, the liquid chaos of the seventh-century Gaelic poem *The Viking Terror:* "Fierce is the wind tonight. It ploughs up the white hair of the sea." The ten-foot craft was nearly swamped. "A bit 'sporty' down there," Glatt said to Widenhouse, employing the term parajumpers use for any dangerous mission. The two PJs flipped a coin and Glatt won. A moment later he had donned his neoprene cold-water gear and jumped through the moaning wind into the 48-degree seas as Widenhouse prepared to lower the Pavehawk's quarter-inch, tensile steel wire rescue hoist, nicknamed The Penetrator.

The helo dropped Glatt up-current, and he finned to the Zodiac. He was afraid that if he boarded it it would capsize from the weight, and none of the fishermen had wet suits, much less dry suits. They had already off-loaded all their salmon catch, their gear had avalanched, and they were taking water fast. So Glatt hung over the gunwale as he harnessed the first man into The Penetrator's basket. Midway through rigging the first fisherman into the harness, the Zodiac was blindsided abeam by a frothing breaker. It was the beginning of the bore tide. Glatt and the half-harnessed fisherman were swept downcurrent. Glatt heard a splash like a horse dropped off a cliff, and swam to the noise. He found the fisherman, secured him, and maneuvered him back to the floundering craft. Now waves were breaking from all directions, rolling over the Zodiac, submerging it for seconds at a time. Glatt knew he was close to having three hypothermic patients on his hands.

Even a limited exposure to cold water is a traumatic experience for the human body. British scientists in the forefront of cold-water immersion study now estimate that two-thirds of British deaths at sea during World War II were caused not by enemy action, but by exposure. Water will conduct heat from the body at about twenty-five times the rate of land-based air temperature. This means when you fall into cold water your body cools four times faster than it does in comparable air temperature. In the mean temperature of Cook Inlet in June, usually between 45 and 50 degrees Fahrenheit, a person without a dry suit will, within moments, experience what researchers call cold shock.

First, the water's temperature affects respiration in much the manner a virus infects a computer. Signals from the central nervous system decelerate, leading the brain to surmise that oxygen is not reaching the lungs. Fearing for your air supply, you begin to gasp uncontrollably, which brings on ungovernable hyperventilation, or overbreathing. As this process begins, the brain's instinctive response is to "order" the body to try to swim to safety. This is a mistake. The physical exertion of swimming quickly circulates the warm blood in the body's core to the muscles of the legs and arms. A human being's limbs have a large surface area but a comparatively small mass. Sending hot blood out into the extremities is an ideal way of losing body heat. Swimming and thrashing about in cold seas not only stirs the water around the body—further increasing the cooling process—but also diverts warm blood that is needed to protect the body's vital organs. In freezing water, arms and legs essentially become heat-losing radiators.

As the body cools, the nerve and muscle functions in the extremities diminish. The cold water acts as an anesthetic, limiting the amount of information coming back to the brain. Even the best swimmers begin to struggle and spasm. A swimmer no longer quite knows where his limbs are moving. Confusion and disorientation follow, presaging the drowning process. Research suggests that to swallow as few as 22 milligrams per kilogram of body weight—for the average person as little as a quart and a half of water—is enough to kick the fatal progression into gear.

These calculations raced through Mark Glatt's mind as he struggled to secure the three stranded fishermen into the hoist basket. Above him the Pavehawk pilot fought to maintain his hover in a busting gale blowing sixty-knot winds. The helicopter's rotors blasted a lily pad of flattened water hundreds of feet behind the Zodiac, despite the fact that the helo was hovering directly overhead. "With wind like that," Glatt smiles at the memory, "well, it was worrisome."

With Widenhouse hanging precariously from the helicopter's left skid to position The Penetrator, Glatt managed to hoist one, and then a second, fisherman. After each hoist, the Pavehawk, unable to buck the gale for more than one airlift, was forced to break off its hover and circle back around the wallowing craft. Between the aircrew, the flight engineer,

Widenhouse manning the hoist, and Glatt in the water, the timing had to be precise. If the tension on the wire hoist is allowed to slack, it can easily send the basket bashing into the head of someone below. Moreover, if there is too much slack in the basket at the crest of a wave, as the wave breaks a stray wire loop can pull off an evacuee's arm, leg, or head.

With one last fisherman left to raise, Glatt was fighting to keep the Zodiac from being swept through the mouth of Turnagain Arm. He gripped the gunwales of the rubber craft and dug his feet into a submerged sandbar he could feel through patches of surface ice as fragile as isinglass. Just as he harnessed the third man into The Penetrator and gave Widenhouse the hoist signal, the tidal bore landed a hammer blow.

"The guy wasn't lifted more than a couple of feet when the boat just disappeared like it was shot out of a cannon," Glatt says. "At first I was afraid it caught him. But when I surfaced I could see that Brent was hauling him into the helicopter." The bore tide had engulfed Glatt, but he was a powerful swimmer supported by fins and warmed by a trilaminate dry suit.

Now, three years later, Glatt recalls the Turnagain "save" with a strain of melancholy. His future with the 210th is looking "tango uniform," or tits up. Despite hours on the treadmill, trying to take off the extra weight is a futile refrain. But he has decided that he will resign before they dismiss him. Melanie and Mark have been discussing his options, and they've reached the mutual conclusion that applying for a job as a paramedic with the Anchorage Fire Department isn't the worst idea in the world. Melanie especially likes the thought. It will give Mark more time to spend with their fourteen-month-old, Jacob. Plus, both have grown weary of the nearly three months Mark spends overseas each year.

Those TDYs in Saudi get old real fast, Glatt rationalizes. The job's perfect for a single guy or young married, but it takes a toll on a family man. Deep in his heart, however, the idea of leaving the 210th saddens him. The team is his second family. He's found a home with the PJs. As Mark Glatt lifts his binoculars again he wears a sad smile.

THREE
The Slough of Despond

So foul a sky clears not without a storm.

—WILLIAM SHAKESPEARE, *KING JOHN*

Steve Ball checks his map. The Englishman has no idea how far he is from seventeen-two high camp. Swirling snow and clouds as thick as spun sugar obscure any landmarks, and there is no movement on the mountain trail known as the Washburn Descent. It is as if he is down-climbing in a dream state through billowy rents of frozen fog along a rocky coastline, snatches of black granite appearing and disappearing like shimmering mirages. But the path is well wanded, and marked by patches of yellow snow. Only a decade ago this route down Denali was a wasteland of ropy, brown turds—frozen where they dropped, unable to decompose—forcing climbers to be wary when gathering snow for their stoves. But since beginning regular mountain rotations in the early 1990s, the Park Service's rangers have enforced laws that keep the mountain's flanks free of human waste. Now all climbing parties face heavy fines if they do not bag their shit and deposit it in authorized crevasses. So Ball is left to navigate his downclimb by bottle-green bamboo tomato plant stakes and splashes of frozen piss fashioned into flamboyant, Dalí-esque shapes.

The forty-three-year-old auto mechanic is dressed warmly enough in an expedition-rated windstopper fleece beneath his insulated jacket, plastic boots, and neoprene overboots. And despite the loss of his right glove, he still has a pair of overmittens. But he feels uncoordinated, and it is hard to concentrate. It has been nearly two days since he's eaten anything save several glucose tablets and a few, small Power Packs. His water is frozen in its jug. Ball has no way of knowing whether or not his climbing partners are still alive. His only hope is to find the mountain rangers' medical bivouac. He hunches a shoulder against the wind and trudges on, a spectral figure hugging the ridgeline. How fucking ironic, he tells himself as he nears a knife-edge crest, we all make a vow that the weather is going to be the last thing to beat us, and now . . .

In midthought, a brittle slab of névé collapses beneath him, and he falls with a soft, showering noise. The earth seems to have opened up, and before he has time to think he is pitchpoling down a sixty-degree slope like a tanker in a typhoon. He reaches for his ice axe, but he can't self-arrest—he's falling too fast. In fact, his ice axe is now a lethal weapon, nicking his thighs as he cartwheels down the ravine. The plunge seems to last forever. He feels his left ankle jam against a rocky outcrop. He hears an awful snap, and everything goes black.

When Ball awakens he is shaken and groggy, although fairly certain he has avoided a concussion. But his ankle is throbbing and he guesses he is going into shock. His rucksack ripped open during the fall, and his gear— overmittens, wristwatch, water bottle, compass—is scattered down the slope, tracing his 1,000-foot passage like Hansel and Gretel's bread crumbs. His ice axe is gone and so is his map, most likely blown off the edge of the world. He begins to crawl back up the shelf on all fours. He makes twenty yards, perhaps thirty, before sliding back down the steep pitch of the gully. He tries to climb again, and then a third time. Each attempt sends him reeling down to his original landing zone, barking the skin off his shins. On his last tumble, he rolls over his missing ice axe, lunges, and grabs it as he flies by. He starts up again, digging the axe hard into the snow.

Twenty yards. Thirty. Now forty. But the couloir proves too steep. He begins to slide down again. His right ankle catches a rock scoured to a marbled sheen by the wind and his foot is bent awkwardly, painfully, behind his knee. Both of Steve Ball's ankles are now screaming in pain, tearing the scabs off unspeakable doubts. His energy flags, and it begins snowing harder. He is not even sure where he is on the mountain; he has truly fallen into the slough of despond.

Ball uses his axe to scrape out a shallow pit in the snow. He manages to snag his torn rucksack and with it lines the bottom of the white crater. He moles into a fetal ball on top of the pack and jams his freezing hands into his pants. The sum of his miseries is finally unendurable, and he sinks into his hole like an animal waiting to die. African hunters say when a lion is fatally wounded it draws a circle around itself with its own blood, lies down in the middle, and waits for the jackals and hyenas to catch the scent. Ball does much the same. In his mind, the only question is what will kill him first, the cold or the snow.

Down on the flatlands in May, miles and miles of mosquito-infested bog and impenetrable bush surround the Denali massif. To reach base camp on the southeast fork of the Kahiltna Glacier, mountaineers are faced with a choice: walk for ten days or hop onto a ski-equipped bush plane in the nearby village of Talkeetna and fly for thirty minutes. Not many hike, and if they do, it is usually on the way out. Climbers often refer to the rutted airstrip abutting base camp at 7,200 feet as "the highest international airport in the world." Now, while a blizzard rages on the mountain two miles above them, PJs Steve Daigle and Karl Grugel enjoy fine, sunny weather as they squat in their idling Pavehawk, inhaling the faint musk of jet fuel, awaiting the recovery of the lost English climber. The two parajumpers watch as a procession of ski planes flies in and out of the wide ravine, disgorging climbers from all points of the globe. After one landing Daigle nudges Grugel, calling his attention to a Japanese hauling brand-new climbing boots and a portable stove that has not even been broken out of its packing crate.

"There's one of our customers now, the idiot," Daigle says. "Didn't even shake down his gear before heading up here."

No good usually comes of parajumpers sitting around and doing nothing, although at Seven-Two camp there really isn't much trouble to find, and the best Daigle and Grugel can do is flirt with "Base Camp Annie," the pretty blonde former flight attendant who returns to Alaska each climbing season to act as an air traffic controller cum den mother for the Park Service rangers and mountaineers gathering to assault Denali. So for the past three hours, while preparing to triage and airlift Steve Ball—if he is ever found—Grugel, who joined the team only two years ago, passed the time wheedling tales of the unit's history from Daigle.

Master Sergeant Steve Daigle is one of the 210th's founding members. Beneath his matinee-idol resemblance to Harrison Ford's Indiana Jones there is a cross-grainedness to Daigle's personality that fascinates the younger PJs. To some of the newcomers to the 210th, he is more like one of them than some of the other veterans. And, to Daigle, preparing these "pups" for the harsh exigencies they will face in Alaska is as much in his job description as free-falling from Hercs or setting fractured tib-fibs. The general consensus among the greener PJs is that if Daigle had been the *Titanic,* the iceberg would have sunk. When the "Daigle Dog" speaks, the raw PJs listen, not least because he is irreverent enough to have the best stories.

Aside from being a sort of North Star of pararescue, Daigle, at forty-one, is perhaps the toughest man on the squad in a barfight, the class clown, the most prodigious beer drinker, the most innovative curser, and the first to volunteer for the hairiest assignments. Like Oscar Wilde, he can resist anything except temptation, and will accept any wager and look forward to winning, whether it involves topping his personal best in a triathlon or sweeping a "friendly" volleyball set on the grass court outside The Section. Daigle was once involved in a can-you-top-this war of pranks while stationed at Fourteen-Two camp with Daryl Miller. It began when the ranger snuck into Daigle's tent each night to deflate his air mattress. It took Daigle, suffering from mild hypoxia, a week to realize his bedding did not have a slow leak. When the PJ discovered the culprit, he punched pinholes in Daryl's steel coffee mug and howled when hot chocolate spilled down the ranger's chin. Miller then rigged the legs of Daigle's cot to collapse when he plopped into bed. Daigle, in turn, ruined Daryl's morning by stuffing the fingers of his favorite gloves with frozen wads of Kleenex.

So at Grugel's instigation Daigle now recounted in glorious gory detail such missions as the Korean expedition rescue of '92, the season eleven climbers died on Denali. "A massive goat fuck," Daigle remembered, employing the gallows humor endemic to the military. "We got trapped in a blizzard at Seventeen-Two for days, and I had dead Koreans stacked up outside my tent like cordwood. I'd go from tent to tent each night asking people if they felt like a little Korean for dinner." He'd reminisced about the time he'd performed "an open-air chest tube" on the Japanese climber who'd tried to snowboard the Messner Col. "A damn, bloody mess," Daigle screeched, hawking a green gob and spitting it into the white snow, "for a damn bloody fool." Grugel, a towheaded twenty-six-year-old Wisconsinite with a Dick Tracy jaw and the thighs of a middle linebacker, hung on every word. But the story the pups were most interested in reliving was the Mount Torbert save. That one was a thunderclap, if you could only get Daigle to tell it. To Grugel and the other newcomers, the Torbert save epitomized what Alaskan pararescue is all about.

Mount Torbert is a prosaic, 12,000-foot peak in the southern reaches of the Alaska Range rising about seventy miles west of Anchorage. The mountain is one of several serving as a natural barrier for the bush pilots shuttling between Anchorage and the state's western coastal villages. Running southwest from Torbert the clusters of glittering spires fade into the netherworld of the Aleutian chain. On the morning of May 27, 1998, a bush pilot operating an eight-seater Cessna 207 contracted to ferry five passengers to Anchorage from a remote Eskimo village near the mouth of the Yukon River. The going rate, usually around $50 per person, is highly negotiable. The pilot had no commercial license, a not unusual occurrence out in the interior. Overflying the Alaska Range, the Cessna smacked into a storm roaring inland off Bristol Bay. The pilot tried to soar above the granite-hued clouds, but was snared by a williwaw, a sudden, 100-mile-per-hour wind shear that builds up on one side of a mountain and spills over the other. The plane got off a Mayday before being yanked down by what seemed like the hand of God. It pancaked onto a glacier at 10,800 feet on Torbert's west flank.

An Air Force AWACS on a training flight intercepted the Cessna's Mayday and called it in to the RCC. By the time the RCC heard from the AWACS flight it was already picking up the bush plane's emergency locator transmitter hit. Every plane is required by law to carry an ELT, a briefcase-sized transmitter set with a spring trigger. When an aircraft crashes, the trigger is released on impact, activating its batteries, and the ELT begins emitting a signal over UHF frequency 121.5. Theoretically, an ELT's radio pings become louder as rescuers approach the downed aircraft, and their position locator system should lead them directly to the site. But a mountain chain often distorts radio waves.

A day alert helo carrying PJs Garth Lenz and Technical Sergeant John Paff executed a grid search over the southern Alaska Range for three hours before pinpointing the crash site. The night alert Pavehawk piloted by Major John Jacobs was dispatched from Kulis. Daigle and Technical Sergeant Greg Hopkins, pulling night alert, were part of the crew. But Jacobs found it impossible to penetrate the four distinct cloud decks he counted lapping Torbert's headwalls like a rising tide. Jacobs put his helo down in a small valley beneath Torbert, and Daigle and Hopkins were joined by Paff and Lenz, whose helo had also landed. The four conferred briefly, and on Lenz's orders began gearing up for a climb. Jacobs told Lenz he could ferry the PJs to a ridge below the cloud cover at 4,000 feet. From there the climbing route would rise nearly straight up over a vertical mile, through a serac-laden ice field with no known routes. The PJs estimated it would take them six hours to reach the downed bush plane. The RCC had dug up the Cessna's flight records and radioed the PJs that the bush plane was carrying a pilot and five passengers. Lenz and his team were debating how much medical equipment and extra clothing to hump for the six freezing survivors when their conversation was drowned out by the blat-blat-blat of the Pavehawk's rotors palping the air.

John Jacobs had received new information from the RCC dispatcher. He told the PJs that the Cessna pilot had been able to get his radio up and had made contact with the RCC. All the passengers, he said, including a young girl and a boy celebrating his thirteenth birthday, were alive and relatively unhurt. But dressed only in jeans, light jackets, and tennis shoes, they were fast succumbing to hypothermia. They would freeze to death before the PJs could reach them on foot. As the officer in command, he was aborting the climb. So Jacobs had disengaged his cerebrum, slipped his limbic midbrain into gear, and decided on a balls-to-the-wall air rescue. To greatly simplify, Jacobs would chance weaving his way through the cloud cover by plotting an ascent according to latitude and longitude readings from the helicopter's global positioning system. Then, using his navigational avionics, he would overlay the GPS points on the cockpit's computerized topography map. A Pavehawk's rotors extend nearly sixty feet in diameter, and Jacobs, studying the topo map and doing the math in his head, dead-reckoned a course through the range's narrow canyons, some no more than one hundred feet wide. He would, in effect, be flying blind, relying on the helo's technology to prevent him from slamming into a mountainside.

If Jacobs wanted to squeeze in any survivors, he knew there was only room in the helo for his co-pilot, navigator, and two of the four PJs. Lenz and Paff reluctantly wished Daigle and Hopkins good luck, and called for another helicopter to extract them. It would be hours before they were picked up. Meanwhile, Daigle and Hopkins scuttled into Jacobs' Pavehawk as the pilot powered up his machine.

Imagine being locked in a coffin hurtling down a raging river, never knowing where the rocks were that could smash your floating box, never knowing if you were approaching a falls. That's how the PJs describe the helicopter's ascent. They were aware of being surrounded by crenellated peaks sharp enough to cut falling silk, some close enough to spit on. But they were blind to any terrain features. All they could see was white. Periodically Jacobs would "mark a hole" in the cloud cover, and in a few brief moments of visibility the five-man crew would snatch a glimpse of a nearby granite headwall. Actually seeing how close they were to the mountains may have been worse than flying blind. In a particular bit of understatement, Greg Hopkins recalls that "all eyes were outboard."

"Jumping" from hole to hole, Jacobs was playing a life-and-death game of Chutes and Ladders. After a midair refueling on the cloud-free east side of the mountain, it took Jacobs two hours to pick a path up the mountainside before leveling off at 10,800 feet. They were now at the same elevation as the crash site, but could see nothing. Two miles away, someone spotted another hole in the cloud deck. Jacobs inched toward it warily. Gradually the crew were able to make out a few jagged battlements, several cornices, a snaking ridgeline—and finally the crumpled Cessna, its nose impaled in the glacier, snow rising to its windows.

"Sheer luck," Hopkins remembers. "Anywhere else and we'd never have seen them."

Jacobs shot a half dozen approaches to the crash site. It was no use. The only potential LZ was a tiny plateau cantilevered over a ridge some six hundred yards from the downed plane. One side of the rock porch sat snug against Torbert's towering headwalls. The other three ended abruptly in sheer drops. As the sun began to edge below the horizon Jacobs dumped five hundred pounds of fuel to lighten his load and powered the helo down. Daigle and Hopkins roped up and took off across the glacier. Hopkins broke trail, cutting it as neatly as a master tailor. Midway to the crash site he noticed a subtle dip in the undulating slope. Probing with his ice axe, he edged too close. His left leg shot through the corn snow and into a crevasse. Daigle hauled him out, and the two continued on.

They reached the Cessna in thirty minutes and began digging out the snowdrifts that had piled around the twisted fuselage. They found every-one conscious. Daigle distributed spare gloves and jackets to the chil-dren while Hopkins examined the woman seated next to the pilot in the cockpit. Her head had slammed into the instrument console during the crash; her nose was shattered and she complained of pain in the back of her neck. Though she insisted she could walk, Hopkins palpated her neck and shoulders and guessed that at least two or three vertebrae were broken. He jerry-rigged a cervical collar from an old sweatshirt he found in the back of the plane and supported her outside.

Entrenched in the parajumpers' memory of the rescue is the Cessna's pilot. He complained throughout the ordeal, in particular demanding to know what had taken the PJs so long to reach them. "He was a real fuckin' trout," says Daigle, employing the colloquial PJ term for the ashen face, droopy eyes, sunken cheeks, and pursed lips of a person they pull out of danger. He was also overweight, yeasty, and had the look of a tax collector or a small-town judge. Before long his incessant whining had driven Daigle barking mad and the parajumper looked as if he wanted to smack the guy.

Roped up for the trek back across the glacier, Daigle took the lead. Behind him, in order, followed the two children, their parents, the bush pilot, and Hopkins in the sweeper position, assisting the injured woman. The pilot insisted on retrieving two duffel bags and a hunting rifle from the wreckage, but it was soon obvious he was too weak to lug their weight. With a sigh, Hopkins heaved the luggage and rifle over his shoul-ders. In a final indignity, halfway to the helo the woman with the broken neck inched past the huffing pilot on the rope line.

When Daigle reached the Pavehawk, he began stowing the passen-gers away. Both children and three of the four adults were safely tucked inside when he heard Hopkins yell for help. Daigle galloped back across the glacier to find the obese pilot wedged into the same mouth of the crevasse—or "slot" in the argot—that had snagged Hopkins on the way over. In fact, he nearly dragged the PJ into the crevasse, but at the last minute Hopkins had buried his ice axe into the glacier to arrest his fall. The PJs managed to extricate the pilot. "If the motherfucker had been a little skinnier he'd be laying at the bottom of that slot right now," Daigle says with an evil grin. "I almost felt like pushing him in myself, he was such a pain in the ass."

With everyone aboard, Jacobs waited for a break in the clouds. The navigator threw a smoke grenade to gauge the ripping wind. Within twenty minutes a hole in the clouds developed, but, carrying so much weight in the thin air of 10,500 feet, all the helo could manage was a five-foot hover. Jacobs checked his power, yanked on the throttle again, and rose no higher than ten feet. The Pavehawk was too heavy. They were stuck. Through his headset Jacobs heard Daigle start to speak, but the pilot cut him short. He knew what was on the PJ's mind. No way he was leaving any of his crew to spend the night on this godforsaken mountain. There was, however, one outside shot.

The Pavehawk had put down perhaps fifty feet from the closest edge of the plateau. If Jacobs could crab-walk his helo toward the abyss, he could hurl it over the cliff and hope to attain air speed and transitional lift to full power as they plummeted. The less distance between a helicopter and the ground, the easier it is for the aircraft to hover. Jacobs was sure the helo's "ground effect" could get it over the rocky rim. Put simply, ground effect is the result of a helicopter's whirling rotors manufacturing a downwash that hits the ground, rebounds to the blades, and creates an artificial lift. (It even happens to commercial airliners when a plane catches air from the tarmac beneath its wings to create the instant of "float" passengers feel just prior to landing.) The difficult part, Jacobs informed his crew, would be maneuvering the helicopter so that its rotors did not clip the plateau's edges as it toppled over the rim. Daigle begged to differ, but held his tongue. The difficult part would be living through the fall so that he could have Major John Jacobs committed to an insane asylum.

Jacobs eased back on the throttle. The two PJs refused to look. "Greg and I pretended we were too busy working on the patients, who, of course, were fat and happy because they had no idea what we were about to try," Daigle says. Once over the edge the Pavehawk dropped 1,500 feet in seconds before regaining its power. An hour later all six survivors were disgorged on the landing pad of Anchorage Regional Hospital.

When Daigle finishes his story all Karl Grugel can say is, "Wow." Jacobs, Daigle, Hopkins, and the rest of the Pavehawk crew were subsequently awarded the MacKay Trophy for their heroism on Mount Torbert, and cited for "gallantry, intrepidity, unusual initiative, and unusual presence of mind." The trophy, presented for "the most meritorious flight of the year," is one of the Air Force's top aviation commendations.

Now, sitting on the Kahiltna Glacier awaiting the recovery of a British mountain climber named Steve Ball, Karl Grugel wonders if he'll ever get a chance to take part in a save anything like Torbert.

From his perch in the King Bird, Mark Glatt monitors the radio chatter all morning. At 11 A.M. a Park Service–contracted Cessna 310 is launched from the 4,000-foot gravel airstrip in Talkeetna with the ranger Joe Reichert riding shotgun. The plane makes twenty passes in a linear pattern over the West Buttress route without spotting Ball. Thirty minutes later the rangers charter a larger bush plane, a private Cessna 185 with more muscle to fight the gathering storm. It is directed to overfly the drainage of several couloirs and ravines at lower elevations. Maybe they'll spot the Brit's body. But the lowering ceiling kills visibility and after two hours the 185 turns back, too.

Glatt is about to concede the climber's death when the radio barks. A private expedition has nearly stumbled over a half-buried body under a mounding snowdrift in a culvert beneath Denali Pass. What the hell were civilians doing out in this weather? Glatt wonders. No matter. They report that the Brit is unconscious, dangerously hypothermic, and has an open fracture of the left tibia and fibula. The Herc is over the scene in seconds. Mark Glatt spots a prone body in a red parka encircled by five people. When the clouds break for an instant, Glatt surveys the Englishman's fall line. The PJ's breath catches in his throat. Not twenty yards further down the couloir, directly in Ball's line of descent, yawns a huge crevasse. A bit more momentum would have carried him right into the slot. Ball had the luck of a Mexican general. His momentum failed to generate that extra revolution.

But they still have to get him out of there, and the weather is deteriorating. As the Herc descends, Glatt can almost feel the whipping snow eating through the plane's paint. Now he listens, transfixed, as messages and instructions fly staccato over the Park Service's radio frequency.

The Lama pilot Jim Hood radios the mountain ranger Kevin Moore at Fourteen-Two camp. He's willing to make a run. Moore relays a go-ahead from Daryl Miller, on station in Talkeetna. Fifty minutes later the helicopter appears out of the white mist and Hood's voice crackles again, telling Moore that the slope is too steep for a landing, "And no way can I handle a shorthaul in this wind." The civilians, the pilot says, will have to try to lower Ball's body to a more level LZ. If they can do that, maybe then he can set his aircraft down.

The high-altitude ranger Billy Shott, on-site at Seven-Two base camp, breaks in on the CB channel. He volunteers to be shorthauled up to the Brit's position with a stretcher-like Miller board. The pilot Hood no-go's that—"Only on flatter ground, buddy"—and buzzes the rescue party to drop radio batteries and a hypo of the anti-inflammatory Decadron to reduce any swelling of Ball's brain from cerebral edema. He bids them good luck and vanishes.

Daryl Miller radios the Herc and asks it to remain aloft as a spotter. The Herc pilot rogers that.

Now Hood makes a second run, looking for a spot to drop a screamer suit and the Miller board, just in case.

Now Kevin Moore, in relay camp, informs Daryl his team is assembled if they're needed to climb.

"Everybody hold on," Daryl finally blurts over the radio. He senses the rescue spinning out of control. "Let's see how far down these civilians can get him before we make any plans. Weather Service is calling for, uh, sporty conditions."

Glatt picks up on the ranger's use of "sporty" and allows himself a tiny smile. Daryl Miller has been spending far too much time with the PJs.

Billy's got the Brit." Steve Daigle punches Karl Grugel hard in the biceps. "Snatched him on a tandem shorthaul. Showtime."

Steve Ball is coming down the mountain in the screamer suit, and the screamer suit is attached by carabiners to the climbing harness of mountain ranger Billy Shott. The civilian rescue party lowered Ball to a small terrace at 17,700 feet, Daigle tells Grugel, and Daryl made the call to send Billy up after one more look at the gnarly forecast.

Five minutes, says Daigle. The two PJs break out their med kits.

. . .

Karl Grugel thinks of the Mount Torbert save as he crams a high-tech thermometer equipped with electronic sensors into Steve Ball's rectum. Hypothermia occurs when the body loses heat faster than it can burn fuel to replace it. The very old and the very young are most vulnerable, but Ball is a middle-aged man in good condition; nonetheless, his core body temperature had dipped dangerously low, below 85 degrees. He has basically been flash-frozen into a human Popsicle. As Grugel removes the shivering climber's hat a long brown ponytail pops out, straight as an icicle. Grugel wonders if it will break off.

The PJ covers Ball's torso with electric blankets and—after chopping away frozen socks—gently packs his limbs in portable heat shields. In hypothermic patients, rough handling or jolts can cause fatally irregular heart rhythms. The Englishman is ranting incoherently as Daigle splints his legs. But Grugel is fairly certain that the British climber will live. Still, something is gnawing at him, something unaddressed, something pitched, like a dog's whistle, too high for explanation.

He knows that the mission will go down on the 210th's logbooks as a "save." But he doesn't feel as if the team deserves it. "Deserve" may be the wrong word. "Earn" is the verb he is looking for.

Ball wasn't recovered by parajumpers on the mountain. Hell, Mark Glatt didn't even spot him from up in the Herc. It bothers Grugel. Ever since he signed on in Alaska he's heard the stories, legends now, some of them hardening into lore. The Torbert save was a motherfucker, on a scale with Glatt's Turnagain save. Loomis and Paff parachuting through a blizzard onto Sparrevohn. Man, verging on pulp fiction. But none loomed larger than Mike Wayt's rescue of the crazy Korean from the high folds of Denali. Grugel wonders why. Most likely because it was the first true test of the newly formed PJ team. That and the fact that it came close to killing a couple of the guys. Whatever the reason, the Wayt mountain saga is the touchstone by which most mountain rescues since have been measured. Grugel would never have made the connection, but Wayt's recovery of the Korean climber is to the Alaska PJ team what the Rubicon was to Caesar's legions. Grugel rechecks Steve Ball's pulse. He'll live.

FOUR

Noble Risks

One hour of life, crowded to the full with
glorious action and filled with noble risks, is
worth whole years of those mean observances
of petty decorum in which men steal through
existence like sluggish waters through a
marsh, without either honor or observation.

—SIR WALTER SCOTT

Mike Wayt remembers thinking that even for a Korean mountain climber, Bin Hong Kim must have been crazy. Not insane crazy. Hubris crazy. Begging for pulmonary edema crazy. "Summit crazy."

How else to fathom why the thirty-year-old Everest veteran broke the first rule of expedition climbing: When in doubt, step back and take a deep breath. Literally. Human organs are not constructed to perform at high altitude, they need time to adapt. Bin Hong Kim ignored this rule as he raced up Denali's West Buttress in the early evening of May 21, 1991.

The West Buttress is one of the most tantalizing "farmer's walks" in the world. Negotiating the route is decidedly nontechnical, although the ridge itself is terribly exposed. Bracing it is like an invitation to sleep with a beautiful woman whose troubles are worse than your own. Instant gratification usually overcomes common sense. With good weather and strong legs an experienced climber knows he can summit Denali via the West Buttress and be back in his tent at Seventeen-Two high camp in less than twenty-four hours. After his body has acclimated to elevation, that is. Unfortunately, intervals of clear, calm conditions around the summit rarely exceed twelve hours. In essence, Bin Hong Kim went up too fast and hung around too long.

Dig into Kim's saga deep enough and you come away with the distinct impression that the South Korean was an accident waiting to happen. Oddly, for such a macho group of men, the parajumpers rarely speak ill of any of the people they rescue. They understand that Alaska is a perilous place in which to play, and probably because each takes advantage of its mountains, rivers, and seas in his own way, the team doesn't hold it against anyone in need of recovery. Unless, of course, the victim displays enough hubris toward nature to confirm that he got what he deserved. So when the topic of Bin Hong Kim arises (as it often will with newcomers to The Section), Mike pauses and lowers his shoulders into an extended shrug, as if trying to burrow into an invisible tortoiseshell. He shoves balled fists deep into the pockets of his pea green flight suit and stares down at the reflection in his spit-shined combat boots. "The true fact is there was bad karma all around the mountain that night," is about as critical as he gets.

And, in fact, luck did not seem to be running down Denali that week. Several days before Kim's accident another Korean expedition had pulled off when most of its members collapsed from altitude sickness at 18,000 feet. Kim and his partner moved into their abandoned tents on May 20. One party staking claim to cast-off equipment is not an unusual occurrence on the mountain. But that same day Kim's climbing partner, suffering badly from frostbite, also turned back. This left Kim to risk a solo summit. Which is how the barely conscious South Korean was discovered crawling across the névé at 18,200 feet, in a cut in the mountain just below Denali Pass, on May 23 by two private expedition guides. Kim had been sick for at least three days, his pulse and respiration were weak, and his hands were blackened by frostbite. He spoke little English, but indicated through signals that his lungs hurt, and vomited as he motioned for water. One of the guides handed him a canteen, but he didn't have the strength to lift it to his mouth, and the water dribbled down his chest.

His discoverers radioed the RCC, which in turn relayed the information to National Park Service rangers. But Bin Hong Kim had picked the worst possible moment to be in need of rescue. In 1991 there were no parajumpers stationed permanently on Denali—the 210th Pararescue Squadron was just over a year old, and the PJs were restricted to working as "adjuncts" in the ranger station in Talkeetna. And though the rangers had had the Lama at their disposal since earlier that spring, they were still unsure of its capabilities. There was no way they were sending it up above 18,000 feet without a couple of trial runs. (Before the Lama's arrival the Park Service would occasionally submit requests for the Alaska Army Air Guard's "rotary wing assets," the sturdy old Chinook 47s. But that was only for extreme emergencies, and from the look of the storm front moving in toward Denali on the night Kim was discovered, even the Chinooks weren't getting up the hill.)

Mountain rangers did maintain a medical tent at 14,200 feet, but the discovery of the semiconscious Kim caught them between a line change. High-altitude ranger Roger Robinson had only just arrived at Fourteen-Two that morning and was not yet acclimated to altitude. It was soon apparent that the South Korean's only hope depended on two PJ patrols that were coincidentally running a month-long high-altitude training exercise across Denali's west flank. The exercises had been devised as a sort of shakedown cruise for new arrivals by the PJ team's founding chief, a shrewd old veteran named Mike McManus. McManus had pulled his new squad together by selecting men from pararescue units around the globe, and he could think of no better environment for a group of relative strangers to assess each other's lifesaving skills than across the slopes of Denali. McManus put Sergeant Skip Kula in charge on the mountain. Although only thirty-one, Kula was a veteran of the 210th's predecessor, Alaska's old 71st Air Rescue Squadron, and had climbed Denali with McManus before.

The PJs split into two groups. One three-man team was camped at 15,000 feet on the West Rib route, separated from the sick Korean by "The Edge of the World," a dizzying outcropping along the rim of a plateau that drops 4,700 feet. They were only about a vertical half mile below Kim, but they may as well have been on Mars. The second team, under Kula's command, was bivouacked at 14,000 feet along the West Buttress below a sheer ice cliff called The Headwall. It consisted of eight men: Kula, the rookie Mike Wayt, and three more parajumpers—Sergeants Garth Lenz, Steve Daigle, and Steve Lupenski—as well as a visiting New York PJ, a Navy SEAL, and a British Royal Marine who had attached themselves to the patrol on their way to the summit. All eight men had been on the mountain for over a week and had acclimated to altitude.

Skip Kula received the emergency call from Daryl Miller, on station in Talkeetna, at 8 A.M. on May 23. Since the PJ team was in the middle of a training mission, they didn't carry their usual consignment of rescue gear, including backup radios, portable Miller boards, and extra rope. Nonetheless Kula broke up his patrol into four separate rope teams and ordered a forced climb up to high camp at 17,200 feet the moment he received the Mayday. It took the eight soldiers five hours to scale The Headwall.

By the time they began their ascent, several other civilian climbers happened upon the expedition guides attending to Kim at Denali Pass, including a second Korean party. Together they formed an ad hoc rescue team, dismantling an abandoned tent to construct a crude sled. They secured Kim to the contraption with a belay line—a safety rope that can be anchored instantaneously in the event of a fall—and lowered him down the thousand feet to high camp. There they gave him oxygen and waited. When the PJ patrol reached high camp the weather had deteriorated to the point where everyone on the ridgeline was in danger, and the parajumpers found not one, but two Koreans in advanced states of high-altitude sickness. Bin Hong Kim was clearly the worse off, and as Garth Lenz tended to the second Korean, Kula examined Kim and made a preliminary diagnosis of high-altitude pulmonary edema, advanced frostbite, and possible high-altitude cerebral edema. He didn't need to spell it out for his teammates. Unless they could immediately lower the South Korean to an altitude from which he could be airlifted out, he was going to die.

While Kula and Lenz treated the two Koreans, the others began digging out snow caves and erecting tents. Conditions were so horrendous that it took them three hours to light a cooking stove to melt snow. In the meantime, the mountain rangers at Fourteen-Two camp had been joined by a unit of volunteers from the Alaska High Mountain Rescue Team. Kula radioed the rangers and together they came up with a plan of sorts. A two-man PJ team would lower Kim down while the unacclimated ranger team, carrying emergency medical supplies, would climb as best they could to meet them. The most direct escape route was straight down a glacial couloir, a 50-degree slope stretching almost 3,000 feet across Denali's west face. The parajumpers were carrying only several hundred feet of rope, and though the rangers had cached two 600-foot spools at high camp, it was going to be dicey. Moreover, Kula had only one working radio. But Kim, now completely immobile, appeared to be getting worse. There was no other choice.

A broad ridgeline snaked along the snowfield at the bottom of the couloir. From the ridge, Kim could conceivably be evacuated to 14,200-foot relay camp. If the weather held down below, a Pavehawk just might be able to put down. High camp was socked in, but Roger Robinson radioed Kula that relay camp wasn't as badly hit. It was just a little overcast, he informed them, with light, ten-knot gusts out of the northwest. The temperature was well below zero, but the forecast called for no increase in the storm raging above him. The PJs bundled Kim in a sleeping bag and lashed him to the makeshift sled with leather chest harnesses. As Kula directed Wayt and Lupenski to tie on to the litter with a fixed line, the thought flashed through his mind that this was not exactly what Chief McManus had in mind when he'd ordered a shakedown cruise. Some of the PJs were veterans, but most were green recruits, and all were new to the arctic. There was also a menacing lack of equipment. Jesus, Kula thought, it was like bringing a knife to a gunfight.

As Wayt and Lupinski roped up to the sledge, Kula laid out his plan. A team on the ridge would secure an anchor line to lower the Korean while they muscled "the patient package" like an overstuffed dogsled down the near-vertical ice gully. At the last minute a Korean from the second climbing party with a passing command of English volunteered to join the PJs and act as an interpreter. Kula also decided to keep the lone radio in order to coordinate logistics with Robinson and the other volunteers ascending from relay camp.

Garth Lenz was in a tent mere yards from the cliff face, treating the second sick Korean. He remembers the wind blowing such solid sheets of snow that as Wayt and Lupenski approached the edge of the cliff, they disappeared from sight. It left Lenz with the eerie sensation that he was alone on the mountain. He had experienced something like this once before when a surfboat he'd skippered was rolled by a rogue wave. In the seconds before the boat righted itself, Lenz sat strapped into the coxswain's chair, hanging upside down beneath several tons of pounding surf, feeling as if he were the only person on earth. Now, a few feet away from Lenz's tent, Wayt and Lupenski shared similar thoughts.

Meanwhile, the PJs on the West Rib, separated by a bottomless chasm, could only huddle in their tents and listen to "dribs and drabs of broken information" coming in on their radios. Technical Sergeant Dalton Maples recalls "the ultimate frustration. We were listening to this adventure unfold, hearing the guys just getting thrashed by the weather, and we were three healthy bodies who couldn't do anything to help."

At 4 P.M., after eight hours of climbing at altitude, Wayt, Lupenski, and the Korean interpreter nudged Kim's litter over the edge of the cliff and began inching it down the couloir. One hour later the weather conditions turned for the worst.

Daryl Miller has a saying about Denali that the PJs have heard too often: "The weather's okay only if it's okay." Now another blasting storm, more fierce than the first, rolled over the mountain unannounced and unexpected. The wind chill dropped to nearly 100 below. But it was the wind, gusting to 80 knots, that every member of the rescue party recalls most vividly. To a man they were certain that the wind would kill Mike Wayt and Steve Lupenski.

Ninety minutes after dropping over the cliff face, the two Americans and the Korean found themselves grappling with Kim's litter while swaying wildly across the black verglas, human kites flapping against the glacier, engulfed in a numbing arctic whiteout. Their erstwhile interpreter had become a liability, and Mike debated sending him back up the slope, but he decided against it when Steve Daigle's tent ripped from its anchor stakes in high camp and flew past them. Wayt motioned to Lupenski and hollered that they had to turn around. The two PJs tried to signal the lowering party, to no avail. They wanted to stop, but without a radio no one heard their cries. Above, Kula's anchoring team continued paying out rope. They had no choice but to go on. Kim was dead weight by now, unconscious, nearly frozen, only the tip of his nose visible through the crust of ice and snow sheathing the litter. It took the three men five hours to pick their way down 1,200 feet. With less than a 600-foot descent remaining, the ridgeline hove into view through the scudding storm clouds. Mike recalls peering down through the whipping snow and offering a silent prayer that the ordeal was nearly over. Then the rope stopped paying out.

To this point, Mike has told friends, the Kim rescue felt like "a drama in slow motion." When his rope line suddenly went taut, it turned into a still life.

The lowering party was stranded, clinging to the icy cliff face in the most horrible conditions imaginable. Wayt and Lupenski didn't know whether they had run out of rope or misjudged the distance to the ridgeline, and climbing back up was out of the question. They had no idea what to do next. The only certainty was that Bin Hong Kim was going to die, and his three rescuers weren't feeling too good about their own chances, either.

But the PJs had not miscalculated the length of their line. The anchored rope had tangled perhaps a hundred feet below the rim of the cliff in a rock-solid, wind-carved snow outcrop climbers call by its ominous Russian name, *sustrugi*. By now, Garth Lenz had finished medicating the second Korean, and had joined Kula's anchor team. Probing the line, Lenz spotted the snarl. He shimmied over the cliff and, facing notoriously hard climbing, followed their trail down through the *sustrugi*. Using his ice axe, he freed the frozen coil. An instant later, Mike Wayt found himself free-falling down the west face of Denali entwined in the ropes of Bin Hong Kim's litter.

In his after action report, Wayt described his plunge in staid, colorless phrasing. "I took a rapid descent with the litter perhaps 100 or 150 feet before I could dig my crampons and ice axe into the ice and arrest our fall. When Steve Lupenski reached us, he employed his ice screws, pitons, and carabiners to secure myself and the litter to the face of the couloir." In real time, Wayt felt as if he were falling through Dante's nine circles, through gales and boiling blood and three-headed cereberi, all the way to Satan's ice. Once pinned to the mountainside, he watched in confusion as the remainder of the now-slack rope whistled by.

But there was another problem. The storm had thrown the litter party off course. Several yawning crevasses bisected the ridgeline directly beneath their position. The ranger rescue patrol, packing food, blankets, down coats, oxygen, and medical supplies, was supposed to be waiting on the south side of these slots. Wayt, Lupenski, and the Koreans were suspended on their north shoulder. In order to bypass the crevasses, they would have to traverse Kim's litter five hundred to six hundred feet across a serac-laden ice field. Mike didn't think anyone had the strength. The Korean interpreter appeared ready to be fitted for a chalk outline. And after so many hours at altitude, the two PJs were also ill to the point of nausea. Mike knew his hands, feet, and face were in the early stages of frostbite, and suspected the others were faring no better. He was over-come with a feeling of implacable loneliness. When he recalls the moment, a subtle tremolo shades his voice. "For the only time in my life I thought, This might be it for me. I mean, we were spent. Totally wiped."

They were also unaware that Garth Lenz was on the way. After he'd disentangled the rope line he continued working his way down the ravine. Two hours later he reached the ragged litter party. Once on-site, he determined that his only option was to unhook from the safety line and attempt a solo downclimb across the ice field to the ranger team below. Maybe he could bring help. Despite the wind and whiteout condi-tions, Garth made it to the ridgeline. There he and Roger Robinson gath-ered what rope they had and completed the delicate climb back across the ice field to the stranded litter party. Buoyed by new blood, all five men cautiously began to belay the litter across the traverse, using a pen-dulum technique to swing Kim no more than two to three feet at a time. At one point Lupenski lost his footing, cheating death only when the lit-ter broke his fall. Then the Korean interpreter slipped. Lenz lunged across the ice and grabbed his flailing arm yards from the edge of a crevasse. Finally back on course, the haggard rescuers succeeded in low-ering Kim's body the final five hundred feet. This was the most danger-ous leg of the descent, for their dearth of rope forced the rescuers to use a "leapfrog" technique, anchoring what line they had to the slope with snow pickets, lowering the litter a hundred feet or so, securing the litter, climbing back to unhook the anchor, and retrieving the rope. Then repeat the entire process.

At 5 A.M. on May 24, nearly twenty-four hours after the pararescue patrol had received the emergency call and thirteen hours after Wayt and Lupenski dragged Bin Hong Kim over a cliff and down one of Denali's steepest aspects, both Koreans were administered oxygen and swathed in down comforters as mountain rangers made frantic calls for an evacu-ation. Lenz got off a final call to Skip Kula to tell him they had made it. Then Kula's radio died.

But within the dramatic rescue lay a hidden tragedy. When Mike had plunged down the mountainside with Kim's litter, the unconscious Korean's hands had broken out of the sleeping bag. At the time, his body was too covered in rime and snow—and his rescuers too exhausted—for anyone to have noticed. Now, as Kim was unwrapped and transferred to a Miller board, the Korean interpreter who had risked his life for his countryman cried at the sight of Kim's frozen, black hands. Both would be amputated, above the wrist, within the week.

As rangers and civilian volunteers from the Alaska High Mountain Rescue Team stomped out a 100-foot runway in the snow, Mike Wayt and Steve Lupenski watched in what seemed like a dream state as a Pavehawk crew took advantage of a narrow window in the storm to touch down at 14,400 feet and airlift Kim to safety. The pilot was then-Major Ron Parkhouse, and no Pavehawk pilot, before or since, ever landed at such altitude. Not that the record meant much to Mike at the time. "By now Steve and I are just a couple of punch-drunk zombies," he remembers. His head ached so much that his vision played tricks, and the snow-blasted icescape morphed into a black-and-white hallucination. He felt as if he wanted to die. He and Lupenski weaved their way to tents at 14,200-foot relay camp, where Mike recalls being handed cups of hot chocolate. "Steve fell asleep sitting up. He spilled his hot chocolate down his chest, where it froze in seconds. But I couldn't sleep. My stomach hurt."

It snowed at relay camp for the next five days, no aircraft could get in, and there was nothing for the civilian climbers to do but ride it out. The PJs continued their training. Several attempted to summit, but were driven back by the fierce winds. All the while Mike's belly felt as if it were on fire. He assumed he was suffering from altitude sickness. A week after the Kim rescue the weather broke and the PJ team hiked back down to Seven-Two base camp on the Kahiltna, where a helicopter awaited to airlift them out. Walking to the LZ, Mike stumbled, collapsed, and had to be helped onto the Pavehawk. He was flown directly to Anchorage General Hospital, where doctors discovered a perforated ulcer and operated immediately.

Mike Wayt had literally busted a gut saving Bin Hong Kim. In the process he had inadvertently set a standard for heroism and bravery that every Alaskan PJ would attempt to live up to.

His exploits may have earned Mike the Airman's Medal—the highest award given by the Air Force for bravery during peacetime—and it certainly solidified his reputation as one of the toughest men in the 210th Rescue Squadron. But it also kept him in the hospital for more than a month, and on restricted duty for almost a year. We're all alpha wolves; we all want to win here, the guys in Mike's unit would say. Then they'd shake their heads. "But Hop Sing, man, he's got some major voltage crackling through his wires. Sometimes, when he's got that oriental mojo working in overdrive, Hop Sing just gets crazy."

It is clear that Mike doesn't like losing, whether at flinting the first fire in wilderness survival school or scoring the highest on the national paramedic's exam or being the first parajumper to nail his groundmark. In fact, he readily admits that he loathes weakness in any form, and drives himself to conquer, not win, any test he sets for himself. His favorite movie characters are the Jedi Knights from the *Star Wars* series, with the fighter pilots from *Top Gun* a close second. Like his fictional heroes, Mike doesn't like to be critiqued or embarrassed and goes to great lengths to ensure the occasion for neither ever arises. It still sticks in his craw that a top kick chewed his ass way back in basic for another recruit's fuck-up. And that was almost seventeen years ago. Now, as he stokes the coals in his backyard barbecue grill, he watches his elder daughter out of the corner of his eye, and feels pride that Stephanie has inherited that gene.

Mike thinks he sees some of his mother in Stephanie. Nobuko Wako grew up fleeing American bombs on Japan's big island of Honshu, and met and fell in love with Chief Master Sergeant Ron Wayt at a USO dance after the war. Because of his work as an intelligence photographer, Ron Wayt couldn't talk about his job to his children. Nobuko Wako just plain wouldn't talk about her childhood. Mike remembers snatches of conversation, but he knows his mom saw a lot during the fighting, maybe too much. The wisdom was in her eyes. She told Mike the story of how her father, a Japanese naval officer whose destroyer was sunk late in the war, had survived by floating on the wreckage and island-hopping his way home. He turned up in Japan a year after being written off for dead. It is this tenaciousness that Mike sees in his older daughter.

In an instant the sunlight in Mike's backyard shifts, and Stephanie is once again a little girl in bell-bottomed jeans and an oversized Nike sweatshirt—an anxious seventh-grader awaiting the arrival of her friends. Mike has promised her this party, an afternoon of burgers and hot dogs and cutthroat volleyball, as a reward for her straight A's. That was before he got the call about the hiker lost up in the bush. The details are sketchy. An American tourist two days overdue at camp. Female. Out hiking alone with her Labrador retriever. The words "bear bait" cross Mike's mind—at least for the dog.

It is Mike's day off, but men from his parajumping team are spread thin all over the globe. With at least seven PJs up on Denali for the Steve Ball recovery, and another three or four pulling TDY over in Spain for the latest space shuttle launch, the 210th's pararescue squad is, in military jargon, "task saturated."

Air Force parajumpers are, perforce, a de facto insurance policy wherever U.S. military planes fly. From a parajumper's point of view, this is both good and bad. Good for the pilots unlucky enough to need rescuing. Bad for the PJs, inherently Type A personalities who too often find themselves droning through endless stateside training runs or riding out their active-duty hitches staring out the spotter's window of a Pavehawk helicopter at the flat Kuwaiti desert.

But the Anchorage-based PJ team prides itself on being perpetually "locked and cocked." It is for this reason that parajumpers crave the liberty afforded by Alaska's civilian rescue authorities. Most peacetime parajumpers, active duty and Air Guard alike, are deterred from taking part in civilian rescue missions on American soil by a combination of red tape and political provincialism. Things are different overseas. PJs, for instance, have pulled countless Icelandic commercial fishermen out of freezing North Atlantic waters. And on the U.S. air base in Incirlik, Turkey, the corps has been known to set up field hospitals for injured and sick local children. But try the same thing in the Lower 48, and there is inevitably hell to pay.

Not long ago, over voluminous cocktails in an Anchorage tavern, a visiting Canadian-based parajumper dumbfounded members of the 210th with the story of a training flight he was part of that happened to overfly a fatal car accident on the New York State Thruway. According to the Canadian, his helo put down near the crash and the two PJs on board dragged several survivors from a burning car. They were administering first aid when the New York State Police arrived. The troopers, instead of expressing their thanks, dressed down the Canadians for operating outside their jurisdiction. "There are two people lying on the side of the road who might have been dead if it weren't for us," the Canadian remembered. He threw down another pint of beer. "And all this goddamn cop wants to know is where in hell we get the authorization. Jesus!"

But Alaska is different in so many ways. The territory defies overstatement, and newcomers to the high north are often stunned by the sheer size of a landscape that, in John McPhee's vivid description, "is wilderness beyond the general understanding of the term." It is a trackless expanse where most valleys contain more bears than people, and where forest and tundra stretch under a light skein of railroad tracks and, at best, casually paved roads. The distance between Juneau and Nome is about the same as that between the tip of the Iberian Peninsula to the shores of the North Sea. And out in the wild interior, local sheriffs' departments, state troopers, native tribal councils, firefighters, the Civil Air patrol, and the Park Service rangers know that daily survival in the bush often depends on small kindnesses and hospitality, virtues considered mere decorum in the Lower 48. Survival in extraordinary circumstances often depends on the airmen from the 210th Rescue Squadron. The locals are not shy about dialing up the Air Force, although sometimes the call isn't even necessary.

Several years ago, on the Friday of Memorial Day weekend, the tiny Alaskan hamlet of Willow was preparing for its annual air show when, late in the afternoon, the pilot of a Twin Beach cargo plane misjudged his approach to the gravel airstrip and crash-landed in a field. A few miles away, vectoring over the Malamute drop zone on the grounds of Fort Richardson Army Base, a stick of pararescuemen were about to leap from the belly of a C-130 on a training exercise when the plane's captain was notified of the emergency in Willow. He canceled the training mission and banked northeast. Ten minutes later the Herc was circling the crash site, and within minutes spectators on the ground saw green, mushroom-cap parachutes popping open above them.

A squad of PJs, six men in all, landed near the downed Twin-Beach and surrounded it. Each appeared to be laden with enough medical and rescue gear to survive for days on a polar ice floe. The parajumpers ascertained that the pilot was not injured and had freed himself from the cockpit. So they nonchalantly watched as the Willow Volunteer Fire Department extinguished the engine fire, radioed for a helicopter extraction, and were gone in a flash. The swiftness of the operation left some civilians wondering aloud if the Air Force's pararescue teams patrolled the malevolent Alaskan skies waiting for disasters to occur.

But, to Mike's chagrin, the spring rescue season has proven uneventful, until now, due in large part to the mild weather on Denali. There have been no heavy missions since they pulled the platoon of Navy SEALs out of the Chugach back in February. That one made some news; the reporters loved the irony. There is a lurking sentiment among Special Ops types that earning the Air Force pararescueman's maroon beret was the backdoor entrance into the Special Operations community. And here were the PJs— backdoor men!—saving the chestnuts of the guys who were supposed to be the toughest hombres on the planet. None of Mike's teammates would admit it in public, but everyone in the 210th got a little extra jolt out of that save. Deep down, however, Mike had felt bad for those frostbitten SEALs. Hell, it was, after all, their first training exercise in a mountain range four times the size of New Jersey. How were those sailor boys to know that their assignment would coincide with Alaska's coldest winter in decades? He could only imagine the AAR, or after action report, that went into that poor SEAL platoon leader's jacket. Guy's career is shot, everyone agreed. Still, it had been one of the quietest springs he could ever remember. The team was having buzzard's luck: "Can't kill nothin', and nothin'll die."

A warm spring always meant downtime, and downtime meant "maintaining currencies." Both the Herc and helo pilots, for instance, had to log minimum hours of takeoffs, landings, and hovers in order to keep themselves classified "proficient." Shooting IPs, or practicing instrument approaches, was the worst. Parajumpers along for the ride despised the boredom. Moreover, once a year the aircrews from the squadron's fleet of Pavehawk helicopters had to qualify in "advanced handling" of their aircraft—that is, simulating real-world combat situations. The Pavehawk would be flown in every conceivable pattern—on its side, nose down, sometimes nearly upside down—in order to mock up combat evasion techniques. And each time any aircraft left Kulis two PJs were always members of the flight crew. This also gave the team the opportunity to get current on "lows and slows," an exercise wherein a helo cruises over water at "double tens"—ten feet and ten knots—while parajumpers throw themselves out the side door. Just the other day John Loomis, who was currently slogging the West Butt in search of Steve Ball, had leapt from a Pavehawk into Cook Inlet when the collar seal on his dry suit broke. It took the helo's flight engineer twenty minutes to fish him out, by which time his feet were two blocks of ice. But at least the downtime gave a couple of the guys a chance to work on their medical proficiencies.

Similarly, the PJs ordinarily had difficulty finding the time to keep themselves proficient on jumps, or, in the vernacular, "drops." Pararescue requirements stipulated at least four drops a year for both round and square chutes, static line and free fall, day drops and night drops. But now the squad was parachuting onto some muddy field, or rappelling into an icy bay, in some godforsaken corner of Alaska nearly twice a day. Such was the lull in rescue missions that a few of the guys even used the extra time to get themselves qualified on tandem chutes.

A month or so ago, a rumor had raced through The Section that the 210th might be called up to backfill some Asian pararescue slots left empty by airmen transferred to the Balkan theater of war—or perhaps even TDY into Kosovo itself. The Air Force had recently implemented a "stop-loss" contingency, which meant that all Air Force personnel, including reservists, were by order of the president constrained from retiring, transferring, or separating from the service at the end of their enlistment. A stop-loss contingency is the step below a call to active duty. With the Kosovo talk, a frisson of electricity coursed through the team. But Skip Kula put the kibosh on that. "Kosovo? Now there's a war that's sputtering out," he'd said. "Seems to me that neither side wants to play anymore." If anyone had the straight dope, it was Skip. He was the team's second in command, wired to parajumpers all over the globe. And sure enough, nothing ever came of the gossip. In any event, Mike figured, there was always enough paperwork to beaver away on.

So after the Kosovo talk fizzled there was nothing much left to do but run on the occasional "trash pickup" of some mail plane down in the interior, take part in training drops, or hunker down in The Section filling out scheduling forms. Until this week. When all hell broke loose. First the two Spaniards stripped off Denali like banana peels, and then the Italian photographer, setting in motion consecutive search-and-recovery sorties. Finally, last night, the squad had gotten the report about the three British climbers lost up near the summit. Now, this—some poor lady tourist mucking about the lichen tundra domes. So much for Mike's day off.

He looks at Stephanie one last time. Their eyes meet and he mouths the words "I love you," before heading into the house to grab his gear.

FIVE

The Edge of the World

Hell no, I ain't goin' out. I didn't lose nothin'
down in the States I have to go back after.

—ERNIE PYLE, "DAMNED GLAD
NOT TO BE IN CHICAGO"

Stephanie Wayt stands on her front porch watching her dad pull out of the driveway. Mike laughs when he sees his daughter flashing him the "V" sign through his rearview mirror. He has always delighted in his daughter's self-assurance, and many are the moments when he's tried to picture her out on her own, independent and self-sufficient. Mike and Lara recently sent Steph and her eight-year-old sister, Emily, on a flight to Washington State, unaccompanied, to visit Lara's parents. The expedition, for that's what it was, involved a layover and airline change in Salt Lake City, and Stephanie handled the responsibility with aplomb. She'd even bought a phone card and called home from the Salt Lake City airport. Mike beamed with pride, for this confirmed his opinion that he and Lara were raising the two most curious, sensitive, and—to Mike's utter gratification—spirited girls in the entire state of Alaska.

Of course, none of Mike's friends had to wonder where the Wayt sisters inherited their strength of character. Mike's cutthroat competitive streak had long been a source of amusement in and out of the Wayt household. "I'll spend hours cleaning my room, not a hair out of place," Stephanie would tell her girlfriends. "And Dad will pull inspection and always find something wrong. One little thing. Always. No matter how long it takes him. He has to win at everything."

Some of Mike's teammates privately wondered to what extent this pneumatic tic in his personality contributed to the perforated ulcer that exploded in Mike's gut after his rescue of Bin Hong Kim. Maybe Stephanie would have, too, if her dad had ever told her the whole story. But he hadn't. So right now she is torn. On the one hand, she sure wants her father at her party. Her friends like Mike, he's a cool dad, they all say, mostly because they love trying to pull exciting wilderness stories out of him. But, on the other hand, she is excited that there is someone out there who needs to be rescued, and is proud it's her father going out as part of the search party.

Like both her parents, Stephanie Wayt grew up an Air Force brat. She knows the drill well. For as long as she can remember her dad had been bolting off to crazy, faraway places after a sudden telephone call—to the Arctic Circle, to the Bering Sea, even to Siberia once—to jump out of airplanes or rappel from helicopters. "Citizen Soldiers," she's heard the men at The Section call themselves when the families get together for cookouts and camping trips. Like the Continental Army she'd studied in American history. Stephanie's eyes follow Mike's truck until it turns the corner at the end of the block. It is at times like this that Stephanie Wayt wishes she could go with her dad.

Stephanie also knows that her father's sudden "alerts" sometimes eat at her mom's insides. Mike and Lara had met at Fairchild Air Base when Mike was an Air Force Survival School instructor. Lara was a lifeguard at the base swimming pool and right off she noticed the taut, sinewy "hunk" with a rolling gait who taught novice pilots how to eat beetles and make wilderness fires and build bridges and boats out of tree branches and reeds. Reared a good Catholic girl, Lara joked to friends that the first time she glimpsed Mike he was wearing a tight bathing suit, and she had impure thoughts. "I saw that rippled, muscular back and it was lust at first sight," she would say. "When he turned around it only got better."

Lara was a catch, and Mike, whose gentle Asian features lend him an almost feminine grace, fell like a cut tree. He chased her like a bird dog and proposed a month later. Now, fourteen years later, they are in Alaska, and he is risking his neck as a member of a rescue outfit no one down in the Lower 48 has ever heard of. Lara teaches math at a local junior high school, and each time Mike leaves on a mission she steels herself to concentrate on long division, or fractions, or root numbers, to think about something else, anything besides what her husband is doing. Since the 210th formed ten years ago, none of its parajumpers had been killed on the job. Still, Lara had seen Mike's boss, Chief Master Sergeant Garth Lenz, fly stateside a half dozen times over the past year alone as the team's representative to other pararescue funerals and memorial services. PJs killed in a helicopter crash in Nevada, or on a training mission in the Canadian Rockies. One had even splatted into the low Nevada desert outside of Las Vegas when his chute failed to open during an instructional jump. She knew the danger was always there, swirling dankly just below the surface.

Lara had never experienced what some of the parajumpers' wives called the "hell vision," though Technical Sergeant Rick Peckham's wife had once described it to her. Diana Peckham had been lying in bed in that hazy state between consciousness and sleep when she was suddenly overcome by "a really weird feeling, more of a sensation than a visualization." She bolted upright in a cold sweat and prayed that her husband was safe. The weird thing was, at about the moment Diana Peckham leapt out of bed with the cold shakes, her husband was out on Cook Inlet off the Kenai Peninsula, part of a four-man squad running exercises on a Zodiac assault boat. Suddenly the craft was struck abeam by a rogue wave. The Zodiac reared straight up, then over on its side, and dumped all four men. Incredibly, the bastard boat then righted itself and, with its pins still turning, headed right for the cluster of men bobbing in the surf. Rick dove just in time, and the prop missed the crown of his head by inches.

Lara knew Diana Peckham was a tough woman. Once, after Rick had called home following a Pavehawk crash, Diana's first words had been "How's the helo?" But her friend's "hell vision" had shaken her, and Lara never wanted to experience one. When Mike returned from a mission, Lara soaked up the details—unlike some of the other wives, who couldn't bear to listen. Oddly, after the first few years there was a weary sameness to the way Mike told the stories, especially if they involved fatalities. No matter how many times you see a dead climber or sailor, Mike would say, you never get used to the experience. The tales still made Lara's skin crawl, and while he was gone she put his job out of her mind. It was as Mike always said, "The minute you start worrying about dying, you're guaranteed to become a statistic."

This method of coping had worked for ten years, and Mike had never failed to come home, if not always in the greatest shape. Lara remembered the telephone call after the Korean climber had been rescued—Mike in the hospital, her heart in her stomach. No, better not to think. Lara knew that thinking too much about what Mike did for a living would only drive her crazy.

But not Stephanie. Stephanie can't help daydreaming about her dad's adventures as she winches the volleyball net tight. In less than an hour, she estimates, he'll be gearing up at The Section, and then heading off to Kulis. She imagines him crouching on the flight line as the Pavehawk shoots its final descent. She sees her dad trussed in Gore-Tex and arctic pile expedition climbing gear, probably lugging a 60-pound rucksack, a medical kit, and God knows what else. Depends on what kind of country that tourist was lost in. Stephanie knows that her dad's unit is always loaded down when they jump; they never go out slick. Stephanie pictures her father waiting to leap through the aft sliding door into the rear spotter's seat, on the left behind the co-pilot. She guesses that by the time she and her mom bring out the burgers and Cokes, the helo will have air-refueled over Fairbanks; and as her party is breaking up, her dad will be off humping the swales of muskeg tundra.

Contemplating the plight of the lost tourist, Mike barely notices the sky spitting a thin mist across the windshield of his Chevy flatbed as he makes the turn onto Spenard Road on the west side of Anchorage. Not so very long ago the Spenard neighborhood had been known as the city's seediest. Mike remembers the old days, when the first parajumper to arrive at The Section each morning was tasked with two duties: raise the American flag on the aluminum pole near the front door, and roust the hookers from the half-ton transport trucks out back near the storage garages.

As he nears the intersection of Spenard and International Airport Road, Mike gazes ruefully at the belching tour buses disgorging scores of blue-haired senior citizens into the parking lot of the Regal Alaskan Hotel. To Mike's outreaching sense of the absurd, the creaking tourists—

clad in pastel golf shirts and plaid shorts, fresh off one of the hundreds of cruise ships that ply Alaskan waters each summer—appear emblematic of what might be called the development hell which has begun to threaten the livelihood of the area's seamy old guard. The sprawling Regal Alaskan, just down the road from The Section, is a case in point. The hotel, with its pricey suites, polished oak-and-slate lobby, and lakeside patio deck and gardens with flowers so improbably colored they look dipped in paint, is the official center of operations for the famous Anchorage-to-Nome Iditarod dogsled race.

Anchorage lies at the same latitude as Helsinki and the same longitude as Honolulu. Equidistant from Tokyo, New York, and—by way of the pole—Paris, it is fast becoming a hub for air cargo carriers. More than a dozen, domestic and international, have set up shop within the last two years. For the Alaskan parajumpers, then, the transformation of Spenard is accompanied by small pangs of regret, like Gauguin's consternation upon discovering empty food tins polluting the ponds of Papeete. Though the area remains home to its share of dilapidated sourdough bars and clubs featuring all-nude reviews (the Anchorage phone book contains twenty-nine listings under the heading "Massage"), the PJs realize that civilization—with its outriders like the fancy Regal Alaskan Hotel—is gradually overhauling what had once been the rowdiest town in the United States.The Regal Alaskan, shoehorned between the airport and a string of seedy motels, serves as a clarion call to the city's business community that no quarter of town is immune to the siren song of urban renewal.

It was bound to happen. Anchorage was growing fast—more than half of Alaska's 610,000 residents live in the city and its suburbs—and, to Mike's eyes, had probably changed more over the past five years than in the first eighty-three of its existence. Jeez, he thought as he watched the tourist buses unload, some of the old-time PJs wouldn't even recognize the neighborhood.

The "pioneer spirit" is what drew Mike to Alaska. He took to the idea of a state so "fresh" that the federal government still owns two-thirds of it. Most of his teammates felt the same way. Alaska's unofficial slogan has long been, "In the High North you do what you feel like doing," and to the hell-bent-for-leather parajumpers that read like a neon-lit invitation. Each newcomer to the squad seemed to have reached the conclusion that a true soldier is not necessarily a man who goes to war or kills people, but rather a man who exhibits integrity in his actions and control over his life. He also realized that a career path is only worth taking if it satisfies the imagination. In Alaska, the mountains, seas, and tundra saw to that.

Back in the early days of the unit, word spread quickly through the parajumpers' grapevine about Mike's recovery of Bin Hong Kim from Denali. Since then there had been much jockeying within pararescue's active-duty ranks to secure a slot on the 210th. All manner of mavericks and berserkers applied, and it had taken Mike McManus some time and effort to winnow the candidates down to men he felt could work together as a well-oiled troop during crises. Even now, nearly a decade after the Kim rescue, the lust to serve in Alaska lingers throughout the career field. Mike remembers the first words of one of the pups, twenty-six-year-old Technical Sergeant Mike Murphy, when he arrived last year. "The whole time I was active duty I had my eye on a spot with the Two-Ten, but, man, it's a bitch getting up here," he beefed. "You have to wait for an opening, and they don't come often. You guys never leave. It's like you homestead up here."

Wayt had just smiled. There are several rationales for this enthusiasm: because of Alaska's remoteness, when the flight crews and parajumpers of the 210th get the call, they begin hunting for people with the ardor of sled dogs ready to start the Iditarod. It is true that they bring a nearly unlimited budget to the search-and-rescue table, but more essentially they are trained to think for themselves on the fly, with no direction from above. This concept, a variation of the Jesuit philosophy of freedom within discipline, is a very nonmilitary notion, like the one articulated by the French statesman Georges Clemenceau, who seemed to have had PJs in mind when he remarked that war is too serious to be left to the generals.

The 210th averages about 65 civilian rescue sorties a year in an "official area of mission opportunities" that extends from the 60th parallel north to the polar ice cap. The squadron stands alert 24 hours a day, 365 days a year. The routine is often described as days of tedium interspersed by hours of terror as action often comes in spurts. Last August, for instance, the unit made 13 saves in 9 days. The men on the team, however, are far from the blood-and-guts Special Forces depicted in popular books and films. Each parajumper has been recruited as much for his fearlessness as for that quality Winston Churchill called "almost repellent common sense." Moreover, a parajumper's allegiance is as much to his teammates as to the flag. During a rescue, it is ultimately the PJ mission leader's call—rank carries no privilege—whether to jump out of an airplane or fast-rope from a helicopter into harm's way.

Like newcomer Mike Murphy, many of the Alaskan PJs began their careers as active-duty parajumpers. Increasingly, however, these airmen have been resigning in droves in order to find a guard unit with a higher action quotient. This leaves the 210th at the top of most wish lists. Despite the occasional spikes in global conflict that might result in a fighter jock shot down over Bosnia, Kurdistan, or one of the Iraqi no-flight zones, most active-duty PJs discover that the bloom soon fades from what the Pentagon calls "forward deployment assignments." Although several of the Alaskan parajumpers can tell off-the-record stories of earning their hazardous-duty pay exchanging fire with Serbian forces on search-and-rescue missions in the Balkans that remain classified to this day, for the most part the degree of excitement in foreign postings is comparable to riding a desk back in the States. Innumerable parajumpers curse the career field when they end up sitting in the Balkans or Kuwait with their thumbs up their asses waiting for something, anything, to run on.

Even worse, training drops off dramatically once an airman is transferred overseas, due to the myriad restrictions put on U.S. troops on foreign soil. Parajumpers rarely get to free-fall, or dive, or climb—all the activities they enlisted in pararescue for in the first place. "Hell, you're lucky if you can find a twenty-five-meter range to maintain your weapons proficiency," Murphy once told Mike Wayt as they discussed his tour of duty in southern Europe. "Mentally, it gets old. You're like a caged tiger."

Whereas active-duty pararescuemen are lucky to get in forty drops over the span of their four-year hitch, the Alaskan PJs average that number per year. Ironically, in an era when occupations such as professional golfer, political consultant, and Wall Street day trader evoke heated analogies to gunslingers and riverboat gamblers, the Alaskan parajumpers are the guys who actually live the beer commercials. Airmen like Wayt, Glatt, and Murphy are emblematic of a unit that projects an intimate, intelligent, yet curiously opaque glow. Though nurtured in the same amniotic fluid that produces smokejumpers, world-class alpinists, underwater demolitions experts, extreme skiers, and inner-city emergency room doctors, dressed in mufti the men of the 210th appear as unprepossessing as an assortment of scoutmasters supervising a suburban Boy Scout jamboree.

There are few archetypal qualities to the Alaska team's components. The squad is predominantly white, by and large married men, about half with young children, with a fondness for four-wheel-drive sports utility vehicles, Labrador retrievers, strong, dark beer, and Harley-Davidson motorcycles. The squad's members average close to fourteen years of experience. In Hollywood terms, they are more Tom Hanks than Tom Cruise, and view pararescue as an art as opposed to a profession. Some got into the rescue business on what might be called a dare—that is, the constant taunting from their boot camp drill instructors that they weren't good enough to make it through the grueling training schools. More than a few are former service brats attracted to the Special Ops community's dual themes of honor and discipline. Some like the steady money and government pension. And others enlisted because they would be good at nothing else. Usually, it is a combination of all of the above.

"Sometimes you can dig too deep for ulterior motives," Mike Wayt often says through a crooked smile. "It just may come down to the fact that we just want the rush of falling out of an airplane two or three times a week."

During his nine years with the team Mike has watched more teammates come than go. And he knows that when an Anchorage parajumper does retire, the clamor to replace him is such that Chief Master Sergeant Garth Lenz, who replaced Mike McManus last year, has the luxury of auditioning a spectrum of replacements. The Alaskan team is like a family on loan, is the way Wayt sees it. When, for instance, one of its members pulls overseas TDY—each Alaskan PJ averages about ninety days per year attached to units ranging from Incirlik, Turkey, to Masawa, Japan—the rest of the guys always make sure his driveway is plowed after snowstorms, or the new deck he started is completed, and that his wife and kids are escorted to team barbecues. It is a special community within the community, and everyone on the team knows that Garth keeps an ear to the pararescue grapevine to cull just the right prospects.

Although parajumpers with the rank of airman exist in the U.S. Air Force, each member of the 210th is a noncommissioned officer between the ages of twenty-five and forty-two. The majority grew up as "tornado bait" in rural America. They represent seventeen states and two foreign countries, with only Detroit-reared Technical Sergeant Dave Thompson and Los Angeles–born newcomer and former Navy SEAL Steve Wolf the products of an urban environment. One theory of why most PJs come from the nation's heartland is that city-bred boys tend to develop a kind of protective, lone-wolf shell about them—an inner radar, one PJ explains, "that directs them to watch their own backs first and foremost. That's a hard habit to break, and out in the bush every member of our team has to be working off the same sheet of music."

No man in the 210th's Pararescue Squadron would have disagreed.

Since time out of mind the sheltered waters surrounding what is now Alaska's largest city have served as a convenient, protected cove for way-faring Russian fur traders, Spanish missionaries, and French explorers on their way to somewhere else. *Anchor-age,* as the name implies, was a safe harbor in which to drop chain under lowering skies and ride out the ferocious squalls that churn the North Pacific. Rising from a broad, con-cave peninsula of moose forest and fox meadow and defined by the two enveloping tidal estuaries, Knik and Turnagain Arms, the site was not even a settlement until 1913. But as the First World War sundered Europe, Congress quietly authorized the construction of a railroad junc-tion across south-central Alaska's prime bottomland to expedite the box-cars of gold and silver flowing south from the interior to the port of Seward, on Prince William Sound. The first railroad workers to arrive feasted on the plentiful game migrating across the stream-severed boreal forest, and marveled at the jagged, snow-capped Chugach Range that pickets the isthmus's eastern flank like the ramparts of Samuel Coleridge's Xanadu. When the railroadmen returned to the Lower 48, they carried with them descriptions of the lush Matanuska Valley that fans north from the rocky coast like an oversized scallop shell.

Throughout the 1930s government-sponsored homesteaders from the Depression-stricken Midwest poured into the Matanuska and Susitna Valleys, or the Mat-Su, hoping to transform its rich, glacial loess into a subarctic Fertile Crescent. Yet despite cool, arable soil and nine-teen-hour summer days that yielded acres of seventy-pound cabbages and carrots the size of saxophones, Alaska's harsh winters took their toll. Oddly enough, the arctic annually receives the same amount of sunshine as Cuba, Senegal, or Thailand, but it comes all at once. Life in the noble, newborn territory moved in an unbearable cycle: three months of fren-zied tilling, sowing, and reaping followed by nine months of cabin fever—"a twelve-foot stare in a ten-foot room"—brought on more by lin-gering darkness than by cold. Sooner rather than later, most of the small farmers who didn't shoot themselves (or someone else) after succumbing to the neurasthenic condition once called prairie derangement in the Old West packed up and returned home.

Trekking south, many congregated at the Anchorage train depot, and a few resolved to eke out a living above the spruce and quaking aspen–covered clay cliffs that loom over the frigid gray waters of Cook Inlet. These settlers transformed the tiny railroad spur into what was gen-erously referred to as a town, although "crossroads" was a more accurate description. Like the sea captains and missionaries before them, immi-grants merely passed through Anchorage, on their way to communities with names like Bearpaw, Chicken, Sleetmute, and Tok. The town's pop-ulation remained well under 2,000 until after World War II.

The war was key in promoting the development of south-central Alaska in general, and Anchorage in particular. Fearing—presciently, as it turned out—a Japanese invasion, the Army broke ground on Fort Richard-son in May 1940 a few miles northwest of the railroad junction. A year later Alaska secured its first National Guard. In the wake of Japan's attack on Pearl Harbor, the state's tactical importance as a staging area for Pa-cific supply routes became evident, and the Defense Department ordered a troop buildup. In order to move men and material overland through Canada, the Army Corps of Engineers began construction on the Alaska-Canada Military Highway, or Alcan Highway, in March 1942. Three months later, in a feint to draw U.S. naval forces away from the looming battle of Midway, the Japanese bombed Dutch Harbor in the Aleutians.

When Halsey's Pacific Fleet crippled Yamamoto's navy at Midway, Japan retaliated with an attack on the Aleutian chain's most westerly islands, Attu and Kiska. This established Japan forever, alongside the Mexican revolutionary Pancho Villa, as the only foreign adversaries to invade U.S. territory in the twentieth century. Unlike Villa, whose 1916 raid on the border town of Columbus, New Mexico, lasted but an afternoon, the Japanese forces in the Aleutians dug in for nearly a year.

Though far from strategic to the overall war effort, foreign occupation was an unthinkable affront, and the campaign to oust the Japanese was directed from Anchorage. It included several bloody skirmishes and, peculiarly, has been generally overlooked in the annals of military history. Although throughout late 1942 and early 1943 the United States lost more airmen to the implacable winds and storms that rake the Aleutians than to Japanese weaponry, 550 Americans (and 2,351 Japanese) were killed during the month-long battle to retake Attu in June 1943. Two months later, Alaska's wicked weather again worked to Japan's advantage when the 5,000-man Japanese garrison evacuated Kiska under dense fog. U.S. forces strafed and shelled the empty island for another three weeks, unaware that the Japanese had retreated. When American troops landed in force in late August, they were confronted by a few stray dogs.

The 1,520-mile Alcan Highway, completed in eight months in 1942, remains the only road into the territory. About the length of the mighty Ganges, the road is one of the world's most daunting testaments to man's mastery of nature and is credited, rightly, with opening Alaska and transforming Anchorage. But even at that, progress was slow. Thirty years after V-J Day—and more than a decade after Alaska became the forty-ninth state—Anchorage's main street was still closed to automobile traffic for several hours each day to allow bush pilots to land and take off. And today, despite its cosmopolitan reputation as Alaska's financial, commercial, and communications center, to its quarter-million residents the city retains a rough, frontier feel.

Sour-smelling saloons, pawnshops, and musty fur outlets form a haphazard checkerboard with glistening shopping malls, modern art galleries, and glass-walled government office buildings that appear to have put down surreptitiously in the middle of the night, like a fleet of gleaming spaceships. In winter a creeping ice fog swaddles the city in a glowing soup. Take-out coffee freezes in its cardboard containers, truck tires square against the ground, and taxi drivers find it more efficient to leave their cabs idling all night rather than constantly jump-start their dead batteries. One hour southeast of the city lies the beautiful Portage Valley, which in mid-May remains buried under twenty-seven feet of snow. Most American municipalities require that their sewer and water pipes be buried at least eighteen inches below ground to keep them from freezing. Alaskan lines are planted ten feet deep.

Conversely, after a few short weeks of "spring," summer nights never achieve that serious dark we all grew up to be afraid of. Instead, as the sun struggles to set, the pellucid subarctic sky softens from a pale yellow to orange to milky green to, finally, a dark mauve twilight that passes for night. On the summer solstice, softball games and golf tournaments throughout Alaska—Fairbanks is home to the three northernmost golf courses in the Western Hemisphere—schedule midnight starts. It is about this time that the foreign-registered cruise ships, most carrying more passengers than Alaskan cities have residents, begin arriving, and hapless tourists are greeted by grinning entrepreneurs hawking necklaces made of hardened moose droppings. The cultural effect is a blatant contradiction, like a Potemkin Village conceived and designed by the team of Davy Crockett and Abbie Hoffman. In Anchorage, owners of American-made four-by-fours with bumper stickers proclaiming "An Armed Society Is a Polite Society" dine in a plethora of New Age vegan cafés. And though the Green Party has more registered voters in Alaska than in any other state in the United States, eco-minded outsiders are soon set straight by a popular T-shirt that depicts a hugely oversized fishing pole, net, and harpoon above a caption exhorting visiting anglers to "Save the Whales—Collect the Whole Set." (The point may soon be moot, as the humpbacks are endangered, and scientists have recently discovered that the huge pods of orcas that migrate through Prince William Sound and the Kenai Fjords each spring are infected with toxic levels of industrial pollutants.)

Meanwhile, sophisticated patrons of the city's opulent orchestra, opera, and symphony halls are routinely stuck in traffic jams initiated by wandering moose. And during the spring and summer salmon runs, the local 7-Elevens advertise specials on sandbags while the banks of Ship Creek in the heart of downtown are lined two-deep with "urban subsistence fishermen" stocking up on the returning reds, kings, and chums that, flash-frozen and vacuum-packed, will provide winter sustenance for both families and dogs. The city has an aroma all its own, the local air heavy and moist with the sense-ravishing smell of fish, sea salt, diesel engines, and wood-burning stoves. Side streets act as fumaroles for the ubiquitous coffee shacks brewing thick, strong roasts.

Anchorage law enforcement and wildlife biologists receive more calls involving problem moose and bears than they do for robberies, bomb scares, liquor violations, escaped criminals, subjects resisting arrests, prostitution, and illegal aliens combined. One savvy entrepreneur recently struck it rich by marketing bottled wolf urine to suburbanites as an invisible shield for vegetable and flower gardens under attack from marauding moose during the fall rut. Fish and game officials, however, prefer to deal with the city's approximately one thousand unruly moose the old-fashioned way, by scaring them off with Roman candles. So far, they've set only one on fire.

The fact that humans are no longer at the top of the food chain in Alaska is a given. The ancient Greeks called the high north Arktikos, "the country of the great bear," and each spring brown bear attacks, about half of them fatal, dominate the headlines of the *Anchorage Daily News*. Recently, an American Legion baseball game on the outskirts of town was called when a silver-tipped grizzly, *Ursus arctos horribilis*, jumped the center field fence. Not too far away, another 800-pounder lumbered up a salmon stream flush with sockeyes as red as poinsettias, pounced on a sow's wandering cub, and devoured him in front of twenty-three horrified tourists. Perhaps what best sums up the city's nonchalant gestalt to sharing bear territory is the reaction of the suburban Anchorite whose beloved Pomeranian ended up a snack for a prowling wolf. "I'm kind of in shock," the man told a local newspaper. "I thought if anything'd ever get ol' Butch, it'd be a griz."

In 1974, six years after the discovery of the vast oil fields on Prudhoe Bay, construction began on the North Slope Haul Road, a gravel strip that runs from Fairbanks through the mighty Brooks Range to the arctic coast. A year later, the first pipe was laid on the $8 billion, 800-mile Trans-Alaska Pipeline, a silver ribbon of noncorrosive steel which snakes from the North Slope to the port of Valdez on Prince George Sound. Its effects are felt throughout the state, most prosaically in the form of the annual cash payment to each Alaskan resident from the interest on what is called the Permanent Fund. In 1976, voters approved a constitutional amendment to establish the Alaska Permanent Fund, in which a percentage of all private oil, gas, and mineral lease rentals and royalties is placed in a trust. This principal must be reinvested annually and cannot be spent without a plebiscite. But a part of the interest dividend from what has grown into a $26 billion pool is distributed yearly to every man, woman, and child who has lived in the state for at least one year. At the turn of the millennium the figure was about $1,700 per person. The Permanent Fund, combined with no state income tax, is not only an incentive for "outsiders" (especially those with large families) to emigrate north, but also makes Alaskans—despite their "Dish Night at the Movies" reputation—perhaps the most knowledgeable Americans when it comes to the minutia of oil and gas fields from Angola to Azerbaijan.

Anchorage and the bush beyond remain by nature a land of immigrants. The Alaskan median age is 31.5 years, second youngest in the country, trailing only Utah. And though whites now make up 78 percent of the state's population, an Alaska-born resident of European heritage over the age of twenty-one is as rare as the musk oxen which once roamed the vast, knobby tundra in herds of thousands. The individuals who emigrate to Anchorage and points north come seeking possibility as much as community. They pride themselves on being a practical, isolated, and, in many cases, anachronistic breed. Like pioneers in the Old West, they were enticed by the territory's natural beauty, employment opportunities, and the prospect of beginning life afresh. Some, naturally, encountered more than they bargained for, perhaps one reason Anchorage ranks fourth among all U.S. cities in the consumption of alcohol. Most, however, adjusted to the north country's rigors. They had no choice.

A virulent strain of libertinism courses through the Alaskan electorate's collective psyche to such an extent that it was once feared that the future state's two elected senators and one congressman would be agents of the Communist Party. This sentiment was somewhat ameliorated when, in 1946—the same year bikinis were unveiled at the Paris fashion shows and Bugsy Siegel opened the Flamingo Hotel in Las Vegas—an anti-labor shiver shot through the state's workforce when steelworkers, coal miners, and railroad workers went on strike down in the Lower 48. Belying their "pink" reputation, Alaskans cheered when Harry Truman seized the coal mines and threatened to snatch the railroad. And though one of the state's major political movements, the Alaska Independence Party, was formed for the expressed purpose of seceding from the Union, most newly minted Alaskans seem content to remain Americans. With good reason.

The state's senior senator, septuagenarian Republican Ted Stevens, has mastered the art of pork barrel legislation. The military has always had a friend in Stevens, whose procurement of money for Air Force bases and Army forts is legendary. But lately Stevens, chairman of the powerful Senate Appropriations Committee, has outdone himself, earmarking approximately $273 in federal funds for every Alaskan man, woman, and child. Some of Stevens' pet projects included $2.5 million to train Russian workers in Alaskan oil management, $15 million for the University of Alaska to study the aurora borealis, $4 million to aid stranded sea lions, $22 million in emergency financing for four tiny panhandle towns suffering from the timber industry's decline, and $5 million to monitor fish in the Bering Sea, a body of water subject to two seasons—four months of fog and eight months of ice—that accounts for 31 percent of the world's commercial catch. The executive director of the Bering Sea Fisheries Association gushed that Stevens has been a "godsend." He also dispelled any Natty Bumppo–like reflection by adding, "You can't lard it on too thick."

By and large, however, Alaskan politicians tend more toward Cincinnatus than the usual assortment of invertebrate Beltway drones. Senators, governors, and local representatives are chosen from a rugged pool of bush pilots, second-generation homesteaders, and trading post operators, and third party presidential candidates usually fare well. Minnesota governor Jesse Ventura may be the peculiar flavor of the month in the Lower 48, but Alaskans will stack him up against their sole congressional representative, Republican Don Young, any day. Young's eccentricity is considerable even by the standards of the state he represents. A former Yukon tugboat captain, he once lost an election to a dead man, and has the unusual habit of interrupting his stump speech to perform an impromptu impersonation of a rabbit dying slowly in a leg trap.

The loopiness is contagious, even within the academic community. The University of Alaska-Anchorage course catalogue recently listed a class on Alaska winter survival that required "good physical condition to allow participation in overnight field trips in below-freezing weather and snow conditions." The catalogue also provided dates for a "makeup weekend" in case the weather was good.

Yet there is an implicit sense of peril underlying every aspect of life in the northern territories, even for something as mundane as a university course in practical outdoorsmanship. Anyone who braves the frontier knows that Alaska can kill you in a million subtle, and not-so-subtle, ways.

Two summers ago, on an unusually warm evening in late June, a class of twelve students and two instructors from the beginner's mountaineering program at the University of Alaska-Anchorage began a descent down the north face of a stubby little mountain in the Chugach called Ptarmigan Peak. Ptarmigan Peak rises near the center of the range, and on a clear day its 4,880-foot crest can be spotted from downtown Anchorage, about fifteen miles away. The mountain, named after Alaska's ubiquitous state bird, looms over a picturesque narrow valley of Sitka spruce and golden dwarf willow named, for evident reason, Powerline Pass.

On this fine summer evening, the class instructors, seasoned and professional by all accounts, had chosen one of Ptarmigan's snow-crusted ravines to demonstrate a fairly rudimentary technique of downclimbing called plunge-stepping—extending a leg out and down with each step while gaining purchase in the snow with the heel of one's boot. The students and teachers were roped together in four teams along a snow chute sloping 45 degrees, not much steeper than an expert ski trail. Then one novice climber on the uppermost team lost his axe-hold and began to tumble down the mountainside, initiating a chain reaction that continued for 2,000 feet. The students peeled off the couloir one by one and, tangled in ropes and climbing gear, plummeted in an accelerating ball of humanity. Survivors recall bouncing from one exposed boulder to another like pebbles in a landslide. The entire class, one student remembers, "finally landed in a big dog pile on a large rock." The fourteen were still roped to one another. Two were dead.

The accident occurred in full daylight, and was reported immediately by several hikers and late-season skiers. Within moments two Pavehawks from the 210th had ferried a squad of eleven pararescuemen, who, fighting the helo's rotor wash, rappelled down to the slender ledge of unstable scree where the class had come to rest. There they were eventually joined by two paramedics from the Anchorage Fire Department and eight volunteers from the volunteer Alaskan High Mountain Rescue Team, including a doctor, Ken Zafren.

"Everyone alive was still basically a critical patient," Dr. Zafren wrote in a subsequent issue of the journal *Alaska Medicine*. "As the PJs arrived, I pointed them to the most severely injured. There were too many for one person to keep straight."

The bloodied survivors were packed so tightly along the ledge that the mission's team leader, PJ Brent Widenhouse, recalls, "It was hard to treat one without stepping on another." The victims were suffering from open head wounds, compound fractures, shock, and concussions. In addition, Dr. Zafren reported, several climbers were asphyxiated by ropes, while others, buried under the pile, were also slowly running out of air. Most were drifting in and out of consciousness, and one student was found splayed across a precariously balanced boulder that had to be secured before any medical treatment could be contemplated. Lashing and airlifting the triaged survivors to Miller board litters proved even more difficult to choreograph. Lives hung in the balance, but almost any movement tended to erode the tenuous rubble slope. In addition, the rotor downwash from the Pavehawk's two giant turboshaft engines not only blew rescuers off their feet, but also coalesced with the cooling night air over the snowfield to put every victim at risk of hypothermia.

"The patients were freezing, but one by one we got them strapped to Miller boards, or to vacuum mattresses, and then into the hoist litters," says Widenhouse, a laconic master sergeant from North Carolina whose thick accent sometimes requires a translator. "Those damn pilots were hovering right above us, with no more than forty feet between the mountain and the tips of their rotors. I was waiting for one to drop on my head."

In addition, Powerline Pass is such a tight pocket valley that the Pavehawks were operating at the end of their 200-foot hoist cables. With so much cable out, a stray gust of wind can send a Stokes litter careening straight into a cliff. The recovery took on an assembly-line rhythm. While one Pavehawk hoisted and ferried injured climbers to Anchorage's Providence Hospital, another was air-refueled by an HC-130 flying high overhead. It took six hours to treat and evacuate every injured climber from the mountainside. All twelve survived.

Today, at the summit of a small hillock along Powerline Pass, a handcrafted cedar bench has been placed as a memorial to forty-year-old Mary Ellen Fogarty and twenty-three-year-old Stephen Brown, the two students killed in the accident. From there one has a magnificent vista of the valley and, beyond, Ptarmigan Peak. Often, when visiting para-jumpers pull TDY in Anchorage, PJs from the 210th will hike them up to the spot, where they will sit amid the dried bouquets, rock cairns, and framed, faded photographs of Fogarty and Brown, contemplating the fragility of life in the bush, absentmindedly popping wild blueberries into their mouths.

Says Widenhouse, his vowels sticking to the tar of his Carolina accent, "Some of the guys tell me they envision that scene—choppers swooping through the air, PJs scrambling all over the mountain, I mean just total pandemonium—every time they head up into the Chugach. Some people think that the bottom line with the military is, if there's no war, nobody really has a job. Which is not a bad thing. Nobody's hoping for people to get in trouble just so we can go rescue them. That's the thing about the team. If we never did another civilian rescue, as unrealistic as it sounds, that'd be fine. But the reason it's unrealistic is because somebody's always falling over the edge out here." He pauses. "Alaska's a big country, you know. It has lots of edges."

Mike Wayt makes the last right turn off Spenard before the exit to International Airport Road—Anchorage is the kind of town where all roads seem to lead to the airport—and pulls into The Section. The twenty-odd parking spaces are jammed with mud-splattered American four-by-fours, interspersed with the occasional Jeep. Three Harley-Davidson Roadmasters stand sheltered beneath the canopy that juts from the front entrance. The building is a rectangular, flat-roofed, cin-derblock structure painted a fading canary yellow. On the front façade, to the right of the volleyball net, someone has painted a beautiful, life-sized angel—wings spread, blonde hair flowing, outstretched arms cradling the earth. Above her, in black block lettering, reads the parares-cue force's slogan: "That Others May Live."

The 36,000-square-foot building once served as an armory for Alaska's Army National Guard, but was abandoned in the 1980s during a cost-cutting campaign. After the 210th was formed in 1990, the PJs leapt at the chance to occupy the depot. Classic self-starters, they set up shop before anybody told them they couldn't. The 210th's official command center is on Kulis Air Base, three miles away, on the far side of Anchorage International Airport. But Colonel Ron Parkhouse, the squadron's CO and the same pilot who holds the Pavehawk altitude record for his rescue of Bin Hong Kim, considers it kismet that his Special Forces outfit found a home near enough to respond immediately to fast-breaking alerts yet far enough away from Kulis that its baser instincts don't contaminate his flight crews and support staff. "It doesn't hurt to sort of keep them penned up over there, all in one place, where you can keep an eye on them," the forty-two-year-old Parkhouse admits as he straddles the hard-backed wooden chair in his tiny office. "I know a lot of commanders who hate the PJs," he continues with a wolfish smile. "PJs are different. They like doing their own thing. They like seeing what they can get away with. But I love PJs. They're the reason we're different. One thing you can say about them: you never have to kick 'em in the butt. Sometimes you have to rein them in, but you never have to kick 'em in the butt."

"McKinley Ron," as he's been dubbed, is the wing commander of the 210th Rescue Squadron of the Alaska Air National Guard, or AKANG, a segment of the United States Pacific Forces. Aside from the 210th, he is in charge of the 144th Airlift Squadron, also based at Kulis. The colonel is a big, gruff man with intense brown laser eyes. Tiny scars form parentheses around his mouth. Qualified as both a fixed-wing and helicopter pilot, he still flies a Pavehawk on a regular alert rotation. And though he secured his MBA after graduating from the Air Force Academy (as the PJs are quick to point out, uttering the word "academy" with the same inflection a Boston longshoreman might say "Harvard"), his demeanor is that of a dignified ice pick. In short, Parkhouse looks as if he could hospitalize a brick.

The parajumpers find their headquarters arrangement much to their liking, and whenever an officer happens to come nosing around The Section, any number of PJs inevitably discover that they have fallen behind on their intravenous injection proficiencies. The call for volunteers to donate a vein acts in much the same manner as an electrified fence or a "Vicious Guard Dog on Premises" sign.

On the sidewalk leading to The Section someone has stenciled two 5-foot Jolly Green Giant footprints, the unofficial insignia of the pararescue service. The roots of this icon are murky, clouded by whiskey and legend. In the generally accepted account, the symbol was born one evening in 1971, when two pararescuemen stationed in Vietnam found themselves in states of questionable sobriety in a joint called the Jolly Dusty Hooch Bar. As luck would have it, the Jolly Dusty was adjacent to a tattoo parlor. After inestimable bottles of the local spirits, both PJs reached the profound conclusion that their career field was in dire need of an emblem that was at once enduring and emblematic of valor. They hit upon the Jolly Green Giant feet—most likely in tribute to the era's HH-3 troop-carrying helicopter whose nickname was the Jolly Green Giant—and later that night had the image tattooed onto their glutei maximi. The tattoo—and its location—has since blossomed into tradition. Like PJs worldwide, most members of the 210th accept the ritual, and in certain circles it is considered a serious breach of etiquette to not display these historic symbols of pride, valor, and commitment to the corps upon the mere asking. There are bartenders and waitresses throughout Anchorage who can describe the tattoo down to its eight stubby green toes.

Before jerking open The Section's double fire doors, Mike eyes a single-engine Cessna floatplane making its final approach onto Lake Hood. The small ribbon of water, chock-a-block to PJ headquarters, is the busiest seaplane base in the world, averaging over 230 daily takeoffs and landings per year. That number rises to around 800 during peak summer months. The bog lake's two acres of shoreline is parceled into 316 float-plane slips; the waiting list to rent one, at $100 a month, is sixteen years long. The bush pilots have been flying off the lake since 1927, and despite the steady encroachment of civilization, it is going to take a lot more than a few three-star hotels and spotless Starbucks franchises to erase the legacy of Alaska's flying lunatics. There is a saying among the PJs about the bush pilots: "Every one a potential customer."

By the Federal Aviation Administration's conservative estimate, Alaska is home to about 8,050 private planes and 10,605 registered pilots, or one for every 58 residents. This is approximately fourteen times as many planes per capita, and six times as many pilots per capita, as the rest of the United States. And the numbers are growing. Yet because there are only 150 FAA inspectors to monitor the entire state, the agency's statistics don't encompass the innumerable aircraft owners who simply "forget" to register their planes or, if registered, fail to maintain them to federal standards. The state has 325 airports, 1,000 recorded landing areas, and 102 seaplane bases, but, in a pinch, any dirt road, glacier, or puddle of bog water will do. There are thus many pilots fending for themselves in a harsh interior larger than Texas and Oklahoma combined who view the FAA's regulations as not only unnecessary but also intrusive. Scores of these bush planes, in the words of one PJ, "are held together with little more than duct tape and baling wire." Moreover, Alaska's 570,374 square miles are graced with only three major highways and crosshatched by a primitive road system frequently washed out or snowed under. Airplanes are the only practical mode of long-distance travel for the vast number of the state's residents—not to mention the million or so tourists who swarm the territory every year.

This sense of isolation is not confined to Eskimo fish camps on the Seward Peninsula or remote wildcatter dormitories on the Beaufort Sea. Juneau, for example, has a population smaller than seventeenth-century Boston, and is the only American state capital inaccessible by road from the rest of the continent. (The Governor's Mansion is mere blocks from a prime grizzly bear habitat.) For an Alaskan citizen interested in observing his state government at work (or at play), a trek to the panhandle by plane, boat, or dogsled is the only option. Given the circumstances, pilots and passengers regard their aircraft in much the same manner "outsiders" from the Lower 48 view automobiles, trains, and buses. This drives FAA regulators crazy. "Alaskans fly everywhere," says a bemused Kent Adams, who manages the flight standards division for the FAA's Anchorage office. "To hunt. To camp. To fish. And three-quarters of them never file flight plans. The aviation community up here is more, shall we say, utilitarian. Combined with our 'last-frontier' attitude, this makes for the diciest flying in the United States."

The nature of the terrain adds to the precariousness of air travel. Alaska is rough and mountainous and wet. Seventeen of the twenty highest peaks in the United States rise within its borders, and ruthless storm fronts the size of small European countries bewitch and disorient even the most experienced pilots. It's the rare PJ who hasn't run a "body drag" out to the abattoir known as Merrill Pass, a winding gap through

the Alaska Range about one hundred miles west of Anchorage intersected by a maze of box canyons and granite parapets. The Tanaina
Indian name for Merrill Pass is *Tutnutl'ech'a Tustes,* or Dark Water Pass,
and there is a saying that the snow along these dead ends runs crimson
with the blood of bush pilots and their passengers. It is not much of an
exaggeration. Yet even over the flatlands, screaming low-pressure areas
pouring in from the sea make an aviator's life hell. In addition, Alaska
has its fair share of "summer fliers," pilots whose skills become rusty during the long, night-shrouded winter. Finally, unlike the Lower 48, Alaska
is too huge to be covered in its entirety by radar stations. Add up these
factors and it is astonishing that the state averages a mere 53 aircraft
crashes and 10 fatalities per year (although those numbers will undoubtedly continue to rise as the growing tourism industry attracts more and
more "flightseeing" outfits).

Mike smiles broadly as a floatplane buzzes the new Marriott Court-
yard Hotel across the street from The Section. The three-story Marriott is
situated precisely beneath the flight line of floatplanes taking off from
and landing on Lake Hood, and the parajumpers amused themselves for
a year when the pilots used the construction site as a target range, lob-
bing beer cans and liquor bottles down the hotel's rooftop garbage chute.
To throw away excess lumber and building materials, construction workers had installed an open chute, the size of a large manhole, that snaked
down the side of the hotel into a green metal Dumpster. They may as well
have painted a bull's-eye on the building. Every few weeks the Dumpster
brimmed with the dregs of Count Smirnoff and empty cans of Alaskan
Amber, and the hotel's owners accused the workers of drinking on the
job. The PJs knew better. They remember it sounding like London during
the Blitz.

The Cessna buzzes The Section and Mike walks through the front
double doors, past the chin-up bar and the two mountain bikes leaning
against the six-foot Inuit totem pole. He strides past the tiny office supply
room and into the larger office area cut into two separate rooms by a
corkboard wall that holds the team's history. The partition is papered
with rosters, daily schedule assignments, briefing notes, etchings of
pararescuemen in action from Vietnam to Desert Storm, after action
reports, climbing posters, calendars with majestic aerial photos of Denali
and the Alaska Range, snapshots of PJs in various states of flight, phone

messages, proficiency memos, announcements about base hockey games and ski outings, jump sign-up lists, triathlon applications, dates for paramedic proficiency courses. Ernest Hemingway wrote that on the battlefield, "there is always much paper about the dead." He should have seen a pararescue section.

The bisected offices are congested with tan head-high file cabinets and sixteen government-issue, gunmetal gray desks. Each workstation is buried under reams of paper, old electric typewriters, telephones, Rolodexes, the occasional laptop computer, yellowing newspapers, and ever more schedules. The veterans have their own desks. The newer PJs share. In the rear of the far office a small, four-foot-by-ten-foot workspace has been carved out. This serves as team leader Garth Lenz's office. Brown wall-to-wall carpeting, threadbare and stained, covers the entire front half of the building.

Lenz is standing outside his office, addressing two men in mufti. "This place looks like such a mess because we're always in crisis management," Mike overhears him telling his two visitors. Mike recognizes one of the civilians as Bob LaPointe, a retired PJ who is researching the military history of the pararescue service for a book he hopes to publish. Mike doesn't know the other, but assumes he's a friend of LaPointe's, probably tagging along for the Cook's Tour.

Mike turns for the day room, and as he walks away catches the end of Garth's spiel. "Let's face it, we're a reactionary force," the chief is saying. "We can't plan for more than two days ahead."

SIX

Thunder Mountain

It is the sins we do not commit we regret.

—ANCIENT GREEK PROVERB

he arctic thermals sweep the scent of fresh snow before them, across the tundra from the Bering Sea, down the cordillera's west face, and out over the glacial bowl. The cold, metallic tendrils flick at Malcolm Daly's cheeks and nose well before he sees the squall. The sky directly above is robin's egg blue, and ice crystals mirroring the bulbous yellow sun wink about the frost like flashbulbs at Yankee Stadium. Malcolm and his climbing partner, Jim Donini, are making their third attempt at the ice wall on Thunder Mountain, and both men are eager to move on to Mount Hunter, the third-highest peak in the Alaska Range and the reason they've come to Denali National Park in the first place. It is Friday, May 21, 1999, and it looks to be a perfect day for climbing. Lifting the tent flap, Malcolm scarcely notices the towering thunderhead, the color of charcoal, draped like bunting upon Thunder's summit.

After eight days at altitude Malcolm's golden beard is nearly full. His thick, reddish-blond curls, going silver at the temples, are greased back from his forehead, as sleek as an otter's belly. At nearly five ten and a lean 165 pounds, Malcolm is buff, if not quite Stallone-ish, with soft, wide gray-green eyes and an aquiline nose. A lifetime of climbing has knotted his shoulder and calf muscles into the hardness of peach pits, and he gives the impression of an overanxious Viking as he thrashes about the cramped four-season tent, squirming into his vapor barrier boots and pulling his Gore-Tex climbing suit over his polypro longjohns and one-piece, polar fleece windbreaker. He flashes an altar boy's grin at his partner. Let's just get this damn ridge out of the way, he says. His voice sounds gargled, as if filtered through river silt.

Jim Donini looks up from his new crampons and manages a narrow, rapid smile, like a sudden crack in ice. When Jim smiles he looks as if he just shot a puppy. He has a long, angular body, sloping shoulders, and a dark cast to his eyes that makes Malcolm think of Clint Eastwood in *Unforgiven*. "Today we do it," Jim says with a grunt, and turns back to examining his crampons.

This is Malcolm's first expedition to Alaska, and his frustration over their struggles on what was supposed to be a "tidy little warm-up" climb is tempered by his appreciation of the sights, sounds, and even smells atop this corner of the world. Reveling in this country's utter wildness, he has come to realize that an Alaskan alpine ascent, as Ambrose Bierce remarked about a hanging, concentrates a man's mind wonderfully on what may come next. Malcolm crawls from the tent and steps into what could be a scene from the last Ice Age—a hostile world of black granite, blinding white snow, and blue ice stretching to the horizon in every direction. Despite the warm morning, perhaps 10 degrees Fahrenheit with steady western gusts dropping the wind chill to near zero, the glacier appears to Malcolm to tremble with frigid intent. Looming above him is the 3,500-foot headwall of Thunder Mountain, speckled with vertical snowfields and riven with ice runnels, twisting couloirs, and daunting snow cornices. Near the summit a rock chimney rises to form a gunsight notch that frames a sheer, snow-crusted gully, its glistening spire reminiscent of a flying buttress adorning the Notre Dame Cathedral.

Malcolm and Jim wolf a breakfast of bread and canned tuna, gulp strong tea, and hike the quarter mile to the base of the headwall. They could be mistaken for mountain wraiths crossing the deserted glare ice, their features hidden by balaclavas, ice axes swinging at their sides, each with a two hundred–foot coil of dynamic, or high-stretch, nylon rope slung over his shoulder. They travel light, casting long shadows under a domed firmament edged with pink and orange. Aside from their climb-

ing rack—ascenders and carabiners, an assortment of ice and rock protection, all hooked into their nylon harnesses—each totes in his rucksack several quarts of water and a handful of Power Bars. Malcolm has
also packed two rolls of duct tape and a vial of painkillers in his emergency medical kit.

Both men know the drill from their earlier attempts at the massif.
They will begin by ascending nearly a thousand feet, varied climbing up a
50-degree slope. This will lead to 1,300 feet of grade six ice steps—technical, near vertical, about as difficult as alpine climbing gets. The route,
laced with icefalls, chutes, and overhanging cliffs, is akin to shinnying up
the Statue of Liberty after it has been doused with water and flash-
frozen. Over the final 1,000 feet the buttress will diminish to a rolling
snowfield, a hikable ridge with no need for a belay.

They climb in tandem, unroped, for six hours, settling into a work-
man-like rhythm and setting small pyramid-shaped stoppers between
free moves over the hard, mixed terrain. They are often out of each
other's sight, and less experienced climbers would have roped up from
the base, but Malcolm and Jim did not feel the need. By nine in the morning they are right on schedule. They have reached the bottom of the ice
wall. The ice is still firm and smooth, what climbers call plastic, and each
swing of the axe resonates with a crisp ping. They judge the chute to be a
seven-pitch climb, each pitch, or stage, constituting perhaps 180 feet.
They set their belay and take turns in the lead. Four hours later, less than
one hundred feet of ice remains. Malcolm twists in his stance and hands
Jim his rock gear. He will be lighter if he leads the final pitch over the last
gnarled swath of shadowed ice without it. The hexcentric chocks and
camming devices will only slow him down.

Before taking the rack Malcolm cocks his ear. Somewhere out over
the glacier, the steady whine of a small, fixed-wing bush plane echoes
through the granite corridors. All day they have listened to an inordinate
amount of air traffic over the range, both fixed wing and rotor. To climbers
in Alaska, the sound is as portentous as a death rattle. And it seems to be
increasing. Malcolm fixes a last ice screw before turning to Jim.

Must be people in trouble over on Denali, he says.

There's always people in trouble over on Denali, Jim murmurs.

.   .   .

Exploration, technology, civilization. Each has diminished the opportunities for adventure in the modern world. Lost are the lands into which our ancestors entered to risk their lives. Of the last perilous places on earth, it is the mythmaking mountains that have lured the most ardent supplicants. Outside of its adherents, the mottled glamour of mountain climbing is little fathomed and less appreciated. It attracts a breed of human being both zealous and vainglorious, men and women whose driving goal is to flow through the spaces humanity has left vacant, to stand atop a portion of the planet where no one else has ever been. World-class mountaineers belong to an exclusive, arrogant, and oddly addictive club, one whose motto may as well be lifted from the provos of the Irish Republican Army: Once in, never out. Malcolm Daly is a charter member.

An accomplished rock hound since the age of fourteen, Malcolm is known throughout the climbing community near his home in Boulder, Colorado, as a man who can handle himself in a pinch. Eight years before he'd incorporated his own climbing equipment company, Great Trango Holdings—named in honor of Pakistan's "unclimbable" tower—and built it from scratch into a multimillion-dollar concern. Along the way he'd scampered up and down both sides of the Rockies, served as a volunteer on myriad mountain rescue teams, and had once led an expedition into the snaggletoothed moonscape of the Patagonian archipelago. Malcolm also possesses the kind of hail-fellow good humor that inspires friends and strangers to gravitate toward his circle, whether it is etched in frozen mountain base camps or at urbane Colorado cocktail parties. With all this he has accrued a small measure of celebrity within the alpine community. But he readily admits that whatever regard he is held in is due less to his abilities than to his longevity in the game, to the fact that he owns a climbing business, and to his reputation as "a nice guy who hasn't made any enemies."

Six months ago, in November, he'd decided to spend his forty-third birthday testing himself against the Alaska Range. Subarctic expedition climbing had long been Malcolm's dream, as neither the Rockies nor Patagonia could offer the magnificent scale, unpredictable weather, or utter isolation he would face in Alaska. Blowing a move on a mountain outside of, say, Vail, was one thing. If a climber was injured, he was never far from an interstate highway and instant first aid. But in Alaska the odds are greater that the ravens will peck your eyes out before a rescue party arrives—if it can find you at all. On their flight into the range he and Jim both took notice of the body of twenty-eight-year-old Josh Hane dangling by his belay line from Hunter's west wall. Hane died in an avalanche three years ago, his corpse unrecoverable.

Now, suspended from the ice wall of Thunder Mountain, Malcolm takes a deep gulp of thin, biting air and exhales a curling stream of breath. As his blood thickens with the altitude, his thoughts flash incongruously to the Flatirons, the symmetric, 65-degree panel of rocks that loom over Boulder like a set of giant marble tombstones. The trail leading up to the Flatirons begins in a parking lot of a municipal park, and after a quarter-mile hike a climber is faced with a 1,000-foot rock wall from base to summit. Mounting the Flatirons requires a lot of traversing and ridge work, and if you rope up every pitch the ascent totals perhaps fourteen pitches in all. Climbers will usually set off around six in the morning and take most of the day to summit. Malcolm has flashed it, round trip without rope, in forty-six minutes flat. Belayed to the wall of this little mountain no one back home has ever heard of, a mountain with its Mickey Mouse name, he is nearing the completion of an ascent nearly four times that length. He pretty much feels that it doesn't get any better than this. Climbing Thunder Mountain requires a mix of every discipline he has ever honed. It takes special skills to be able to move smoothly and efficiently over the variety of ice, rock, and snow Alaska throws at you in the course of one climb. Malcolm had grown weary of making excuses to himself for never having tried. He knows in his heart he'll be good at it.

Just after Christmas he'd approached his friend Jim Donini about partnering up. Donini is a weathered technical climber who had pioneered first ascents from the Himalayas to China to Pakistan. Cranky old Jim, whom one climbing magazine dubbed "Donini-a-saurus," has led annual expeditions into Alaska for two decades. His north country résumé includes pioneer ascents up Mounts Foraker and Barrille, and in 1989 he just missed completing the first ascent of the avalanche-prone east ridge of Mount Wake on the Ruth Gorge, a route veteran climbers liken to free-climbing a pissed-off white rhino. When alpinists recount his climbs, the word "epic" becomes a verb. In contrast to Malcolm's natural good humor, Jim projects the countenance of an alpine Ichabod Crane—a gaunt, fifty-five-year-old with a face as craggy and pinched as the Matterhorn, deep-set blue eyes the color of glacial ice, and a high, sloping forehead set beneath grizzled tufts of hair the tint and texture of iron filings. A former Green Beret and self-described "purist" who sneers at the "yuppie peak-baggers" slogging up Denali for mere summit bragging rights, Jim is renowned for his all-out assaults on the world's most difficult technical routes, as well as his desperate descents. It is his contention that peak-bagging and climbing are two different activities requiring two different mentalities. The first measures success by notches in a belt. Everest, Aconcagua, Denali, Kilimanjaro. The latter is a cerebral test of one's uncertain will, an experience for experience's sake. At some points the skills, naturally, overlap. But what Jim and Malcolm have planned in Alaska is vastly different from anyone churning up the West Buttress.

Jim is notorious for his refusal to pack what other climbers view as necessary, backup safety equipment. "Superfluous bullshit" is his phrase for radios, portaledges, the odd spare tent, or even extra rope on his hazardous ascents. To him, the most important aspect of expedition climbing isn't choosing a mountain or packing the right gear, but selecting a partner. He's made it his habit, as often as possible, to climb with only one other person. He's watched too many climbers fail because of what he considered a lack of character that stoked a primal fear: fear of running out of food or fuel, fear that climbing conditions weren't perfect, fear of being out of contact with rescue parties. "You have to recognize when your imagination is cooking up excuses," he warns his climbing mates. "You have to force yourself to go on, no matter the circumstances." It is easier to preach this sermon to a congregation of one—to instill in a single partner the ethos of all or nothing.

Paramount to Jim's climbing character is his abhorrence of communication with the outside world. His credo is as simple as it is absolute: if you are set on conquering a mountain, sportsmanship demands that the mountain be given equal opportunity to conquer you back. To Jim, radios and satellite phones aren't what climbing is all about. He's proud of his "minimalism," and anyone who cares to climb with him will have to live with it. Although married three times and the father of two, Jim boasts of staring long hours at the Weather Channel upon checking into a hotel room on the road. He claims to be that rare human being who can be alone without being lonely. He earns his living as a sales rep, hustling climbing gear—including the Trango brand—to sports shops and outdoor stores throughout the central Rockies, and his reputation works to enhance his sales. But his passion is climbing; the more technically difficult the mountain, the happier he is. He once spent twenty-six days trapped in a storm on the western rampart of Karakoram in the shadow of K2, the second-highest mountain in the world, with only fourteen days' worth of food. He escaped by rappelling 8,000 vertical feet. "One of the best times in my life," he calls the experience. If Jim Donini were weather, he'd be sleet.

Five years ago Jim and his wife, Angela, had moved to Colorado from Washington State. In the incestuous climbing community centered around Boulder and Fort Collins, they sparked a friendship with Malcolm and Karen Daly, a fetching elementary school principal with a soft, lilting voice.

"You just have to get to know Jim, he's really a great guy," Karen Daly would tell friends put off by—or perhaps terrified of—his deadpan scowl. She'd winced as he once baited a pair of German climbers by insisting that Western Europe had turned into a backwater of civilization that would soon serve no purpose other than as a sort of quaint theme park for American and Japanese tourists. "You don't make anything we need anymore," Jim sneered. "And your small wars have no global implications." When he realized they were insulted, his idea of an apology was to add that he meant no offense, as they'd presently be joined in global insignificance by the eastern seaboard of the United States. But in her husband's eyes, Jim Donini was an icon. Malcolm stood in awe of his friend's strength and determination, and often repeated the story of how, two years earlier, Jim spent fifty-three hours, one for each year of his life, rappelling down Patagonia's mile-high, rapier-like Torre Cerro in a howling storm, buffeted by 100-knot gales, rime ice encrusting his body, his eyelids nearly frozen shut. Karen even noticed her husband adopting Jim's disdain for technology. Every time you add a layer of safety to a climb, she heard Malcolm tell his climbing crowd, you subtract some of the value of that climb. "I choose not to have a radio because it solidifies my commitment to what I'm trying to do up there." His friends rolled their eyes. Malcolm knew people thought he was crazy. He didn't care.

Jim was enthusiastic when Malcolm suggested an expedition to Alaska's Mount Hunter. Hunter is a broad, complicated mountain, with several extensive technical faces. Unlike the more celebrated Denali, there is no easy route to the summit. Fourteen years earlier Jim had pulled the first ascent up Hunter's Diamond Arete with the prominent Alaskan climber Jack Tackle, who just a few days before had given advice to Antony Hollingshead, Nigel Vardy, and Steve Ball as they struggled up Denali's West Rib. Jim hadn't been back on the mountain since. He considered Malcolm "an extremely strong partner" and told his wife, Angela, he liked "the cut of Malcom's jib." So, like Stradivarius approaching the worktable, Jim repaired to the library of the Boulder Alpine Club to fashion a virgin ascent up Mount Hunter, a 14,573-foot slab of granite experienced mountaineers consider the most arduous "fourteener" in North America.

During his research Jim happened upon an unclimbed route up the southwest shoulder of Mount Hunter. Although organically a part of the Hunter massif, the 10,970-foot cantilevered promontory was known locally as Thunder Mountain. "Thunder will be a tidy little warm-up," Jim enthusiastically told Malcolm. From the topographical maps he consulted, the route struck Jim as both a technical adventure and an aesthetically pleasing tune-up. He and Malcolm had planned on a three-week expedition, and Jim reckoned the Thunder ascent would give them time to acclimate to elevation before attacking Mount Hunter. The Thunder route would also furnish Malcolm with a suitable introduction to alpine Alaska. Jim favored the exploratory nature and problem-solving trials of first ascents, and in a rare burst of self-deprecation he'd advised Malcolm not to worry, "because if you bail on a first ascent it's not that embarrassing, since no one else has ever done it either."

Still, when presented with their itinerary, Malcolm had turned to Karen in mock disbelief. "Thunder Mountain? C'mon, what is this, some Disneyland ride?" Now, however, after two unsuccessful cracks at the near-vertical wall of black rock and ice, Malcolm was affording the prosaic peak its due respect.

Back in Colorado, some of Malcolm's closest friends questioned the motivation for his excursion. He had lately seemed out of sorts, and several wondered—quietly, and with concern, for everyone loved Malcolm and Karen—about the welfare of the Dalys' fifteen-year marriage. When Malcolm told her about this trip, Karen's first reaction was that, somehow, such a journey would be healthy for her husband's spirit. She couldn't articulate what had changed in their relationship—exactly when, where, or how the fragile fault lines of love and dependence had buckled and shifted. But she knew something was wrong. She found herself casually probing her girlfriends about their knowledge of mid-life crises. Lord, how she hated that hackneyed phrase. Still, her heart ached knowing that even their two young sons, Mason and Kitt, had sensed the ennui between their mother and father.

Deep down she knew her husband required this experience. His soul needs it, she told herself, like one of those characters in John Bunyan's *Pilgrim's Progress* seeking the path through the valley of Despond to the Celestial City. To go up onto that glacier and be alone with his friend, to talk about love and marriage and kids, to decide where he wanted to go with it all. Karen was only a casual climber, more of a hiker, really, but she instinctively grasped the hormonal drumbeat to which Malcolm periodically marched as he set off assaulting mountains. Without artificially constructed challenges, she knew, modern life was appallingly safe. Malcolm was genetically hardwired to abhor such constrictions. However this adventure turned out, whatever revelations Malcolm would come upon in those peaks, Karen assured herself that it could only have a positive effect on their lives.

Malcolm wouldn't have put it in quite those terms. In fact, for all his glibness he wasn't sure how he would have put it. When you're climbing, and climbing well, his argument ran, there is nothing else in your brain. Everything else takes a backseat. What I am doing in Alaska is pure and clean, and that in itself is its own biggest reward. No other sports "washed" his mind like a climb. Nothing else compelled him to put every thought aside and achieve that signal state of clarity. Even when he was on a pair of Nordic skis or chugging up a hill on his bicycle until his muscles cried out in anguish, it was impossible to stop thinking linearly, competitively. About going hard. About technique. About his standing in the race. But climbing for Malcolm was like meditation, like yoga, each aspect of the ascent a purifying experience.

Thus far, Alaska had not let him down.

.   .   .

Before heading into the mountains, Malcolm spent his first few days gearing up in the tiny village of Talkeetna, once the supply center of a gold mining district and now the staging area for 90 percent of the expeditions heading up onto Denali. Wedged into the confluence of the Chulitna, Susitna, and Talkeetna Rivers—the Tanaina Indian word "Talkeetna" roughly translates to "three rivers"—the 450 or so year-round residents of Talkeetna are civilization's outriders even by Alaskan bush standards. The town has a Unabomber feel to it, and it is rumored, only half jokingly, that the FBI could clear a passel of outstanding warrants if it raided Talkeetna's three jumping roadhouses on a Saturday night and ordered all the men to shave. Scalawags include the women. Now, during climbing season, Malcolm picked up snatches of conversation in Korean, French, Italian, Spanish, and Japanese as he hiked the town's Main Street. In the Latitude 62 barroom he stopped to study what at first appeared to be a wanted poster. Upon closer inspection he saw it was a flyer with a picture of a half-naked old geezer bathing in a river. The hand-lettered caption read, "Lost. Ole Jim. If seen, call Beau." Below the local phone number, in giant block letters, read the caveat, "DO NOT APPROACH!"

While in town Malcolm also renewed his old friendship with Park Service ranger Daryl Miller, with whom he went back nearly twenty years. In the early 1980s, Malcolm had founded the Experiential Learning Center at Colorado State University in Fort Collins. Its curricula, funded by the university and similar to the Outward Bound programs, consisted of noncredit courses from pottery making to aerobics to more strenuous field trips to climb Mexico's volcanoes or bike through the redrock canyons of southern Utah. In 1985, Daryl succeeded Malcolm as the program's director. Daryl had even shared an apartment with Sari Nichol, a climber and outdoor clothing designer who later became Malcolm's business partner in Great Trango Holdings.

At fifty-five, Daryl resembles a more compact version of the actor Jon Voight, down to the floppy, silver-hued bangs and chipmunk cheeks. He hadn't seen Malcolm in years, but he'd kept sketchy tabs on him through Sari and mutual friends who'd passed through Alaska. In the weeks before Malcolm's trip the two had exchanged e-mail and phone messages like old war buddies, and Daryl had thrown together plans for a salmon-fishing trip downvalley after Malcolm's return from Mount Hunter. For some reason, Daryl had even stuffed into his wallet the last phone message Malcolm left him prior to his arrival. Dated May 10, it read, "Your worst nightmare is approaching."

There is a saying among the PJs that relaxing with Daryl Miller is an exhausting experience. His physical strength is legendary. In the winter of 1995 he circumnavigated the Denali and Foraker massifs with the Alaskan backwoodsman Mark Stasik. Daryl wrecked his skis 100 miles into the 45-day, 350-mile traverse, and snowshoed the remainder of the course over twelve separate glaciers. He even broke through the ice into the Chulitna River. Glacier trekking notwithstanding, however, Daryl is the first to admit that he's done a "lot of stupid things in my life." Included in this résumé of imprudence is volunteering for two tours of duty in Vietnam with the Marine Corps (where he took shrapnel in a friendly-fire incident), deciding to become a hang-gliding pilot, getting hooked on mountain climbing, and spending a good portion of his youth as the "world's slowest rodeo clown."

In one memorable confrontation, an ornery Brama named Rattler pinned Daryl to a corral fence and raked his horns until Daryl's back vertebrae, spleen, and kidney were ruptured, several ribs cracked, and his skull concussed. "The riders loved me," he admits. "I was just so easy for the bulls to catch." After his first week on the job one of the cowboys predicted, "You'll be dead by Friday." And though he hung on for three more years, Rattler's goring was the final straw, and Daryl's rodeo days were over.

But none of his "hobbies," not even the 100-mile ultramarathons, have been quite so unwise as his stint with the three man-fighting chimps Congo, Butch, and Joe, the lead—and sometimes only—act in a broken-down, one-truck carnival called Noel's Ark, which Daryl nicknamed The Banana Warriors. This backwater roadshow was the brainchild of a former Greek sponge diver with the build and disposition of a cannon-ball named Bob Noel, whom Daryl met near Parris Island shortly after returning from his second tour in 'Nam in 1969. Somehow the effervescent carnie talked the Marine into signing on with his outfit. Noel would point his eighteen-wheeler throughout Georgia, Alabama, the Carolinas, and northern Florida, and in each new town he'd drop the broadsides of his truck to expose a wire-mesh cage holding his three chimps before heading for the nearest saloon. After sizing up the loudest drunk in the joint, he'd make a grand show out of daring the local tough guy to step in with one of his monkeys. He'd offer $25 to anyone who could go three minutes with Congo, Butch, or Joe, including a bonus of $100 per second for every second anyone could pin one. The only catch was a $1 admission fee for anyone who cared to watch their local heroes stomp a fellow primate.

To the indigenous pugilists, generally bullies fueled by Noel's copious rounds for the house, the offer appeared too good to be true. Once they saw their adversaries, it looked even better. None of the chimps, a flea-bitten lot, weighed much over 150 pounds. As Daryl remembers, "The general reaction would be, 'I'm gonna kill that fuckin' monkey.'" While gulling his marks, Noel made sure to keep his key chain out of sight. Attached to it were his four fingers that Congo had bitten off.

Come fight day, Noel made each contestant sign a dubious medical waiver before stepping into his caged rig. Then he would issue plastic hockey helmets to the human combatants and equip the fighting chimps with muzzles. "There's two ways you can't win a fight," Daryl says knowingly. "One is if you can't hurt the other guy. Two is if you can't hit the other guy. You couldn't hit or hurt these chimps."

When Noel blew his whistle Congo, Butch, or Joe charged across the cage like a hairy, black typhoon. The chimp would kick his human challenger full force in the head, rip off the helmet to use as a cudgel, and pick up the stunned human by the ankle and swing him over his head until he screamed for help. After the first fight there were rarely more takers. Of course, given the hooched-up disposition of many of the paying customers, they often felt they'd been snookered out of their admission fee by both the length and outcome of the competition. This is where Daryl came in. Before the unruly customers turned into a mob, Bob Noel would suit up Daryl, send him into the cage, and have him take a beating from one of the chimps. Hard experience had taught Noel that seeing a stranger monkey-handled, particularly a stranger who was a part of the outfit that had just relieved them of their entry fee, had a settling effect on the locals.

Yet despite Daryl's seemingly rough-and-tumble character, Denali's lead high-altitude mountain ranger has a blue spiritual side that he wears on his sleeve. Like his psychic forebears Jim Bridger and Jeremiah Johnson, Daryl has come to believe that it is easier to "get along" up in the mountains than it is down on the flatlands. "There's no false hopes of anyone caring about you up there," he says soulfully, much like his friend Malcolm Day. "It's just you versus nature."

Daryl once thought he would never do anything as mind-numbingly idiotic as fight a chimpanzee—until in 1981, at the age of thirty-six, he found himself heaving lung cookies down a sheer rock wall on the north face of Denali, stuck in one of the worst storms ever recorded in the Alaska Range. He'd climbed a few mountains in the Lower 48, Mexico, and South America, but this was his first Alaskan ascent. He remembers the experience as "a forty-four-day epic where I saw Jesus Christ at nineteen-six. I won the lottery and met the ayatollah, the mother of all storms. And I haven't seen one as brutal since."

Daryl had done "everything wrong that you can do wrong on a climb," from failing to adequately acclimate to altitude to forgetting to pack lip balm or wear his glacier goggles all the time. As he was to learn, on Denali even a broken microscrew on your sunglasses or a cracked ruck strap becomes a matter of life and death. "They brought me back down a rag doll. It was only after I *had* climbed Denali that I decided to learn how to climb Denali." He took every lesson to heart and two years later he climbed Wyoming's Devils Tower with his eleven-year-old son, Chan, who became the youngest person to reach the top. In 1985, four years after his first, disastrous Denali ascent and on his eighth attempt, Daryl not only summited the highest mountain in North America but also discovered his calling as a mountain ranger. He had always thought of himself as a square peg lacking even a round hole. In Denali National Park and Preserve, an area more than twice the size of Yellowstone, a restless Daryl Miller finally found his fief.

"I always thought that climbers were crazy," he says with a sharp laugh, explaining how he gladly substituted a sort of cultural vertigo for the real thing. "I was scared of heights. Christ, I'm still scared of heights. But fear is fine. All courage is controlled fear. It's when you are not afraid that the problems arise. If you lose complete fear of anything, you can't make good judgments. Still, if you'd told me twenty years ago I'd end up discovering my life's work on the highest mountain in North America, I'd've said you were nuts."

Like pararescuemen, high-altitude rangers like to say they aren't paid so much for what they do as for what they can do. Daryl settled down in Talkeetna and in 1991 was hired as one of the four permanent Park Service high-altitude rangers who patrol Denali. He was immediately tempered by the crucible of rescue. That July he was leading a patrol when a Polish climber, Krzystof Wiecha, became weathered in at 19,900 feet on his descent from the summit and sent a Mayday. Daryl and ranger Jim Phillips responded. The storm that kept Wiecha trapped in a snow cave for three days without food, water, or a sleeping bag also prevented the rangers from reaching him. When the gale broke Miller and Phillips were shuttled by the Lama from 14,200-foot relay camp to a ledge of unstable névé at 19,500 feet. They scrambled to Wiecha, now nearly comatose, strapped him into a litter basket, and spent more than three unacclimated hours making a series of technical rope-and-anchor descents over ice cliffs and around crevasses to a spot where the Lama could land and shorthaul Wiecha to safety. They saved the Pole's life, but could not save his feet. Both were amputated.

It takes some wheedling to drag it out of him, but by Daryl's unofficial count he's helped rescue close to forty stranded climbers and has administered lifesaving medical care to another two dozen over his decade in the mountains. He attributes this to his being "unlucky enough" to have patrolled the peaks during some of Denali's worst storms. But he hasn't been able to save every climber, and the losses have left their mark on his soul. Two Park Service patrol volunteers have died on Daryl's watch, and the year after the Wiecha rescue he again found himself plowing through a raging snowstorm in search of four Canadian climbers trapped on the Messner Couloir at 19,000 feet. Daryl and his patrol made it as far as 18,000 feet, where dangerous weather conditions led him to shut down the rescue. The Canadians, barely visible above through the scud and gale, were roped up, and Daryl watched from a ridgeline as the lead man in the expedition tripped and dragged his partners 3,000 feet to their deaths.

"It was my call to stop," he recalls haltingly, achingly, as if he were somehow complicit in their deaths. "We were in the middle of a whiteout, fifty-knot winds, at some points maybe fifteen feet of visibility. I didn't feel I could risk the lives of the volunteers under me. But watching them fall, the trauma they must have suffered, I still live with that. I sealed their coffins that afternoon by saying, 'No, it's too dangerous to go any further.' But it was the right decision. If we'd gone after those Canucks, somebody'd be up there looking for *our* bodies pretty quick after that."

Two seasons later, in 1994, two South Koreans climbing the West Buttress headwall, including a climber on an exchange program with the National Park Service, were flash-frozen by a sudden furious storm at 16,000 feet. To old Denali hands, the Koreans are considered the Irish of Asia: belligerent, tenacious, prone to showing off, but a boon if they're in your foxhole. But these two had deliberately walked into a maelstrom any sane man would have avoided. The next day Daryl and parajumper Steve Daigle discovered the body of one, still clinging to his rope line. "He was just hanging there, swinging, dead. I was shouting at him, hoping against hope he'd lift his head or wave an arm. It was haunting. I was up there shouting his name. And the echoes were bouncing off the mountain." The other climber's body was found the next day in the rocks at 16,000 feet.

But perhaps the hardest punch Daryl took was the death in 1998 of his good friend, thirty-three-year-old Park Service volunteer Mike Vanderbeek. For three-week stints each climbing season, Park Service Volunteers-in-Park, or VIPs, help the mountain rangers in organizing Denali's various camps and assist them on patrol. Mike, an expert climber who had grown up in Talkeetna, had been a VIP once before on Denali. Daryl had known Mike for eight years. He'd been his rope partner, his tent partner, and one of his best friends. On May 24, nearly a year to the day before Malcom Daly arrived in Talkeetna, Mike disappeared shortly after making a frantic call to Daryl at 14,200 camp, where he was standing patrol. It had been a good day for climbing and Vanderbeek was descending the West Buttress at 16,900 feet when he witnessed a Canadian peel off a ridge toward the Peters Glacier. Mike radioed the incident to Daryl, and said he was going after him. Witnesses later reported watching Vanderbeek lose his footing on the downclimb and plummet down a couloir. Daryl organized the search party that scoured the high cols for four days. They found the dead Canadian. Vanderbeek's body was never recovered.

After the search for Vanderbeek's body was called off, Daryl came off the mountain and spent three hours with Mike's parents over coffee in the Talkeetna Roadhouse, going through every aspect of the search mission. After that, he went into seclusion. Steve Daigle, his best friend on the pararescue squad, was one of several PJs who called him daily. "Mike's death just took the fire right out of me," he told Daigle. And, in fact, it was several weeks before he could bring himself to see anyone, even his partner, Judy Alderson. It still hangs over Daryl like Banquo's ghost. Since the tragedy he has seemed constitutionally heavy of heart, and to this day he admits to friends in a slow, deliberate voice that he cannot bear to attend funerals or memorial services. As he told Malcolm Daly upon his arrival in Talkeetna, "I'm so sensitive now it doesn't take much to set me off. I've seen people die, in Vietnam, even occasionally on the rodeo circuit. But until I started working on Denali, I was never so emotionally vulnerable."

Following Vanderbeek's accident, Daryl, who had spent each climbing season since 1991 virtually living at 14,200 relay camp, decided it was time to give up being a ground pounder and accepted the open position as Denali's lead mountaineering ranger, which meant riding a desk down in Talkeetna. There was more to the choice than Vanderbeek's death. Despite rigorous daily workouts, Daryl's six knee operations, torn rotator cuff, several herniated disks, and the wounds and injuries from his rodeo days were catching up with him. Where once he could nearly jog up to Fourteen-Two from base camp lugging an overstuffed pack in under five days, now the thought of scurrying to the summit to drag some dumb cheechako to safety, well, Daryl knows he'd only end up doing what he hates most: putting his fellow rescuers in danger. And at this point he feels he can be of more service "down below," where his experience makes him an invaluable resource for the next generation of high-altitude rangers.

"You gotta have somebody sitting back in the ranger station who has the respect, who has the credibility, with the younger guys," he says, sounding as if he is trying to convince himself that he made the right decision. "Somebody who knows where the fall line is. Somebody who knows what kind of protection you need on what kind of rescue. Somebody who knows a slope angle, or the best place for a helo LZ. Some-body who knows the conditions in the range in May as opposed to the conditions in July. Somebody who's worked with PJs and guide outfits and volunteers. Somebody who knows when a climber's out of radio range, or how to call in a C-130. Somebody who knows the difference between a full bird and a lieutenant colonel, and knows how to talk to each. I think that's me."

Once, when asked if the rush he gets from being in the clouds might be called spiritual, Daryl assumed a hangdog look and thought for a while. His face was a mask of intolerable regrets and hope. "No, it's more of a sadness over the tragedies," he finally answered. "A deep sadness over all the people who have lost their lives up there."

Daryl now spends his off-seasons lecturing at alpine and rescue schools, composing safety letters and e-mail, traveling the world with his slide show to warn of Denali's cruel moods. Despite the sedentary job, he envisions working on the mountain's slopes for another half dozen years. "I'll still be out evaluating sites on the bigger rescues," he says. "And they're always going to need an incident commander, which I believe is my strength." And after Denali? "Then I want to just become a gardener. I don't want to do anything that involves risk. I want to work with my hands. I like trees, gentle things. My ego doesn't need to be fed anymore. I know who I am. If anything, I want to become less, not more."

As his friends and associates attest, Daryl Miller's defining strength lies both in his willingness to say "Go" on a rescue as well as in his know-ing when to say "No," when a recovery appears too hazardous. His abil-ity to call off a search, to manage risk instead of taking it, is the ultimate measure of a mountain ranger.

Because of its perilous character, climbers testing Denali are required to register their route with the Talkeetna-based rangers. They must also fill out a perfunctory mountaineering résumé and attend a short indoctrina-tion class. This course provides Daryl with an opportunity to dissuade the ill equipped and foolhardy.

Further prompting comes from a two-page warning he has put together under the heading "Field Notes from a Denali Ranger."

Daryl's experiential axioms include:

- "In the wilderness democratic societies do not exist and your rights do not exist."
- "As a rule, if you die in the wilderness you made a mistake. Negligent judgment has a sharp learning curve."
- "The prerequisite to misadventure is the belief that you are invincible and that the wilderness cares about you," and, finally,
- "When deciding what your best resources in the wilderness are, you should be looking no further than yourself. If you aren't, you should reconsider your trip and go do something where at least a mistake may not mean your life."

Legally, the National Park Service cannot prohibit any U.S. citizen with the $150 registration fee from climbing the mountain. But Daryl and the other mountain rangers have developed a pre-climb slide show of such bone-chilling verisimilitude that most idiots who arrive in Talkeetna on bar bets inevitably catch the next flight out of town.

No pre-registration, however, is required to climb any of the other peaks in the Alaska Range, including Mounts Hunter and Foraker. And as Daryl and Malcolm shared beers and old times in the Talkeetna Roadhouse, the ranger took note of how cryptic his friend was about the Hunter route he and Donini had selected. All Malcolm would say is that after the warm-up on Thunder Mountain they had mapped out a challenging first ascent. The thought briefly crossed Daryl's mind that Malcolm might not have completely thought through his expedition in relation to his family. He'd seen this before. It's one thing to be willing to risk your life on these badass climbs, to buy into the concept that you might not be coming back; if you're a single guy, the chain of pain stops with you. But too many times married men just didn't stop to consider all the ramifications. Daryl often wondered if some of these climbers would still attack a hazardous route if they had to sit down beforehand with their wives and children, or even with their moms and dads, and explain that there was a chance they might get in deep shit on this particular adventure, and that they might not get rescued. Would they all sign a waiver slip agreeing to those terms? He knew the answer. No fucking way. Daryl liked to say that good judgment was often the lightest thing in a climber's backpack.

He remembered one of his first trips up Denali, back in 1989 when he was still an arctic greenhorn. He'd made it to 19,500 when his climbing party saw weather moving in. They turned around, and the downclimb to high camp took them seven hours. On their descent they'd met three Englishmen, Everest veterans no less, at 18,800 feet. Daryl and his partner tried to convince the Brits to fall back. They'd laughed and called the Americans pussies. Daryl still remembers their laughter echoing off Denali's black granite. Two days later he was a volunteer on the body drag detail that climbed to recover their corpses. At the end of the day, though Daryl found Malcolm's coyness vaguely unsettling, it raised no red flag. He chalked up his friend's evasiveness to Jim Donini's paranoia. Jim was an odd duck, but he was also one hell of a climber, by Alaskan standards one of the finest in the world. Malcolm was in good hands.

Malcolm Daly and Jim Donini had arrived at the base of Thunder Mountain via bush pilot Paul Roderick, who'd ferried them the sixty miles to the Tokositna Glacier, 7,500 feet above sea level, on Wednesday, May 12. Roderick flies a single-engine Cessna, and between climbers and tourists, business is good for the Talkeetna bush pilots. The lines outside the flightseeing outfits ringing the town's airstrip grow each year, even if some of the old-timers bemoan the gaudy tableau of overweight vacationers herded into the Alaska Range by guides reeling off mechanical spiels about the rugged days gone by. They see it as a depressing preview of what is to come: a kind of virtual frontier experience with minimal physical risk and discomfort. But nobody with an airplane is turning down any fares.

Roderick set Malcolm and Jim down on a remote southwest fork, no more than a crevasse-laden cul-de-sac, of the Tokositna. The Tokositna is the fifth largest of the seven major glaciers flowing down from the high cols of Denali like the snakes from Gorgon's head.

Of the nearly 100,000 glaciers geologists have charted in Alaska, thousands alone crisscross the Alaska Range. Constituting 54 percent of the earth's glacial fresh water, they also cover about 5 percent of the state, and a permanent stratum of snow and ice cloaks about a fifth of the almost 5 million acres of the "American Serengeti," Denali National Park and Preserve. The park is a riotous tract of subarctic boreal forest and withered taiga, dun tundra, and alabaster mountains carved into the belly of south-central Alaska. But the extent of ice present today would have constituted no more than a skating pond 3 to 5 million years ago, when the entire, newly formed Alaska Range was entombed in a vast ocean of frozen water. A visitor from another world flying over the southern half of the state at the culmination of the Pliocene epoch would have viewed not a mountain chain but a few pathetic mounds—including the summits of Denali, Foraker, and, perhaps, Hunter—breaching a miles-thick mantle of peacock blue ice extending south for hundreds of miles to the shores of Cook Inlet and Prince William Sound. Of such volume was the northern ice pack that even a scant 17,000 years ago, the planet's ocean level was 330 feet lower, exposing an arctic grassland 900 miles wide known as Beringia, the geological term for the Bering Land Bridge.

What remains of this frozen desert is what geologists call the "back waste," or retreat, of this ice cover, though even today Denali's glaciers surge and retract on a regular basis. Throughout 1956 and 1957, for instance, ice elevations on the Muldrow Glacier dropped by 300 feet as the slow-motion river gushed at velocities approaching 1,500 feet a day. By the time the surge ended, the terminus of the Muldrow had advanced about four miles. Similarly, over the winter of 1986–87, the snout of the Peters Glacier extended almost three miles at speeds of up to 336 feet per day. The joke in Talkeetna was that an adventurous man with time on his hands could scale Denali and surf the Peters out.

Despite the occasional spike, however, Denali's glaciers are shrinking. One research data program set up in 1991 on the largest, the mighty Kahiltna—a curling tongue of ice two miles across and forty miles long that moves at a rate of about eight inches per day—concluded that a "negative net mass balance" has occurred on the glacier over the last decade. In other words, the Kahiltna's ice is melting faster than snowpack can replace it. None of these glaciers will disappear soon, though. Geologists have yet to measure any absolute depths on the frozen rivers snaking down Denali. But seismic soundings near the base of Mount Dickey in the Ruth Gorge suggest that if the ice on the Ruth Glacier suddenly were to melt, the gorge would become the deepest in North America. For comparison's sake, the exposed headwall of the heretofore nondescript Mount Dickey would dwarf Yosemite's El Capitan by a factor of three.

A glacier creeping down a mountain valley will flow around some obstructions, and bulldoze others in its path. However, when corners are too narrow to be negotiated, or icefalls too steep, a glacier "tears" like a ripped radiator hose, opening a crevasse. On the surface, the slots can range from a few inches to thirty yards across. Beneath surface ice, however, they often bell out into caverns large enough to hold the Taj Mahal. Although crevasses can conceivably extend miles to the earth's bedrock, on most of the planet's glaciers they rarely exceed a hundred feet in depth—except on Denali, where explorers routinely descend to twice that pitch and beyond. (Crevasses also close as suddenly as they open; it is not a good idea to tarry in one.)

In a deep, steep-walled valley in the middle of the French alpine province of Haute-Savoie sits the headquarters of the Peloton de Gendarmerie de Haute-Montagne, or High Mountain Gendarme Squad. The gendarmes of Haute Savoie are charged with the rescue of stranded climbers—or, in worst-case scenarios, the recovery of their bodies. In the basement storage room of the Gendarmerie sits a musty file cabinet crammed with cracked and yellowed legal pads filled with the descriptions, transcribed from witnesses and relatives, of missing climbers dating back to the late 1950s. Each spring the glaciers flowing out of the spiky Aiguille Rouge and the Mont Blanc massif spit a mangled body or two out onto the valley floor. If the gendarmes can match a description on file with a frozen corpse clad in, say, a unique pair of lederhosen, they have the grim satisfaction of notifying any living next of kin. By contrast, anyone tumbling into a crevasse in the Alaska Range can expect to be expelled from the glacier's terminus, in the form of fine glacial dust, in approximately 1,000 millennia.

The first two recorded deaths on Denali, in fact, were neither the result of falls nor avalanches, but of crevasses. They occurred in May 1932, when two scientists gathering data on the nature of cosmic rays for the University of Chicago lost their trail in an occluding snowstorm while searching for overdue teammates. Both plunged into a slot. One researcher managed to climb out before expiring from exposure. The body of the other, Dr. Allen Carpe, was never—and will never be—recovered. Moreover, as glaciers cascade over particularly steep icefalls, they do not course smoothly, in one continuous motion. Silo-sized blocks of ice called seracs pile atop one another at the ledge of the fall, tipping precipitously outward. Gravity eventually sends these slabs crashing down with the destructive force of small meteorites. The geologist Michael Collier describes a chunk of ice "the size of a gas station" that broke from a high ridge, ricocheted off a ledge, and tobogganed down the face of Mount Hunter, "trailing snow in a veil two thousand feet long." The avalanche occurred not far from the route Malcolm and Jim intended to climb.

South-central Alaska is a relatively young landmass. The Pacific Ocean once lapped upon what is now the southern margin of the Brooks Range, one thousand miles of crumpled peaks molded by a process of continental drift and tectonic compression somewhere between 90 million and 120 million years ago. If, early in the Pliocene epoch, one had installed a time exposure camera on a space station and aimed it toward Alaska, an observer could have seen the state build incrementally. That said, it must be added that geologists have been known to declare war over the nuances of Alaska's origin. In crude summary, however, they do agree that the state sits at the nexus of several continental and oceanic fault lines where "floating" plates of land crashed together. As the bottom of these plates "subducted" back into the magma of the earth's core, their tops sheared off, or "obducted," and hove against each other like giant ocean liners violently docking in succession against a coastline. This is how south-central Alaska was formed. Scientists have also determined that along the Denali Fault System, the largest crustal break in North America, Canada's Yukon is still inexorably moving east and south while the bulk of the Alaskan subcontinent moves west and north. Over millions of years the two landmasses intersected, and as they collided the Alaska Range was "accordioned up."

Unlike the Brooks Range, or even the smaller, 90-million-year-old Chugach, the Alaska Range is a relatively new chain of mountains. By examining pollen fossils and through thermal dating, geologists have determined that 10 million years ago the land where the range now rises was a flat, natural drainage basin. The menacing towers of the Denali,

Foraker, and Hunter massifs were no more than great masses of granite entombed in a softer, sandstone-based rock called flysch, like watermelon seeds buried in the fruit's pulpy flesh. The presence of this flysch, spiked with micas and fine clay, accounts for Denali's near-vertical ramparts. The Alaska Range sits atop what is called a strike slip fault, and as the earth buckled and piled up along this fault, the flysch, inherently more malleable than granite's interlocking potassium and sodium crystals, weathered and spalled, leaving the geodesic granite to stand alone. As wind and ice further carved away at the cordillera, over the ages it left sheer structures like Denali's jarring Wickersham Wall.

The Alaska Range is only 5 to 6 million years old, and frequent earthquakes speak of a land still in the making. Further, unlike the Rockies or the Appalachians, the mountain chain is still growing heartily at a rate of nearly three-quarters of an inch per year. This means, for one, that Denali was 1,000 feet shorter when the Athabascan Indians first gave it its name twelve millennia ago. As opposed to the north-south contours of the Western Hemisphere's great mountain chains—the Andes, the Rockies, the Appalachians—the near-perfect east-west configuration of the Alaska Range forms a natural weather barrier creating distinctly different climate zones on each flank of the Denali massif. The southern ramparts, which include Mounts Foraker and Hunter, trap most of the weather systems sweeping up from the North Pacific, and receive roughly twice as much precipitation. Thus, the bulk of the chain's great glaciers, including six of the seven largest, fall to the south. The southern glaciers—the Kahiltna, Tokositna, Ruth, Eldridge, Yentna, and Dall—are used as the main thoroughfares for the air taxis and flightseeing tour planes negotiating their way through the central Alaska Range. The Muldrow, which flows north to Wonder Lake, and to a lesser extent the smaller Peters, which falls west, serve the same function.

Although the earth's temperate-zone glaciers represent just 2.2 percent of the planet's water, they account for 75 percent of its fresh water. To greatly simplify, most glaciers are formed as massive snowpack warms in summer months, consolidates, and compresses into ice. This ice absorbs every color of the spectrum except blue, which is scattered back and gives each glacier its sapphire sheen. In Denali, however, the length and severity of the Alaskan winter combine with the extremely cold ambient temperature to retard this welding and consolidation process. Thus, Alaskan glaciers are less stable than those elsewhere on the globe, and subject to devastating avalanches that routinely bury not only climbers in the high altitudes of the Alaska Range, but also snow machiners and day hikers in the foothills of the Chugach Range just outside of Anchorage. During one six-week period last spring, thirteen Alaskans perished in snowslides.

Not long after the worst, a killer slide that took six lives in Turnagain Pass, PJs Mike Wayt and Greg Hopkins set out on a training climb to the 3,500-foot summit of Flattop Mountain, a popular hiking destination in the rugged hills where the Anchorage city limits bleed into wilderness. On their descent a slab of névé cleaved from the soft corn snow at its base and engulfed Hopkins, who was glissading down the middle of the snowfield when he suddenly saw a scimitar-shaped crack rip off the crown face of the mountain in front of him. He turned to warn Wayt, but was buried before he got the words out.

Mike, who had managed to jump to a rib of granite near the edge of the snowfield, watched in horror as Hopkins swam with the cascading white tsunami, his dark blue parka bobbing up and down like a sailor caught between the crests and troughs of a weather sea. Hopkins was completely covered over three times during the snowslide. On each occasion he managed to raise his head for a gulp of air just before being interred again. After plummeting 700 feet Hopkins was swirled out of the main body of the avalanche by an eddy-like tributary near the curving seam of a couloir. It left him in a standing position, buried waist-deep, beyond the pull of the main current. He was lucky.

Between the Alps, Caucasus, Andes, Rockies, Urals, and Himalayas, high mountains cover 20 percent of the earth's landmass. Across these ranges, scientists estimate there are close to 3 million avalanches per year. An avalanche can travel at a speed of 200 miles per hour for a mile or more *on level ground,* and the velocity of the compressed air forced from its flanks has been known to rip the clothes off climbers and hikers standing a half mile away. Those caught head-on in a major avalanche have their bodies broken and pulped to such an extent that rescuers refer to them as being "Maytagged." Once, just outside of Anchorage, a squad of PJs disinterred an errant snowmobiler caught in a snowslide after he'd ridden too close to an unstable cornice of snow. "When we pulled the corpse out," recalls one parajumper, "every bone in this guy's body was broken, and his face was an unrecognizable sack."

Finally, because the Alaskan snowpack consolidates at so slow a pace, when warmer weather finally arrives during the high north's short spring, insidious snow bridges—made of surface hoarfrost that has barely congealed into weight-bearing spans—tend to rot faster from both the top and bottom.

This was the deceptively frozen world into which Malcolm and Jim stepped when Paul Roderick's ski plane landed on the Tokositna. The strategy to bring their climbing chops up to speed on Thunder Mountain's southwest buttress before tackling Mount Hunter had looked solid on paper. But almost from the start, the "tune-up" turned out to be more devious than either anticipated.

By his fourth day on the Tokositna, Malcolm Daly is beginning to rethink Jim Donini's policy of packing no radios. He isn't concerned with a rescue scenario. Rather, he is afraid he and Jim have become too great a pain in the ass to the bush pilot Paul Roderick. Roderick is a veteran climber himself, and thus more sympathetic than most to the sport's lonely vigils. He makes it a habit to try to overfly his clients' campsites at least once a day whenever the range's unpredictable weather permits. Yet it seems whenever Roderick buzzes Malcolm and Jim, they always have a favor to ask, and because they won't carry communications, he has to land.

On their first morning in country the two overslept when their alarm clock malfunctioned. By the time they reached the snow gully at Thunder Mountain's base the sun was already high, slopping the ice and loosening the rock overhead. Passage proved impossible. When Roderick appeared overhead later in the day they'd signaled him to land and requested an overfly of their route up the mountain. The next morning they'd flagged him down again when Jim discovered they hadn't packed enough white gas for the stove. Paul picked some up in Talkeetna and bombed it into camp that night. Finally, on day 3 they hit the headwall at 2 A.M., and made steady progress well past noon. By mid-afternoon, however, a flash snowstorm engulfed the ridge and they floundered through a whiteout halfway up the ice field. Worse, Jim had been wearing new crampons, a sample pair borrowed from his sales kit, and the steel had not yet been tempered. Late in the climb the front points on his right foot crumpled in, rendering them useless. After nineteen hours on the face they rappelled down to regroup. The afternoon of his crampon mishap Jim had managed to signal Roderick on his afternoon flyby, and, after setting down yet again, the pilot promised to get back as soon as possible with new spikes. When he returned later Malcolm half thought he'd aim the shoebox at their tent.

Now Jim and Malcolm are both frustrated and a little cranky, and over a supper of ramen, bouillon, and chunks of canned tuna Malcolm says, "It would have been so much more efficient to tell him about the gas or the crampons by radio." Jim just shrugs.

With Jim outfitted with new crampons, they set off for their third crack at Thunder on Thursday, May 20. They'd left a single fixed line halfway up the lower ravine, so the early climbing is easier. Jim is leading on the second pitch up the chute when a slab of chunky ice comes crashing down onto Malcolm's right shoulder. The collision numbs his arm for five or ten minutes. Malcolm is sufficiently shaken that, after securing more fixed line, they decide to call it a day. That night Jim hunches in their tent voraciously eyeing the sack of limes and bottle of Cuervo Gold he's packed. The deal is not to crack the seal until they've conquered Thunder Mountain. But now he is anxious, and thirsty. Before drifting off to sleep he tells Malcolm—again—that frozen margaritas made with glacier ice always taste better after a triumphant first ascent. Malcolm thinks he's trying to convince himself.

At 2 A.M.—neither slept much—Malcolm is struggling into his climbing gear when he promises his partner, "Today we do it." And by midday Friday his words seem prophetic.

There are fewer than 100 feet of grade six ice steps remaining as Jim hands Malcolm the rack. "We got this puppy in the bag," he says. Malcolm, too, feels as if they have broken the back of the route. They are 2,400 feet above their base camp, nearly two miles above sea level, with less than three pitches remaining before reaching the soft, final, up-slope of snow. Jim can practically taste the margaritas. He is still thinking about them as Malcolm disappears up and around the sharp corner of a massive snow cornice. The rope plays out haltingly for perhaps 70 feet before it stops and fist-sized chunks of ice begin pinging off his fiberglass helmet. He knows that the ice atop the overhang must have changed from plastic to brittle. Malcolm is chipping away at the insubstantial feathers of frost, trying to gain a purchase in good ice before moving on.

Up above, Malcolm is perhaps two moves away, three at the most, from reaching the soft snow ridge. Yet here he is, frustratingly, dead-ended. The afternoon sun beating down on the ice above the cornice has turned it so sloshy that he is having trouble finding a patch to hold his ice screws. Not far from his perch he spots a long vein of granite with a vertical crack crying out for a saddle chock. He curses himself for leaving his rock protection with Jim. "God, I wish I had some rock gear with me," he hollers down the cliff face. But Jim doesn't answer, and Malcolm is left to make due.

Malcolm scrapes off a veneer of weak ice and prepares to insert one final screw. He reassures himself, Christ, I can almost spit over to that snow ridge. Then he pauses one last time to look up, drawn to a low, distant growl in the sky. The pitch and echo—a deep, sonorous drone—are unmistakably that of a powerful aircraft, perhaps one of the hulking cargo planes the Alaska Air National Guard's mountain rescue team use as spotters. This time, he figures, someone's hauling out the big guns.

Yup, he thinks, someone's in deep trouble over on Denali. Malcolm has no way of knowing that the synchronous growl he hears is an Air Force C-130 scouring the massif for Steve Ball, nor that PJ Mark Glatt is at this moment training his binoculars on the squall gathering over Thunder Mountain. Malcolm turns back to insert the ice screw.

SEVEN

The PLO Climbing Club

If you want to get something done in the military,
classify it.

—SENIOR MASTER SERGEANT
BOB LaPOINTE (RET.)

What's the word from Glatt? The Herc pick up anything yet?" Mike Wayt approaches Chief Master Sergeant Garth Lenz, leaning against a wall outside his tiny office in The Section. Lenz breaks off his conversation with ex-parajumper Bob LaPointe and unconsciously brushes away a few wispy strands of cornsilk hair that have fallen across his broad forehead, nearly to his pebble gray eyes.

"You mean with the Brit?" Lenz says. "The rangers got him. The Daigle Dog and Grugel evac-ed him off the mountain couple minutes ago."

"And some lost tourist up on the tundra?"

Garth tells him Mike Murphy's got the latest intel on that. Murphy's somewhere in the back, maybe in the scuba room. Wayt makes some chitchat with LaPointe before nodding to Garth and heading off in search of Murphy. It dawns on Wayt that Garth Lenz always looks anxious, as if he's itching for a mission. Like a kid with ten bucks in a video arcade.

As Mike walks away LaPointe turns back to Garth. "People lost up in the outback?"

"Just one. Lady trekker. Overdue. But I got six people on the mountain looking for a British climber, Glatt up in a Herc, and another four or five over in Spain for the shuttle launch. It's Wayt's day off, but I had to call him in."

Bob LaPointe nods. He knows the drill. "If it's a bad time," he says.

Garth waves him off. LaPointe has invited a buddy over for the fiddler's tour of The Section. And yeah, it is a bad time, but when is it a good time? Besides, one does not easily blow off a former PJ chief. Anyway, Garth enjoys LaPointe's visits. The old Combat Smurf ran the 210th's predecessor, the 71st Rescue Squadron, and Garth's relationship with him has acquired a certain symbiotic property. LaPointe shares Garth's passion for rescue history, and relies on the new chief's network of PJ contacts to keep his hand in the game. Conversely, Garth is relatively new at running the team, and he finds in LaPointe a natural sounding board off which to bounce command principles, particularly those involving new hires. Twenty years ago it was LaPointe who nearly single-handedly rewrote the pararescue mission statement that allowed PJs to become players in the Alaskan mountain rescue business, and no member of the 210th is likely to forget that debt.

As Garth speaks, he absentmindedly picks up an avalanche shovel someone has stored in the corner of the room. Every year, the 210th runs joint SAREXs, or search-and-rescue exercises, with its Russian and Canadian counterparts. The shovel is Russian-made, its refined titanium blade soldered to a cheap broomstick handle. To Garth the tool stands as a metaphor for the schizophrenia of the former Soviet Union. It also calls a story to Garth's mind.

"Did you know that early in World War II the Soviet Air Force experimented in their jump schools with conscripts who would actually drop from three hundred feet into snowbanks?" Lenz runs his fingers over the edge of the cold titanium while he sets up the punch line. "Without parachutes?"

Garth says he's seen the pirated videotapes. "The mortality rate was close to 30 percent." Pause. "An acceptable figure to the Russians."

Soldiers say that a unit invariably becomes a reflection of its ranking officer. Less often noted is that a ranking officer often becomes a reflection of the warriors he commands. If this is indeed the case, Garth Lenz is as diverse an emblem of an eclectic crowd as any army could ask for. Even for a parajumper, the long, lean Lenz cuts an enigmatic figure. With the unyielding posture of a British Beefeater and a proclivity toward uttering cornball oaths along the lines of "criminy" and "hokey smokes," the 210th's team leader does not especially summon the Sergeant Rock persona associated with the warrior code of the Special Forces. Though he smiles regularly, there is the hint of northern grimness about the chief master sergeant, as well as occasions when his six-foot two-inch frame somehow manages to fade into the geography, inexplicably disappearing into itself as in a painting by Maurits Escher.

Some of this is undoubtedly due to Garth's relatively recent promotion to team leader. He has held the title for only seven months, and he sometimes leaves the impression that he is still wringing the rigidity from his new authority, like a rescue swimmer breaking in a stiff new wet suit. Garth is only the second chief in the 210th's short history, having replaced the legendary Mike McManus, who founded the unit in 1990. Garth vied with several other veterans still on the squad for McManus' vacated position, and is still tentatively feeling his way into the job. He has tried not to alter his demeanor or his routine, but the fact that he now outranks former colleagues certainly underlies his command scenario. Outwardly, he shows no hint of anxiety, and he continues to pull his regular rotation on alert. "But," one PJ allows, "you can sense something different about him, sometimes even see it in his eyes."

More than likely it is the subtle shroud of weariness worn by men responsible for the fate of others. Like all military leaders, particularly top kicks promoted from within, Garth trod a fine line between being one of the guys and being the man who might have to order the guys out to risk their lives. Yet even prior to his promotion, there was an air of the dilettante, the dabbler, about the new chief. Some of this may be because of his Coast Guard background. Historically, when Marines and Army grunts look down their collective noses at their Air Force colleagues as the pretty-boy flyboys, well, at least the Air Force has always had the Coast Guard to sneer at. Although, in Garth's case, he belies the standard cliché.

Garth's off-duty activities include competing in 100-mile Arctic Man races, snowbound Ironman-like events run on a course from Skagway to Whitehorse, and he has the odd habit of denying himself food after a slow day at the office. He tells astounded friends that if he hasn't worked hard enough he doesn't feel he's earned the right to eat. On the other hand, he represents a strain of what might be described as idiosyncratic primness that does indeed run through Alaska's pararescue community. Mike Wayt, the erstwhile Hop Sing, earned the nickname Daisy early in his Alaskan tenure for his habit of checking out books from the base library on edible plants and flowers. Mark Glatt looks and acts more like a university professor than a seasoned bush soldier. And several members of the team are studying to become that very personification of sissiness in macho circles, the male nurse. A parajumper's interests are varied and, sometimes, inscrutable. Only last night a group of PJs, including Staff Sergeant Chris Keen—a Hollywood handsome, All American decathlete from Florida State with a degree in mechanical engineering—huffed about the day room for hours engaged in a spirited, stream-of-consciousness discourse involving the application of the quantum physics of terminal velocity to a hypothetical climbing rope stretched between downtown Anchorage and the planet Venus.

Yet even among the assorted quirks of the 210th, there are moments when the forty-two-year-old Lenz would appear to be more comfortable in the eighteenth century than on the eighteenth green. One of his preferred pastimes is to tromp through the boreal forest with his wife, biologist Julia Moor, each calling out the Latin genus of various trees, shrubs, and flowers. And his taste in literature runs from dog-eared rescue manuals to the obscure English dramatist Christopher Fry, a favorite of his mother's. Fry's most successful work, *The Lady's Not for Burning*, is a wry comedy set in the Middle Ages in which love overcomes prejudice and hypocrisy. Not exactly foxhole reading.

Asked what his future holds after his PJ career, Garth grunts out a laugh and protests that he's got a good seven or eight more years before he has to think about that. Press him, however, and the former Coast Guard coxswain concedes that he is still a creature of the sea. After pararescue, he says he'd love to go to work for a volunteer organization like Doctors Without Borders, perhaps on a hospital ship, "preferably one with a helicopter." In a unit that to some outsiders might seem no more than a bunch of rescue-obsessed nuts, Garth is the unqualified champ of collecting rescue memorabilia, and his knowledge of military history is encyclopedic. The fixation extends to his vacation sites, which he and Julia select with an eye toward search-and-rescue, or SAR, esoterica. Julia jokes that if Garth encounters a lighthouse anywhere in the world it will be days before the poor lighthouse keeper is allowed to come up for air. Then again, rescue has been in the chief's blood for a long time.

Garth grew up on the outskirts of Lake Tahoe, Nevada, his backyard the high folds of the Sierra Nevadas. His father, a farmer–turned commodities broker "of good, Midwest German-Lutheran stock," instilled the ethos of discipline in his oldest son. Garth's whimsy must have come from his mother, who published her poems under a nom de plume she kept secret even from her family. His parents met as undergraduates at Cal-Berkeley, and in order to bequeath an appreciation of nature to their four young children, Clifton and Mary Ellen Lenz took jobs as concession-stand managers in Yellowstone National Park for several summers. The effort worked perhaps too well with Garth. "I'm the lone rescue nut in the family," he admits. "Dad thought there were smarter things to do in life, like join the Rotary Club."

In school he inclined toward math and the natural sciences; even today he laces casual conversations with words and phrases such as "granitic" and "homoclinal ridges." After class he water-skied, enrolled in survival courses, and honed his alpine ability as a thirteen-year-old volunteer to the local Nordic mountain rescue squad. His respect for nature's fury ratcheted up a notch when he was a member of a search party that recovered the bodies of two young boys buried in an avalanche. Later, when his parents deemed Lake Tahoe "too crowded," the Lenz family moved to a small town on Puget Sound. Flanked by the Cascades and the sea, young Garth was in heaven. It was here that he began collecting rescue memorabilia, mostly old radios and Coast Guard paraphernalia. It was also at about this time that his Mr. Rogers-meets-John Muir persona emerged.

"I'd do crazy things as a kid, sure, rock climbing, jumping off mountains, but it was always after thoroughly researching them. I wouldn't necessarily go out for the thrill. In fact, I'm not sure if I've ever felt thrilled by any of that stuff. But I feel it's my medium, I have an aptitude for it, so I do it and love it. But I don't get off on it." He confesses to having a test pilot's sensibility in a profession renowned for its "fighter pilot's mentality." Grinning wide, he also allows "that parajumpers are known to jump into any situation with both feet. Well, I jump in with both feet—but only after giving it a little thought."

Garth enrolled in Cal-Berkeley in 1976, and joined the Coast Guard

Reserve while working toward a double major in forestry and pre-med. In his junior year he discovered he could design his own curriculum, and became the first Berkeley student to devise and graduate with a degree in search and rescue management. It was solid on the physical sciences: meteorology, celestial navigation, geomorphology, topographic map interpretation, landform analysis, what Garth calls "all that good stuff." Following graduation he mustered through Coast Guard boot camp in Alameda, California, and set his sights on a leadership position somewhere in the service. As a "reserve bum," he could pick and choose assignments. At the time, the Coast Guard was at a technological crossroads, replacing their old wooden surfboats with sleeker, larger craft. The historian in Garth managed to wrangle an assignment to Oregon's Depot Bay, a keyhole harbor and one of the last Coast Guard bases still sailing aged, cigar-shaped thirty-six-foot lifeboats. The memory evokes a dreamy expression. "Those wooden lifeboats only went six knots, but they were living history." Over the next eight years he "bummed" through eleven different Coast Guard bases, from the Chesapeake Bay (where he served on an ancient cuyahoga cutter, the kind once used to chase rum runners) to the San Juan Islands off Washington State, running "surf boats," the tug-like, self-righting craft built to barrel-roll through, and under, high seas. Along the way he earned his commercial pilot's license.

A Coast Guard superior introduced him to the Air Force's pararescue career field, and he was immediately attracted to its unconventional disciplines. He enlisted and completed the PJ Pipeline in 1986. His first posting was to the 129th Rescue Squadron at Moffett Naval Base, where his love of the esoteric followed him like a talisman shellacked to his sea chest. His teammates dubbed the new guy as upright as a T square Mr. Spock. Three years later he learned of the unit being formed up by the Alaska Air Guard, and became one of Mike McManus' first hires.

PJs are traditionally the Air Force's wild bunch, and one of McManus' legacies was his ability to cull just the right candidates from a never-ending slew of applicants. By all accounts his judgment was uncanny; the 210th could take their motto from Dumas *père*: "All for one, one for all." This is the responsibility Garth now takes most seriously. He is discovering that having an eye for group dynamics is not as simple as it looked under the old chief. Last year, for instance, after an adventure magazine published an article on the 210th, Garth was besieged by calls, letters, and e-mail from men and boys wanting to know how they could join. But the story concentrated on a mountain rescue, and most of the applicants turned out to be climbers. "The first question most of them had was when could they get up there on Denali and do the big, dramatic rescues," he says with a wave of his hand. "I had to explain to them that we don't just do climbing rescues, and not all our missions are quite so dramatic. It's my job to make sure the people I bring in here are more well rounded. It's just like the guys who go through The Pipeline. They might be expert swimmers, but if they can't do the jungle run, they're out. Our strength lies in our integration, more socially than rescue-wise."

Including McManus, no more than half a dozen PJs have retired since the 210th's formation. Nonetheless, Garth is always on the look-out, in the catchphrase, for a few good men. "A high degree of team orientation," is what intrigues him most during meetings with recruits—PJs who talk about their units, as opposed to themselves. "My interviewing technique is all so subjective, and not very scientific," he says, clearing his throat. "But so far things seemed to have worked out okay."

Like McManus, Garth relies on input from each team member regarding prospective replacements. He expects everyone under his command to get a feel for "outside" colleagues while pulling TDY. And though he has served in Alaska with veteran parajumpers, he sometimes gives more weight to personnel suggestions from the squad's younger members on the theory that they are more familiar with fresh pups spewing out of The Pipeline. The men of the 210th do not need to be reminded that they are going to have to live with their recommendations for years to come. As Garth says, "No one's out scouting for drinking partners, for good ol' boys. They're looking for somebody that will haul their butts off the top of Denali when they're injured or sick." But, he adds, "At the end of the day I take all the responsibility for who joins this team."

His reasoning is straightforward. If he learned one thing from McManus and LaPointe, it is that executive decisions are rarely, if ever, well made by committee. To that end he has cultivated a network of "spies"—friends at indoctrination school down in Lackland; colleagues spread around the globe—whom he regularly pumps for small-bore intelligence. When bringing on new PJs, Garth must also take into account certain military expediencies such as rank. Peacetime military promotions generally occur at a glacial pace, and there are plenty of young staff and technical sergeants in the 210th who have been waiting on another stripe for years. Throwing a new master sergeant into the mix inevitably bumps them down a rung on the promotional ladder. It's not something Garth likes to do. So far he has avoided it.

Given these complexities—not to mention the more mundane tasks of command such as formulating budgets, juggling TDY schedules, and running interference with the brass—there are team members who, sotto voce, believe Garth should begin easing himself into more of an administrative role. He appears oblivious of the sentiment despite the fact that he has broken his right arm, right hand, tailbone, and right heel on various drops. He realizes that the unique thing about pararescue is that you have to stay in it to do it right. It isn't necessarily the physical activity or the danger that will force you out of the career. It's the calling itself. The problem with pararescue is that you get beat up so young. It's true that some of the old-timers want to stay on and on when it's well past the time to go. But there is a saying in pararescue that resonates: it isn't the kind of job where you can retire and announce it three years later.

"I believe the younger guys, no matter what they say, respect a veteran who participates, who doesn't just totally slip into a management position," Garth says. "As for me, well hokey smokes, I'd hate being just an administrator. If that happened, it'd probably be time for me to pass the reins to somebody here who can still take a regular turn pulling alert."

Right now the last thing on his mind is whether he is ready for that retirement hospital ship. He suspects that the travails of the three British climbers on Denali are only the beginning of a long rescue season. Moreover, he has learned from his daily weather update that there is a huge low front forming out over the Aleutians, which is likely to raise hell over the Alaska Range. He confesses to LaPointe that he feels uneasy about his plans to leave for the East Coast tomorrow on an inspection tour of the 102nd Rescue Squadron on Long Island, New York. Between official duties he hopes to satisfy his rescue jones with stops at the Mystic Submarine Base in Connecticut and the Sandy Hook, New Jersey, Coast Guard Station, one of the oldest in the nation. He has also been invited to Warsaw to take part in a water-drop demonstration with Poland's nascent search-and-rescue special forces. The assignment is right up his alley. Yet, as much as he's looking forward to the experience, it gnaws at him to abandon Alaska in the middle of mountain rescue season.

"It's nothing I can put my finger on," he admits to LaPointe. "You know, I've just got a feeling I should be sticking around."

LaPointe is nonplussed. "Don't flatter yourself. You got three senior master sergeants and six master sergeants here, any one of whom can run this section just as smooth as you. Probably smoother. Go. Jump. Have fun. Come back and tell me how Stash and Yash pull people out of the Baltic."

This breaks what was creeping perilously close to becoming a sober mood, and Garth resumes his tour. As the three head toward The Section's parachute room, he earnestly describes for LaPointe's friend how the aerodynamic theory of the parachute dates back to the rudimentary sketches in Leonardo da Vinci's celebrated codex. "A particular sign of Leonardo's genius is that when he outlined the general construct of the world's first parachute, he didn't find it necessary to throw himself off the Tower of Pisa to test it."

Both his visitors laugh.

As it happened, the first successful parachute test jump was indeed made from a tower, in 1783, by the French physicist and aeronaut Louis-Sebastien Lenormand. Several years later the brothers Joseph-Michel and Jacques-Etienne Montgolfier—Lenormand's countrymen and the practical inventors of the hot air balloon—proved the practical efficacy of the parachute when they discovered their linen bag afire one afternoon over a field near Lyons. They were forced to bail out and, amazing themselves, they lived to tell about it. The next advancement in rescue flight occurred nearly a century later, during the Franco-Prussian War, when French balloonists recovered 160 wounded soldiers from a besieged Paris in what is believed to be the first air medevac in history.

Yet despite (or perhaps because of) Gallic advancements in parachute aerodynamics and rescue techniques, the world's nascent air forces were slow to keep pace. During the First World War few aviators on either side stowed away parachutes on their biplanes. In fact, it was considered noblesse oblige during the Red Baron era for pilots to go down with their ships after losing dogfights or taking ack-ack. Moreover, in the early days of motorized flight the notion of inserting troops or rescue teams behind enemy lines by parachute was never broached.

It was not until the early 1920s that the idea of incorporating the parachute into standard military strategy began to gain adherents. In the United States, the man most responsible for advancing the theory was legendary U.S. Army Brigadier General William "Billy" Mitchell. A veteran of the Spanish-American War, Mitchell commanded the American Expeditionary Air Force during the First World War, when U.S. military planes and pilots were under the Army's command. After the armistice Mitchell became a vocal proponent of the nascent concept of military airpower, and advocated establishing the Air Force as a separate branch of the services. To promote his plan, Mitchell staged a small display of America's potential airborne might at Kelly Airfield in Texas. Pentagon brass and foreign military observers were invited to watch six infantrymen drop from a Martin bomber over the airfield. Less than three minutes after deploying, Mitchell's parachute commandos had assembled their weapons and were ready for combat. A few months later, in October 1922, U.S. Army Lieutenant Harold R. Harris became the first American airman to be saved by his parachute when he bailed out of his disabled plane over Dayton, Ohio.

Billy Mitchell, however, was not one of Washington's favorite generals. The army high command was dominated by aging horse soldiers, and Mitchell's increasingly critical arguments in favor of an independent U.S. Air Force were construed as bordering on treason. In 1925 he was court-martialed, suspended from duty, and forced into retirement. But if the hidebound American brass weren't listening, the Germans were. Their military observers had been present at Kelly Airfield, and by the early 1930s, Nazi Germany had incorporated the air construct into its burgeoning war machine. During the Spanish Civil War the Luftwaffe dropped pararescue teams to recover downed Stuka dive-bomber pilots on the theory that an airman was worth salvaging both for his flight expertise and any military intelligence he might have picked up on the ground. The German tactics spread. As World War II approached, the Royal Air Force commissioned a pararescue team to fish downed RAF airmen out of the English Channel, the Soviet Air Force trained a

squadron of jumping female nurses, and almost a year before U.S. paratroops dropped into France on D-Day, ninety German parachute commandos freed Italian dictator Benito Mussolini from his two-month
imprisonment in the Abruzzi Mountains.

The seminal moment in American pararescue occurred in early
August 1943, when an Army C-46 transport plane took off from Chabua,
India, ferrying seventeen passengers and a crew of four on a secret mission to China over the Himalayan route known to U.S. airmen as the
Hump. Almost two hundred miles into the flight, the C-46 developed
engine trouble and all twenty-one men were forced to bail out into
uncharted jungle near Burma's Chindwin River, where Japanese patrols
were known to be operating. The downing of this particular C-46 was
not your average wartime calamity. Among the survivors were several
high-ranking Chinese Army officials, the war correspondent Eric
Sevareid, and delegations from the U.S. State Department and the Office
of Strategic Intelligence. Not only did these spooks have intimate knowledge of the forthcoming Allied campaign against the Japanese in North
Burma, they were carrying documents to General Joseph "Vinegar Joe"
Stilwell that laid out the battle plans.

The wing operations officer in India in charge of the rescue was
Colonel Richard T. Kight. Poring over sketchy topography maps, Kight
fixed the C-46's last radio transmission somewhere near the northern
escarpment of Burma's rugged Naga Hills, which put the crash site
somewhere between the Japanese-controlled village of Pangsha—a tiny
dot on the not-always-reliable topo maps—and a vast tract of jungle
known to be the territory of the head-hunting Naga tribe. Kight suspected the only way to reach the survivors, while they were still survivors, was by parachute. Three medical corpsmen, including Kight's
wing surgeon, Lieutenant Colonel Don "Doc" Flickinger, volunteered
for the mission. Flickinger had made a parachute jump exactly once, two
years earlier, while testing rescue and survival gear in Hawaii. The other
two corpsmen—Sergeant Harold Passey and Corporal William
MacKenzie—had never stepped out of a plane unless it was sitting on a
runway.

The three medics were airlifted to the point where Kight surmised the
survivors had bailed out. Three hours into their vector pattern, Flickinger
spotted a ground-to-air signal panel through the jungle canopy. These

blue-and-yellow sheets had only recently been installed on U.S. aircraft. The panel was encoded and the translated message read: "Need urgent medical care." Ironically, when the signal panels were introduced, wartime fliers groused about having to learn what they considered yet more bureaucratic bushwa. But the new equipment was paying almost instant dividends.

Flickinger radioed Kight that his earliest suspicions had been confirmed. Men were injured down in headhunter territory, and it would take a ground party close to three weeks to reach them. Flickinger volunteered to jump and Kight agreed. The colonel informed Passey and MacKenzie of his plans, and ordered them to remain aloft. The two corpsmen were less than delighted with this decision, and sidestepped Flickinger's orders by utilizing a ruse employed by combat soldiers since time immemorial: they disobeyed orders by obeying them. Before Colonel Flickinger jumped, he'd left Sergeant Passey in charge of the mission. Once Flickinger was out the bombay door, Passey reasoned, he was in command. So Passey issued new orders, and he and MacKenzie followed the colonel into the sky from eight hundred feet. Modern PJs will tell you that Passey's quick, independent decision making is the basis for the parajumper's credo today: it is left up to each PJ to calculate the risk of whether to jump or not.

When the rescue team reached the crash survivors' makeshift camp they found twenty of the twenty-one men alive and in relatively good shape. The C-46's co-pilot was dead, and the most seriously injured was the transport's radio operator, who suffered a broken leg. Over the next thirty days the limping and bruised party skirted Japanese patrols and headhunters on their trek back to India and safety.

The precedent had been established. Never before had so many passengers successfully bailed out of a crippled airplane and returned alive. In addition, Eric Sevareid's subsequent public validation of the pararescue concept went a long way toward prompting the Pentagon to consider institutionalizing a permanent pararescue unit within the armed services. "Gallant is a precious word," Sevareid wrote of his rescuers. "They deserve it." But one paean from a war correspondent was not quite enough to convince the brass back in Washington. That took an army general finding himself in harm's way.

The general was Nathan F. Twining, and in 1943 he was commander of the Pacific Theater's Thirteenth Air Force when his plane went down during a routine flight from Guadalcanal to the atoll of Espíritu Santo. The massive rescue effort diverted combat resources from the Pacific front, siphoning ships and aircraft from the Army, Navy, and Marine Air Corps. After floating about the South Pacific for six days, Twining and fourteen others in his life raft were recovered by a Navy PBY near the New Hebrides Islands. This got the Pentagon's attention, and became the official rationalization when several American flying squadrons were subsequently devoted exclusively to emergency rescue. The unofficial explanation has a greater ring of truth: a week on a raft in the middle of the open ocean has a way of crystallizing a four-star's thought process.

In February 1944, the Army Air Force's newly activated 1st Emergency Rescue Squadron departed the United States for Casablanca, Morocco. The squad remained stationed in the Mediterranean until after the Normandy invasion, when it was transferred to the Pacific Theater. Simultaneously, the 2nd and 3rd Emergency Rescue Squadrons were formed in the Pacific under the aegis of the Fifth Army Air Force, and soon reached group status. Between July 1943 and April 1945, nearly 2,000 U.S. soldiers, sailors, and airmen were recovered by these units.

Such was the reaction to these dramatic rescues—throughout the rank and file and with the public—that after the war the Pentagon began studying the equipment and techniques being advanced by the U.S. Forest Service's budding smokejumping school in Missoula, Montana. The first American smokejumpers dropped into a forest fire four years earlier, and had since tinkered with all manner of improvements in both tactics and equipment. For instance, they had learned a painful lesson from one too many errant landings on tree branches, and now wore custom-made jumpsuits equipped with heavy canvas crotch liners and leather chaps. (Forest Service instructors enjoyed startling army observers by kicking each other full-force in the balls during inspections.) The smokejumpers were also experimenting with new, streamlined parachute harnesses and risers that allowed for easier steering into clearings on heavily wooded mountainsides. The Army liked what it saw, and began incorporating smokejumping techniques into its pararescue training. Moreover, about half of the postwar soldiers trained as parajumpers were flight surgeons. By the end of the 1940s three "paradoctors" remained on call twenty-four hours a day for rescue coverage in an area stretching from the Gulf of Mexico to the Canadian border, and from the Mississippi River to the western boundaries of Arizona, Utah, Wyoming, and Montana. At about the same time, the U.S. Coast Guard began establishing pararescue units along America's seacoasts. Their original base was located in the pulp mill town of Ketchikan, along Alaska's Inside Passage, whose waters had been patrolled since the mid-nineteenth century by the Coast Guard's predecessor agency, the Revenue Cutter Service.

Still, a turf feud prevented any distinct national rescue service from being formed. The Coast Guard, backed by the Navy, argued that since it had been charged with air and sea rescue since 1915, any national rescue agency should be under its aegis. The Army Air Force countered that its pararescue capability, tempered in the crucible of war, far outpaced the Navy's. After the usual backroom wrangling and logrolling, the Army prevailed. On May 29, 1946, the Army Air Force formally established a national Air Rescue Service (ARS). Its mandate was to unify the Army Air Force's global rescue operations as well as to upgrade and refine parajumping techniques and equipment. Colonel Richard T. Kight, back from India, was named the ARS's first commander. The Army's political triumph, however, was short-lived. Less than a year later (and a decade after General Billy Mitchell's death), the U.S. Air Force was split from the Army Air Force and officially designated a separate branch of the armed services.

Authorization was soon granted to this new Air Force to train and equip six pararescue teams, each composed of a doctor, two medics, and two survival specialists who, in theory, would be available for worldwide military rescue operations. An ARS command post was opened at MacDill Airfield in Tampa, Florida, and pararescue survival schools sprang up from the Mojave to the Cascades. As might be expected, this exotic subbranch of the services attracted some diverse recruits. One graduate of the first ARS class was a doctor named Stanley Bear, who was the first on the scene in 1963 when test pilot Chuck Yeager ejected from his flaming, rocket-powered F-104 at 104,000 feet. Bear went on to become President Richard Nixon's personal physician.

More in keeping with the modern PJ's eclectic temperament was another early graduate, Norwegian-born Colonel Bernt Balchen. Balchen, a protean figure, was a former Olympic athlete as well as a reputable painter and author whose service record included hitches in the

French Foreign Legion, the Norwegian Army, the Finnish Army, the Norwegian Navy, and the Royal Air Force. He headed one of the North Pole search parties for Roald Amundsen and Lincoln Ellsworth in 1925, and a year later signed on as a member of their next arctic expedition. In 1926 he was introduced to Admiral Richard Byrd, who made him his second pilot on his historic 1927 transatlantic flight. Balchen was also the chief pilot on Byrd's 1928 antarctic voyage, and he served in the U.S. Air Force with distinction during World War II. When Balchen died in 1973 he was buried in Arlington Cemetery, becoming the first foreigner since the Marquis de Lafayette to receive his U.S. citizenship through a special act of Congress. Because of his dashing reputation and arctic expertise, Balchen has become a sort of historic touchstone to the parajumpers of Alaska's 210th Squadron, who have adopted his catch phrase, "Vee go now, yah," as their unofficial slogan.

Alaska was of strategic importance during the Cold War—the Alaskan island of Little Diomede is only three miles from Russian territory—and the Air Force maintained a gridwork of Strategic Air Command bases and lonely radar stations throughout the wilderness. These included the famous DEW Line, or Distant Early Warning Line, along Alaska's arctic coast. Where there are planes there are pilots, and where there are pilots there are PJs. In 1952, Alaska's 10th Air Rescue Squadron achieved group status under Balchen's command. It went by two nicknames, Guardians of the North Pole and The Sourdough Savers. The group was inactivated in 1958, although one of its rescue squadrons, the 71st, remained on duty. This active-duty squad was succeeded in 1990 by the Air National Guard's 210th—or the Second 10th.

Pararescue evolved with the killing machines of the world's belligerent nations. The carnage in Korea and Vietnam served as a prod to upgrade the ARS's medical proficiency, and by the mid-1960s all new recruits were required to pass a certified nurses course. Parajumpers were now capable of treating the battlefield's most egregious medical emergencies: shock, bleeding, shattered bones, and blocked airways. (In pararescue schools, triage training was demonstrated on anesthetized goats, probably the source of the armed services–wide tendency to refer to any hairy situation as a "goat fuck.") Such was the reputation of PJ rescue teams that, during the Vietnam War, a parajumper's money was no good if there were U.S. pilots or flight crews drinking in the same bar. Of the nineteen Air Force Crosses—decorations of valor second only to the Congressional Medal of Honor—awarded to enlisted personnel during the conflict, ten were given to pararescuemen.

After Vietnam, as the draft was abolished and the American military went through a services-wide "drawdown," pararescue became a career field in search of a mission. The number of parajumpers shrank from a Vietnam-era high of over 600 to today's 400 or so, including a lonely baker's dozen attached to the Air Force's 71st Air Rescue Squadron at Elmendorf Air Base outside of Anchorage.

There had been U.S. Army rescue outfits—if not yet parajumpers in name, then emphatically in job description—stationed in Alaska for over three decades. Prior to 1941 the state served as a junction for thousands of aircraft flown to Russia on FDR's lend-lease program. And one month after D-Day, the Army Air Force reconstituted the 924th Quartermaster Company, Boat (Aviation) as the 10th Army Air Force Emergency Rescue Boat Squadron. Two years later the 10th Air Rescue Squadron succeeded the boat squad. In yellowing photographs, hard-eyed men of the 10th ARS wear faces that look as if they've been left out in a sandstorm. Pilots from the 10th flew every manner of aircraft, from Grumman Ducks to PBYs to Sikorsky H-5s, Alaska's first operational helicopters. The pararescuemen jumped with dogsleds, weasel tractors, miniature gliders, and trained parachuting dogs. During the Second World War's Aleutian campaign the unit's spotter planes and crash boats were blessed sights to downed airmen bobbing in the frozen slurry of the Bering Sea.

By the mid-1970s, the Air Force's command structure saw Alaska's vast interior not only as a natural barrier between the Soviet Union and the contiguous United States, but also as a convenient dumping ground for a returning cadre of disaffected Vietnam vets. One of those men was a two-tour veteran parajumper named Bob LaPointe—who discovered that his calling in life was to turn the parajumping career field into civilian rescue.

When Bob LaPointe returned from Vietnam, he was named chief of a thirteen-man PJ team assigned to the 71st ARS at Elmendorf Air Base (where he still works, part time, as a flight instructor). These veterans soon came to suspect that their transfer to Alaska had been merely an excuse "to sweep us under the rug." With few plane crashes to run on, the PJs naturally looked around at their new environment and devised alternative means of training.

"When I came up here in 1975 pararescue was sort of in search of a mission." LaPointe enunciates each word as if it were a bullet fired from a Sten gun. "I mean, we still had a job to do—air rescue, should any military planes go down. But the combat mission didn't exist anymore. And there were major-league hard feelings about the war and how it ended. PJs had done great things in Vietnam, but to be quite honest, our commanders didn't trust us when we came back. They thought we were some sort of psychotic unit. They'd watched one too many war movies that portrayed Vietnam vets, particularly Special Forces vets, as, you know, Loony Toons. They even took all our rifles away. Really! They gave us wooden guns to train with, to run around with and go bang-bang. It was the craziest thing you ever saw.

"So I'm sitting in Alaska with a bunch of high-energy PJs, trying to figure out what to do with them when there are no rescue missions. And suddenly it dawns on me: what could be more natural in a state with thirty-nine mountain ranges than a training regimen based on mountaineering?" In essence, he explains, he "conned" the Pentagon into initiating the PJ mountaineering program.

Previously, nearly all of America's military mountaineering needs had been served by the Army's Ranger battalions. In the 1950s and 1960s a PJ's stop along The Pipeline included the Army's Mountain Ranger School at Fort Benning, Georgia. The training was low-tech and rudimentary, essentially designed to get troops up a hostile cliff as fast as possible. The teaching model still in use was the attack on Utah Beach during the Normandy invasion. But when the sport of mountaineering exploded in the late 1960s and 1970s, civilian technology leapfrogged over the military's obsolete mindset and equipment. While the Army still issued heavy iron climbing tools, for instance, European manufacturers began marketing aluminum carabiners and pitons made from tempered steel. Soon civilian climbers were experimenting with foam-filled helmets molded from polymer plastics and fiberglass while U.S. Army alpinists continued to use combat-issue helmet liners.

"Not even the steel helmet, just the plastic liners," LaPointe remembers with a belly laugh. "Which, by the way, would crack when hit by even a small rock. It wasn't even a hard plastic. The only thing it was good for was as a place to put a number on your head, so they could say, 'Number Seven, get up that mountain.'" As outdoor-equipment companies brought out new products ranging from multi-fuel portable stoves to synthetic-based climbing ropes, the U.S. military lagged dangerously behind. "They may as well have still been issuing tweed knickers, cashmere puttees, and tins of pemmican."

Sitting in the middle of Alaska's burgeoning climbing scene, LaPointe decided to personally upgrade the military's mountain-rescue capabilities. It was a brilliant stroke. Not only would it give the PJs a new mission statement but, he reasoned, he could also use the state's forbidding peaks as his high-tech testing grounds. All he needed was a plan to sell to Washington.

LaPointe began by requisitioning as much of the more advanced, civilian-made climbing gear as he could slip under the quartermaster's radar. If their equipment so far outpaced the military's, he reasoned, perhaps civilian mountaineers had evolved better methods of climbing as well. So next he started digging through the few alpining books he could find. Just as he had suspected, there were precious few military climbing stratagems beyond, "Number Seven, get up that mountain." Essentially, military climbing techniques had not changed since Hernando Cortés ordered his lieutenant Diego de Ordaz on a scouting mission up Mexico's erupting, 17,887-foot Mount Popocatépetl in 1519. Then one day, visiting the Anchorage library, LaPointe came upon an instructional mountaineering manual entitled *The Freedom of the Hills,* published in 1960 by the Puget Sounders, an amateur climbing club in Seattle. The book's premise, according to its dedication, was "to encourage the spirit of good fellowship among all lovers of the outdoor life." To this day LaPointe refers to it as "the bible of pararescue mountaineering."

"I took it back to my squad and we absorbed their techniques—everything from knot tying to traversing a glacial ridge. And when we decided to put together our own official Air Force climbing manual, we basically just cloned everything from *Freedom of the Hills.* Virtually word for word. I mean, we weren't writers. We were soldiers. And we were in a hurry." At least, he adds, the PJs didn't sink so low as to xerox the Puget Sounders' instructional diagrams. "Those we redrew ourselves before we had our version printed up."

Few of the 71st Squadron's PJs had much mountain experience beyond passing the basic alpine courses in Army Ranger school. LaPointe himself had once climbed New Hampshire's 6,288-foot Mount Washington, which conferred upon him virtual Sherpa status within the unit. "We were all low-altitude, low-tech climbers," he recalls. "After we'd all read *Freedom of the Hills,* we went over to Mount Spurr just west of the base and climbed around. That's when we really discovered just how little we knew."

LaPointe's PJs became self-taught mountaineers. Every afternoon he would lead a platoon over to Matanuska Glacier, just north of Anchorage, and use the viscous river as a training ground. On each occasion he was reminded of the old Alaska saying: There is no law above the Yukon River, and no God above the Arctic Circle.

"When we could get away for days at a time, we threw people out into the woods in the middle of winter. We spent days and days out in the valley under Mount Susitna. I mean, it's cold out there. Meanwhile, military aircraft may not have been crashing, but bush pilots were another story. Civilian search and rescue was going gangbusters up here. Planes were going down all the time, landing on glaciers, hitting mountains. But nobody—including us—was very effective at these high-altitude rescues."

LaPointe and his unit discovered that there is more to mountaineering than developing stamina and learning a few alpine techniques. Only experience can teach the little tricks and quirks that may mean the difference between life and death at elevation. Veteran climbers, for just one innocuous example, never pack childproof lighters with them to cauterize the tips of their climbing or tent ropes. Even a bout of mild hypoxia will leave them daft enough to be snapping the lighter for hours without producing a flame. Further, aside from the predominantly Asian climbers who smoke incessantly at altitude, no mountaineer with any sense chaws above the tree line. Many PJs are tobacco chewers, yet nicotine in any form is a vasoconstrictive drug that narrows the lumen of the blood vessels and prevents the flow of oxygen. Sunblock? First-timers are often flabbergasted to see wizened climbers spreading it up their nostrils and across the roofs of their mouths. They get it, however, after a day's hard climb, when the sun's cosmic rays have pierced the thin, pollution-free air and bounced off the blinding snow into their noses and gasping mouths.

There is also the delicate process of cleaning yourself. A whore's bath at fifty below is less than inviting. Yet the PJs learned that dirt is noninsulating, especially any caked around the anus. Fluffy, freshly washed hair also provides tiny air pockets that trap body heat. It takes uncommon willpower to dip your head—or your ass—into a pot of water that is already coalescing into icy slush seconds after it's been boiled. But it may save your life.

Then there's food. No climber ever knows what he'll be able to hold down at altitude. Everyone plans for diarrhea. Above 10,000 feet or so, red meat goes through most people like water through a drainpipe, the body retaining none of its protein. Some, like the ill-fated Naomi Uemura, develop an affinity for Eskimo food such as blubber and raw caribou. Others, mostly Europeans, subsist on chocolate. Most pack a variety of freeze-dried meals and experiment with what their stomachs can keep down. There is a famous story about one Swiss climber at 17,000 feet on Denali surviving on nothing but sticks of butter. LaPointe has never been tempted to try that diet himself.

Suddenly it all came together. Now that the parajumpers possessed a semblance of proper civilian equipment and techniques, their mountain skills showed quantum improvement. The next logical step was somehow to insinuate themselves into the civilian rescue business. And given the fact that they were, after all, PJs, LaPointe concluded, "Well, if we're gonna climb, let's climb the biggest thing there is to climb. Hell, we're sitting right next to Denali. Let's get our asses on up to the top of that mountain."

In 1975, LaPointe approached his superior officers with research showing that even routine military missions on small mountains had traditionally given U.S. forces fits. Why not form a unit that honed its alpine techniques on the meanest mountain of them all, Denali? He contended that rescuing civilians would increase the Air Force's real-world combat proficiency. "It's impossible to simulate the stress of a real-world mission in a training exercise," he argued. Plus, if the PJs could conquer Denali, anything else would be a piece of cake. His ace in the hole? He told his bosses he'd only come up with the idea after overhearing two visiting generals discussing it during an inspection tour of Alaska's air defenses. In order to buck the military's inherent conformity, it never hurts to let the brass believe that they were the men who conceived of a new idea in the first place.

It almost worked. If two generals were intrigued, then LaPointe's bosses were interested. Unfortunately, the timing was awful. The post-Vietnam military industrial complex was under attack from Congress. The Pentagon was downsizing. Finally, it didn't help that the majority of civilian mountain recoveries at the time tended to be "body drags"—that is, pulling corpses off the windswept peaks. LaPointe got his answer: The Air Force wasn't funded for civilian SAR. Recovering dead civilians was not only "negative cost-effective" but it was also not worth the risk to military personnel.

LaPointe regrouped. If the Air Force refuses to fund a unit dedicated exclusively to civilian SAR, perhaps they would come across with the money if he could demonstrate how such a program would reap reams of positive publicity. The following year, 1976, LaPointe returned to his superiors with a new proposal that painted a patriotic Bicentennial por- trait of a squad of handsome, all-American PJs standing tall atop Denali's summit, the Stars and Stripes fluttering over their heads. The media would trip over themselves for the story. It was dramatic enough to earn LaPointe an audience with several wing commanders at ARS headquarters in Illinois. They seriously weighed the scenario until one officer brought up the deleterious public relations effect a squad of dead PJs draped across Mount McKinley's barren heights might have on America's self-congratulatory birthday party. Recalls LaPointe, "The main reason that one didn't fly was because I couldn't guarantee them that we'd even make it to the top, much less live to tell about it. They pointed out, correctly, that none of us had ever even climbed a peak as high as Denali, and kicked me back to Elmendorf. I couldn't disagree with their logic. But if you ask me, I was making progress."

Upon his return to Alaska, LaPointe doggedly began brainstorming with his unit about ways to overcome the dead-PJ scenario. Voilà! If the generals wanted high-mountain experience, then Bob LaPointe would give them high-mountain experience. He applied for a thirty-day leave, and signed up as an assistant guide with an outfitting group called Mountain Trip that, for a fee, shepherded climbers up Denali. That May, Bob LaPointe ascended the West Buttress route and descended across the Muldrow Glacier. There would be no more excuses about inexperi- enced PJs. LaPointe returned to his superiors at Elmendorf and racked the slide. Look, he said, climbing Denali isn't exactly rocket science. "I told them all it took was a couple of guys with some smarts who were in great shape. Like PJs." He also shifted his emphasis from positive public relations to enhancing the career field's arctic training, evoking the dashing reputation of Bernt Balchen for emphasis.

"You can't ask for a better cold-weather training ground than the Alaska Range," he maintained. "If you can survive Denali, you can survive anywhere in the world. I told them we'd cut down drastically on our injury rates. Plus, if we ever invade Siberia or Finland, man, would we be prepared."

LaPointe's determination impressed the brass, but convincing any military hierarchy to take a flier on groundbreaking tactics is harder than boning a marlin. They turned down LaPointe's proposals yet again. A year later, in 1977, LaPointe was browsing through secret military dispatches at Elmendorf Air Base, and noticed that many concerned Palestinian commando encroachments into Israeli territory. An idea hit him like a bolt from Odin. "I'd been approaching them from the wrong angle all along. I was using too much logic. I told myself to pick a line of attack that might not be quite as logical as civilian rescue, or even good publicity, but might be a little bit more dramatic."

Bob LaPointe's eureka moment was the invention of the Palestine Liberation Organization Climbing Club. What if a U.S. bomber or fighter jet carrying classified material or "sensitive munitions"—the code phrase for nuclear warheads—were to slam into a mountaintop somewhere on the globe? And what if the PLO Climbing Club decided to go hiking precisely in that area? Does the United States really want to face the prospect of one of its portable nukes ending up in some basement in Beirut? LaPointe's scenario resounded through Washington. Today, the erstwhile Combat Smurf shakes his head slowly at the symmetric simplicity of the pitch. With his short-cropped black bangs and a tight T-shirt pulled over a taut chest, the animated, wiry LaPointe must have resembled a Caucasian Bruce Lee as he pitched his idea.

"It was the height of the Cold War, Strategic Air Command had money galore, and they loved these James Bond–type ideas. And that's how we sold the concept. We had to classify the whole thing, of course. If you want to get something done in the military, classify it. We had a cover story—a classified ops plan—on the books for a decade after we dreamed up the idea. It had something to do with the PJs donning civvies and posing as civilian mountaineers."

LaPointe admits that even he could have countered his cockamamie scenario "in a million different ways"—beginning with the prosaic detail that the PLO did not have a climbing club. Moreover, the odds of *anyone* recovering "sensitive munitions" from a crash sight as severe as Denali were astronomical. In 1997, for instance, an Air Force A-10 crashed into a row of eminently climbable peaks in the Colorado Rockies, instigating a massive search for its payload of 500-pound bombs. They were never recovered. But the idea is father to the deed, which is how, in the spring of 1977, the Air Force authorized permission for Bob LaPointe to lead a squad of six parajumpers on an ascent of Denali. The mountain was empty. The PJs went days without seeing another climber. All six members reached the top late in May, and Bob LaPointe recalls the intense solitude he found there. The parajumpers took a few triumphant photos and returned to Elmendorf.

The press was waiting. The Air Force expedition (for it was no longer merely a PJ operation) triggered front-page newspaper headlines across the nation. The PJs were feted like astronauts. Newsmagazines dispatched battalions of profile writers and photographers to the 71st's lonely corner of the arctic. The Pentagon basked in the publicity. And a larger PJ ascent of twelve men was planned for the following year, with LaPointe again in command. He realized that if he was going to successfully exploit this public relations hiccup into an ongoing high-mountain SAR program, he would have to include guard and reserve PJs on his next climb. He put word out over the PJ wire, and spent the next year culling suitable candidates from the reserve units in California and New York.

The 1978 ascent did not run quite as smoothly as the climb the year before. Two PJs fell ill. One suffered from a case of mild hypoxia; the other nearly died from pulmonary edema. Luckily, the weather cooperated, and both were airlifted out from 18,000 feet by Army CH-47 Chinook helicopters. It remains the U.S. military's highest helicopter mountain rescue. The Air Force had ordered a cameraman from their documentary unit to accompany the expedition, but when it became obvious early in the climb that the technician was woefully out of shape, LaPointe abandoned him at base camp. The parajumpers filmed their own conquest, and the documentary was distributed to Air Force bases around the world. This second ascent erased any doubt about the PJs' ability to perform high-mountain civilian rescues.

But a hitch remained. The 71st was authorized to run immediately on any military SAR. Run they did. Between 1984 and 1989, for instance, the squad flew on seven F-15 crashes. Response time on civilian rescues, however, still depended upon authorization from Washington. It was rarely given; when it was, the civilians in need of rescue were usually either already recovered or dead. In 1987 the 71st's capacity was curbed even further when its C-130 tankers were transferred out of state. Without midflight refueling capability, the squad's helicopters were limited to round trips within the range of their gas tanks, a few hundred miles.

Federal budget cuts sounded the death knell for the 71st ARS in 1989. The unit was deactivated, its remaining eight helicopters transferred to Arizona. In its keening wake the always-helpful Senator Ted Stevens secured $73 million from state finances to man and equip a new Air National Guard Rescue Squadron. The 210th was born on January 1, 1990. Many of the PJs from the old 71st, including Chief Master Sergeant Mike McManus, were separated from active duty and signed up with the "Second 10th." Several still serve on the current team. But Bob LaPointe, with sixteen years of active duty, was two years over the limit to transfer from active duty to a guard unit, and the state wouldn't pick up his pension. He retired in 1996, and these days, on any given afternoon, the fifty-year-old former PJ can be found hunched over his computer or shuffling through yellowing reams of squadron rosters, hand-scrawled notes to himself, and piles of military history books in the living room of his tidy ranch house on the outskirts of Anchorage. He has been compiling what he hopes will be the first official history of the PJs, with an emphasis on their Vietnam experiences.

LaPointe, sitting at Elmendorf Air Base, followed the brand-new Alaska Air Guard's 210th Rescue Squadron's first official mission in the winter of 1990 by short-wave radio. Two Pavehawk helicopters, with PJs serving as flight crews, hammered through a whiteout blizzard, refueling midflight over Prince William Sound, to save the lives of four civilians trapped in a plane crash near the town of Cordova. They did not have to await official permission from Washington.

I suppose the 210th has sort of become the apex of pararescue," Garth Lenz says, standing near The Section's front entrance with Bob

LaPointe, his arm draped over the Inuit totem pole. He goes on to note that since the unit's formation, it has saved the lives of close to six hundred civilians. "There's a lot less red tape to cut through up here. A lot less than there used to be, anyway."

LaPointe cracks a small smile. Garth jerks a thumb toward the Chugach Range, mantled with snow. The peaks resemble the blades of a ripsaw dipped in cream. "Plus, it's still pretty wide open out there. People can be really, really stupid about nature. You learn that fast on this job . . . at least you better. In a way, we're like the Eskimos. Each PJ passes his knowledge along to the newer recruits. The Eskimos learn from their elders that in order to survive, you have to take this country seriously. If you do stupid things . . . well, let's just say there are no stupid elders in Alaska."

Lenz turns toward his office. "You know, I suppose if there's one major difference between us and the Eskimos, it's that we're more mountain-oriented. The Eskimos know better than to be larking about these hills in bad weather."

EIGHT

The Weathermaker

When I saw Elton slide past I braced myself to be able to hold the point. In seconds he was pulled loose and my belay was not strong enough to hold two men. After that, I only remember tumbling end over end in the loose snow.

—Excerpt from the 1954 National Park Service report on the first park ranger to be killed on Mount McKinley

Jim Donini assumes from the debris crashing down on his helmet that Malcolm Daly is struggling to find solid placement for his ice screws above the cornice. He reckons that fourteen hours of sunlight has turned the ice soft. Though he can't see his partner, he figures Malcolm is about seventy feet above him.

Suddenly he hears a sharp crack, like a phone book dropping to a marble floor. He jerks his head and sees both ropes, the haul line and the belay line, whip past him in a shower of rock and ice. "Oh my God!" he screams. Then Malcolm's flailing body hurtles over the cornice, aimed right for his head. Jim ducks into a fetal position and takes Malcolm's full weight on his right shoulder. He feels a searing pain in his right leg. He doesn't hear Malcolm cry out.

A wave of nausea roils Jim's stomach, and as he fights it he sees bright flashes before his eyes, like neon fireworks. They slowly coalesce, and for several moments everything is a parching white. He begins to hallucinate. The world around him is completely, utterly silent. He feels an eerie sense of cold detachment, as if he were observing himself from afar. He's in a desert. Staring at rolling sand dunes. But why is it so frigid? And why does his leg feel as if it's on fire?

The white begins to fade. It comes back to him. He is hanging from an ice step on Thunder Mountain. With Malcolm. Where is Malcolm? He looks down. Jim can see his partner dangling from the belay line, perhaps fifty feet below. Malcolm is unconscious, slumped in his harness, twisting like a marionette held by a single string. Now Jim remembers the sickening thuds that echoed through the couloir as Malcolm's body banged and slammed off the rock and ice, a noise like a pumpkin being smashed by a club. Jim figures that he must have bounced off the mountain at least a good 120 feet. The thought sucks the air out of him, as if he's been mule-kicked in the gut.

Jim's first clearheaded thought is that his friend is most likely dead, and he is shackled to a corpse.

He takes a moment to compose himself and finally notices the puncture wound in his thigh. Blood is pumping from a deep hole, neat and circular, almost surgical, about six inches above his right knee. One of Malcolm's crampons must have gotten him. He jams his neckerchief into the tear in his Gore-Tex suit to try to stanch the bleeding. He yells down to Malcolm. There is no answer. He yells again, and again. Malcolm's head jerks spasmodically. He is still alive. Get focused, Jim tells himself. Get fucking focused.

It takes Malcolm several minutes to figure out where he is. His head feels thick and fuzzy, as if his brain's synapses are misfiring. Like a rummy trying to cadge a drink, he cranes his neck and spots Jim hanging by an ice screw less than a hundred feet above. Jim is yelling something. Yelling at him.

"Did I fall?" Malcolm hollers back. "Was I leading?"

Jim yells, but his voice blows away in ribbons.

"Jim, tell me! Was I leading?"

This is ridiculous, Malcolm thinks. When he turns in his harness to get a better vantage, it feels as if someone has driven railroad spikes into the hollows behind his knees. He howls in agony, but screaming makes the pain even worse. Tentatively, Malcolm forces himself to look down to his feet. Jesus! They're both dangling from his shins, literally blowing in the wind. Like a rag doll's. Instinctively he reaches for his legs. It is then that he notices his left pinkie, bent back from his hand at a 90-degree angle. Good Lord—now the mere act of thinking seems to drive the railroad spikes even deeper—both my ankles are broken. He feels a steady trickle of warmth flowing over his left foot. His own blood is filling his boot. He guesses he has at least one compound fracture to his tibia, maybe his fibula, maybe both.

From far away, Jim Donini's voice sweeps over him. "Malcolm! Malcolm, you have to stabilize yourself. I can't get down to you until you stabilize yourself." The words come slow and blowzy, as if from a tape recording whose batteries are winding down.

Malcolm forces himself to ignore the pain in his legs. What the hell went wrong? He has to think. He can't remember anything about the fall. My ice protection must have pulled out. Either that or my foothold broke. It doesn't seem likely, given my position, that I was knocked off by falling ice. No, it must have been the screw in that ice. That pin below must have saved my life.

"Malcolm! You have to stabilize yourself."

Stabilize myself? Of course. Malcolm is being held by the belay rope, his lifeline to Jim. And Jim can't move until Malcolm attaches himself to the ice wall. He retrieves his ice axe, still clipped to his harness, and chops out a mini-ledge in the mountainside. The effort takes him half an hour. He inserts two ice anchors and ties himself in. He ventures a glance at his misshapen ankles, but quickly looks away. With his good hand he signals Jim to climb down.

Adrenaline muting the pain in his thigh, Jim gingerly makes his way down to Malcolm. It takes him forty minutes. He blanches at the sight of Malcolm's feet. Both ankles are smashed and swaths of blood smear the ice near his left foot. His crampons must have caught in several places during the fall. Malcolm repeatedly asks if he had been leading, and Jim guesses he is also suffering from a mild concussion. He doesn't notice the broken finger. Jim knows enough first aid to pat his partner down. Thank God, Malcolm doesn't appear to be suffering from any internal injuries.

He is wedged into the middle of an ice runnel, as if stuck between the pages of a half-open book. It is a position, Jim knows, from which a rescue will be impossible. "We gotta get you out of here, pal. We gotta move you down."

Malcolm strains to think straight through the pain. Like Jim, he has worked with enough volunteer rescue squads to realize his position is tenuous. Even on the off chance that Jim can contact a rescue team, there is no way a helicopter can get close enough in this ravine to haul him out on a line.

"Right, Jim. We have to get down. But first we got to do something about my legs."

Malcolm hands Jim his small medical kit. Jim rips open a vial of Vicodin tablets and hands two back, along with a bottle of water. While Malcolm is forcing the pills down, Jim grabs the duct tape. He wedges Malcolm's ice axe between his shattered ankles and begins taping them around the ice axe, constructing what he hopes will be a serviceable shin splint. Malcolm is still bleeding from his left foot, and soon Jim's hands are covered in blood, exactly as salty as the sea. With each circumnaviga-tion of the tape, Malcolm cries out in pain. When Jim has used up both rolls of tape they huddle on the side of the ice ledge. He tells Malcolm he is going to try to lower him the 2,600 vertical feet. Then, for the first time, he notices the belay line. The rope is a 9.5-millimeter nylon dynamic, manufactured precisely for these conditions. Dynamic rope has more give to it, more stretch, so if a climber falls he will bob just a bit at the end of the line. Tauter rope will break a climber's neck. Jim holds a section of the rope up for Malcolm to examine. It is cut more than halfway through, held together by threads. It must have slowly severed on the ice cliff as Malcolm dangled unconscious. Neither man says a word.

Jim fashions a loop knot to bypass the frayed section of rope and belays Malcolm in. He begins lowering him; ten, fifteen, twenty feet at a clip. Whenever any part of Malcolm's feet brush the ice wall he yelps in pain. After one hundred feet it is apparent that the makeshift splint is not holding, but there is no more tape to refasten the splint more securely. After two hundred feet they reach the upper rim of a small vertical snow-field framed by the gunsight notch. Both men realize further lowering attempts are futile. Malcolm can feel that he is still bleeding.

He speaks first. "Jim, we gotta get a rescue. If I keep trying to go down in this condition . . ."—the words catch in his throat—"I'm gonna die."

Jim doesn't answer. Instead, he takes out his ice axe and begins chop-ping a ledge in the sheer couloir. Within an hour he has hacked out a platform eighteen inches wide by five feet long. Together they secure anchors in the crunchy snow, loop the belay line over a horn of rock above Malcolm's right shoulder, and clip him tightly to the ledge. Jim cuts the laces on his inner and outer boots to ease the pain of the swelling, empties his own rucksack, and places Malcolm's feet inside it. He strips off his wind jacket and fits it over Malcom's upper torso and arms. Then he hands him two quarts of water, all he has left, a few Power Bars, and the vial of painkillers.

The two men stare at each other wordlessly. Finally, Malcolm reaches out and wraps Jim in a bear hug. "Man, be safe."

I'll be back, Jim says, and scrambles down the snowfield.

Malcolm watches as Jim fixes his rappel line and vanishes over the rim of the cut. He knows that downclimbing this chute with a wounded thigh and bad shoulder, even with the fixed lines they left below, will be a formidable task. Craning his neck and looking through the gunsight notch, Malcolm can barely make out the snow gully that leads to the Tokositna Glacier at the base of the mountain. He trains his eyes on the spot. His greatest fear is that any moment he will see Jim's lifeless form shooting across that gloom and talus at two hundred miles per hour.

Two hours later his partner staggers from the shadows out onto the glacier. Jim is limping, but to Malcolm he moves with an inspiring grace and confidence. The spire of granite that forms the western margin of the gunsight blocks Malcolm's view to their campsite, but he follows Jim's movement across the white ice as far as possible. He thinks he sees Jim turn and wave just before disappearing behind the rock chimney.

Malcolm starts to bunker in. He is in less pain now, the Vicodins having kicked in. He checks his left wrist; his watch is gone. He must have lost it during the fall. He glances at the curving shadows and guesses at the time. Early evening, he thinks, studying the pale peppermint sky. Maybe five hours 'til sunset. He calculates that any rescue attempt will be, at best, twenty-four hours away. He is positive he can keep himself alive that long. But what if it takes longer? Blood continues to weep into his left boot.

He straddles the snow ledge and maneuvers his body into a half-sitting position. He begins shoveling loose snow, the consistency of mashed potatoes, into the rucksack around his feet. Ten minutes later he hears the distant whine of a bush plane. At that very instant the first snowflakes whisper past his face.

Just over a hundred miles southeast of Thunder Mountain, a jolly snowball of a man negotiates his way through the fifth-floor offices of the Anchorage Bureau of the National Weather Service, a warren of cubicles cluttered with weather forecasts, tide tables, meteorological charts, satellite photographs, and computer printouts. Dr. Gary Hufford, whose thick white beard leaves the impression that he might have sailed with Vitus Bering, is the National Weather Service's chief scientist for the Alaska region—or, as he is fond of saying, the Cassandra of the arctic.

Hufford and the battalion of meteorologists who work out of Anchorage's government building share space with the governor's staff, the U.S. Marshals, the federal prosecutor's attorneys, several grand jury rooms, and sundry other state satraps. Hufford, a weather junkie and ardent outdoorsman who moonlights as a fishing guide and bush outfitter, is looking forward to a weekend rendezvous with a half dozen king salmon. But before he lights out for the weekend he's decided to take one last peek at the images coming in from the GOES and POES.

The National Weather Service operates a swarm of satellites racing around the globe, including the geosynchronous operational environment satellites, or GOES, that track the earth at 22,000 miles above the equator, and two polar operational environment satellites, the POES, that orbit from pole to pole just 450 miles above the planet's surface. Each relays a real-time photo of the earth's weather to the service's dozens of bureaus. Now, as Hufford scans the computer screen superimposed with the faint, pale outline of Alaska's borders, he absentmindedly lets out a long, low purr. "Holy Toledo," he says to no one in particular. "I wonder if the Park Service guys know about this."

Pulsing on the screen's upper-left corner, a neon green blotch indicates a high-pressure front roaring south out of the Bering Sea and bearing down on Denali. This in itself is not unusual or worrisome. When the front slams into the massif, it will, of course, build some weather, most likely a lenticular cap. It has no choice. As Hufford says often, the Asiatic peoples who crossed the Bering Land Bridge sure didn't know from barometric pressure or Doppler radar, but they had the damn good sense to intuit that geography is destiny. And they discovered early that if you set up a barrier as tall as Denali in front of the natural flow of air, that barrier does indeed become a weathermaker.

From a strict geological point of view—that is, measured from base to summit—at 20,230 feet Denali is the highest mountain on earth. Denali rises out of the Susitna Valley at 80 feet above sea level, and its northwest face consists largely of the 15,000-foot Wickersham Wall, the sheerest vertical drop in the world. By comparison, 29,028-foot Mount Everest rises from the Tibetan plateau 12,400 feet above sea level. By this standard, Everest is a *mere* 16,628-foot mountain. (There are seamounts, such as Guam and the big island of Hawaii, that, measured from their base on the ocean floor, dwarf every mountain on the earth's crust.) Moreover, by a quirk of geography, Denali sits directly in the path of several natural storm movements, and intercepts all the weather aimed at it. There are only two things moving air can do when confronted by an obstruction the size of Denali: go around it or be lifted over it. But there is no going around Denali. So Hufford is fairly certain that the high-pressure front he is viewing on his computer screen will generate an inertial force on the mountain equivalent to a category 3 hurricane. But that is not what has caught his attention.

Down in the left-hand corner of the screen sits a ruby red swirl, a huge, low-pressure front gaining strength out over the Aleutians. When the dense high-pressure front eventually clears Denali and resumes its southern tack, it will collide with this tropical low racing up from the South Pacific and, like Grendel "wearing God's anger," begin its advance on southern Alaska.

Put in its simplest terms, when cold air from the arctic meets warm air from the tropics, the only possible result is a maelstrom that will gather momentum with the fury of a typhoon. This meteorological phenomenon is particularly endemic to the Western Hemisphere, where natural north-south "weather pathways" exist. (If the Rockies ran parallel to the Mason-Dixon line, Oklahoma would be tornado-free.) Similarly, on the lee side of the North American continent there are no natural obstructions to stop cold air from rushing down out of Canada, Greenland, and Norway and colliding with hurricanes swirling up from Bermuda to create perfect storms over the fishing grounds of the North Atlantic. Meteorologists call these areas of liquid chaos "generation sites." The Aleutian Islands off Alaska's southwestern coast are a traditional storm epicenter, where high- and low-pressure fronts inevitably collide. One primary generation site surrounds the island of Attu, the last island in the archipelago. There, tropical lows conceived off Tahiti ride the Japan Current north and collide with immense cold fronts streaming south from the shores of Siberia. It is the weather equivalent of a train wreck, and it occurs quite frequently. Dutch Harbor, a perpetually misty fishing village on the island of Unalaska—about five stops beyond the rim of the world—averages 309 cloudy days a year and is the perfect realization of the poet Siegfried Sassoon's description of "death's gray land." When the sun comes out, residents drop everything and congregate in the town square to stare upward, like the children in "Village of the Damned."

As these storms intensify, they ride the prevailing winds on a north-easterly track and slam into the backbone of Alaska's panhandle, the Wrangell and St. Elias chain, the tallest coastal mountains in the world. One of two things will then occur. The storm will either jump the mountains and continue east into Canada—in which case, as Hufford says, "it becomes the Yukon's problem"—or Alaska's coastal ranges will act as a barricade and, like a pinball being smacked from flipper to flipper, the tempest will ricochet north-by-northwest around the inside of the Wrangell and St. Elias Range, the Chugach Range, and the Talkeetna Range, until it is passed off to the 700-mile-long Alaska Range. From there the pendulum will swing back west toward Denali, accumulating moisture—and force— from the small lakes, ponds, and muskeg swamps it sweeps across. In south-central Alaska, this is called a backdoor low, or backdoor weather, and it bodes ill for anyone mountain climbing in the vicinity.

The weather that wracks the Denali massif is unique. At 63 degrees north latitude—the same latitudinal coordinates as northern Hudson Bay and central Scandinavia—it rises just two hundred miles south of the Arctic Circle. The position of Mounts McKinley, Foraker, and Hunter at the northern extreme of the planet means that the climate around their summits presents some of the most severe year-round averages of any location on earth. It is weather wretched enough to kill wolverines and freeze a human's eyeballs in their sockets. The Himalayas are tropical by comparison, and only the 16,864-foot Vinson Massif, the highest point in Antarctica, approaches the Alaska Range's brutality. In essence, weather on Denali is not much different from weather at the North Pole—albeit in three dimensions—and it transforms the environment at incredible speed. Thus, at Denali's 7,200-foot base camp climbers often find themselves tent-bound in a ravaged environment, subject to sudden, deadly changes in wind and temperature. Conversely, in the shadow of Mont Blanc, at about the same altitude in the Alps, mountaineers can be found enjoying a 1989 Bourgogne Rouge in the French village of Chamonix, ogling the bronzed Swedish trekkers two tables away. The effect is that Denali's austere setting combines with the deceptively thin air of the northern latitudes to lay low even the most experienced climbers.

Put simply, the atmosphere that encases our planet is made up of a swirling collection of gases held in place by the earth's gravity. It is composed of 78.09 percent nitrogen, 20.95 percent oxygen, and trace elements of argon, neon, helium, methane, hydrogen, krypton, xenon, ozone, and, increasingly, carbon dioxide. The underside of this thermal umbrella is called the troposphere, which extends from sea level to roughly five to ten miles above the planet's surface before reaching, in succession, the stratosphere, mesosphere, thermosphere, and the exosphere, which gradually trails off into space. Because of the pull of gravity, the further one journeys from the earth's surface, the fewer oxygen molecules circulate. (Although in the magnetosphere 600 miles above the earth, the odd nitrogen and oxygen molecules do ping around the space shuttle.)

The troposphere, whose temperature cools with elevation, is where weather happens. At the top of the troposphere is a temperature-based line of demarcation called the tropopause, usually found at around -70 degrees Fahrenheit, where King Hell weather happens. But the troposphere's boundaries are not distributed equally around the planet. In warmer air over the equator, the troposphere expands to become twice as thick as it is over the poles. Near the equator, the tropopause may occur at around 50,000 feet. Over Denali it is closer to 30,000 feet. There is thus less oxygen in the air in the Alaska Range at, say, 15,000 feet than there is at the same altitude in the Himalayas or the Swiss Alps. To human lungs, 19,000 feet on Denali feels like 21,000 or 22,000 feet on Everest.

In addition, as the earth spins eastward on its axis at nearly 1,000 miles per hour, the troposphere swirls in great eddies and vortices, giving it an unstable consistency similar to a sloshing bowl of Jell-O. When this Jell-O-like casing folds inward, the jet stream, which screams around the world at up to 200 miles per hour, descends with it. Over most of the planet's mountainous regions, this has little effect. If the troposphere creases, say, 10,000 feet above Argentina's Mount Aconcagua (at 22,834 feet the highest mountain in South America), it remains several miles distant from the mountain's peak. In Alaska, however, the jet stream— with wind velocities analogous to a tornado's—has been known to touch down on Denali's summit. Thus, when the neon green splotch on Hufford's computer screen collides with that ruby red swirl, there will be hell to pay for anyone climbing near Denali. Hufford guesses that the brunt of the storm will hit the Alaska Range in no less than thirty-six hours. With this in mind, he thumbs through his Rolodex, searching for the mountain rangers' number.

One hundred miles to the north, on a deserted section of the Tokositna Glacier, Jim Donini slumps into his tent and glances at his watch. It is 7:15. It has taken him two hours to downclimb from Malcolm's position. He can vaguely make out the drone of air traffic across the cul-de-sac and out over the nearby Kahiltna Glacier. At this time of year it stays light until close to midnight, but Jim knows that none of the flightseeing tours will be overflying this desolate fork. He resigns himself to spending the night in the tent.

His thigh aches, although at least it has stopped bleeding. He shucks his mango orange Gore-Tex climbing suit and examines the thick crust of blood where Malcolm's crampon punctured him. He is about to tie off a makeshift tourniquet, in case the blood starts to flow again, and settle in for the night when he hears the approaching engine. At first Jim can't believe his ears. In a flash he is out of the tent, sprinting as best he can across the glacial ice, madly waving his climbing suit at Paul Roderick's approaching Cessna.

Paul Roderick usually planned his flybys over Jim and Malcolm's campsite sometime for mid-afternoon. If he didn't spot them, he assumed they were off in the mountains. But today the bad weather high on Denali has backed up his schedule, and Paul has fallen behind while ferrying climbers up and down the range. He thought he'd probably skip Jim and Malcolm today. But he is on his way down to Little Switzerland to pick up a group of glacier trekkers due to return to Talkeetna when he decides, since it is only 7:30 P.M., to bank into the Tokositna's southwest spur for a quick look.

The first thing he sees against the backdrop of the white and blue glacier is Jim Donini running in circles waving that damn orange jumpsuit over his head.

Jesus Christ, Roderick thinks, what the hell do these guys want now?

NINE

Real Bullets

The professional is the guy who can do it twice.

—DIZZY GILLESPIE

Mike Wayt pops his head into the day room looking for Mike Murphy. Several teammates, a few coming off or going on alert duty, some on their way to lift and work out, are gathered about an ash blond bar rubbed to a gleam by years of propped elbows. They are slurping Yuban, checking jump schedules, and buzzing about the British climber Karl Grugel and Steve Daigle are airlifting from Denali to Anchorage. Rumors have been flying through The Section since Steve Ball's extraction. Someone's heard that he has already lost a hand, and that both his feet will have to go below the knee. There's a story floating around that Daigle had to medicate the guy after he went into a psychotropic fit, and another that Grugel shocked him back to life when his ticker gave out.

"Hell, why doesn't somebody just give Daryl a call up in Talkeetna to see what's going on with the Brit," says Staff Sergeant Mario Romero, who is coming on alert. "That way we can update the whereabouts of Loomis and Grabill on the mountain, too." The PJs treat Daryl Miller as if their mutual bonds of bravery and lunatic restlessness extend beyond the official boundaries of the 210th. He is one of the few "civilians" with an open invitation to all of their barbecues and team parties, and he returns the camaraderie by acting as their eyes and ears on the mountain.

"Naw, no way Daryl's back at the ranger station yet," says Technical Sergeant Dave Thompson, checking his watch. "He's still up at base camp, battening things down. Weather Service says there's a storm on the way. Could either jump the Wrangells or back-door into Denali. Either way, Daryl won't be back down 'til tonight. But no matter. Glatt's due back in soon. His Herc should be wheels down any minute. He'll have the straight skinny."

Mock groans arise at the prospect of Mark Glatt relating another of his windy stories. Then Thompson notices Mike Wayt for the first time. His eyebrows lift quizzically. "What are you doin' here? Thought you were off."

Thompson is one of the five "Traditional Guard" members on the team, and even in his nondescript flight suit the thirty-three-year-old cuts an elegant figure in a *West Side Story* sort of way. Thick wavy black pompadour. Roman nose. Classic V shoulders. Along with Mike and one or two other vets, he is acknowledged as one of the team's most proficient mountain men, especially on ice, and has picked up the affectionate nickname Sardog—SAR being the military acronym for search and rescue.

"Got called in," Mike says with a brusque shake of his head. "They were short a team for a hiker lost up north of Fairbanks."

"You better double-check that." Thompson's smile is dazzling, as if his teeth were dipped in white paint. "I think I heard they found that woman. Fell and broke her ankle on the muskeg. Other than that, she's all right. Airlifted out."

Mike snatches a bottle of Gatorade from the refrigerator and picks up an in-house loudspeaker phone. His voice resonates through The Section. "Hey, Mike Murphy. You in the building? It's Wayt. I'm in the day room looking for you. Give me a holler."

The day room floor is covered with the same, shit-brown carpet as The Section's office area, and holds three couches in various states of disrepair, one of which Mike Wayt plops down on. Surrounding him are a twenty-four-inch television and VCR, and a soda machine wedged between a regular refrigerator and an industrial-strength model like the kind found in restaurants. The smaller one is filled with microwavable junk food: Hot Pockets pepperoni pizza, Campbell's chicken teriyaki bowls, individually wrapped beef, cheese, and green chile burritos. Its freezer holds innumerable cartons of fresh-fruit Popsicles. The larger refrigerator is stocked with enough Gatorade to slake the thirst of a Berber tribe, piles of packaged hot dogs and hamburger patties, moldering processed lunch meat of indeterminable origin, tubs of butter, saran-wrapped hunks of cheese, and countless jars of mustard, catsup, and mayonnaise. The team's greenest rookie is traditionally assigned two essential culinary tasks upon his arrival in Alaska: ensure that the squad never, ever, runs out of Popsicles, and make certain that the bottom two chutes of the soda machine are continually stocked with beer. It is a serious responsibility, and there is hell to pay from the veterans should the unit run short of either. Yet the last ninety-six hours have been so hectic that no one seems to notice that the soda machine holds nothing but soda.

The day room's faux cedar paneling is covered with a haphazard assortment of plaques, testimonials, commemorative hats, embossed canoe paddles, framed cartoons, and military and civilian awards and citations. The PJs have had more medals showered on them than Zeus' golden rain on Danae. An autographed photo of George and Barbara Bush shares a wall with the skin of a six-foot eastern diamondback rattlesnake smoothed and shellacked to an oaken frame. Tacked above both is a ribald poem in honor of a "virgin" parajumper's dearth of rescue missions. Nearby are "26 Thoughts to Get You Through Almost Any Crisis," among them, "Happiness is merely the remission of pain"; "The careful application of terror is also a form of communication"; and "Anything worth fighting for is also worth fighting dirty for."

Linoleum has been laid over a culvert in one corner, and the niche serves as a kitchen. A half dozen five-gallon jugs of Alaska Best spring water are piled beside a water cooler adjacent to a double sink. The cabinets and drawers are a riot of microwave popcorn bags, cardboard coffee cups and paper plates, jars of peanut butter, hot dog and hamburger buns, plastic kitchen utensils, cans of dog food, packets of Cup-A-Soup, half-eaten bags of pretzels and potato chips, and meticulously stacked 35-ounce cans of Yuban coffee and Maxwell House espresso. There is no decaf. The microwave is serviceably clean, but the coffee machine has the encrusted look of Korean War surplus. This is said to come in handy should the PJs ever run out of fresh grounds. All they'd have to do is fill the glass ewer with hot water and shake.

"Check out my new wheels on your way in?" Thompson asks Mike

Wayt, who nods yes he sure did. Thompson is the team's Harley freak, as the bumper sticker affixed to his locker attests—"My Wife and Harley-Davidson Are Missing. Reward for Information Leading to the Harley." Over a varied fifteen-year pararescue career he has served active duty, full-time reserve, and now traditional guard. This means he pulls alert perhaps four days or nights a week between shifts at the powder-coating company he recently started. Born in Detroit and reared just outside the city, Dave Thompson's reputation as a nonpareil ice monkey strikes some new teammates as incongruous; the Motor City has never been particularly known as a breeding ground for alpinists. But when Dave was small his parents took him to visit his great-grandmother, who owned a cottage in Calistoga, California, in the Napa wine country. He remembers sitting on her front porch gaping at the Sierras. The mountains looked as if they were right across the street, and Dave's desire to climb them was overwhelming.

Thompson cut photographs and drawings of the Himalayas and Alps from magazines and newspapers, and salted them away in a scrapbook he stored under his bed. A typical teenager of the seventies, he grew up "drinkin' beer and chasin' girls with my high school buddies." But deep down something told him there was more to life than six-packs and love in the backseat of his father's car. When his friends went off to college to continue the lifestyle, Dave visited the local Air Force recruiting station. He figured a four-year hitch would give him time to decide on a career. At the recruiting office he happened across a pamphlet about pararescue. His eyes widened. Scuba diving? Parachuting? Mountain climbing! "Where do I sign up?" The recruiter just laughed. "That's for the big boys." Thompson stretched to his full five-ten height, and asked again. Dave Thompson turned to pararescue in much the same spirit others turn to cloth and cowl. Working as a PJ was perfection personified.

He served a four-year active duty hitch, alternating between the now-defunct 305th Squadron in Michigan and pararescue headquarters in New Mexico. And he pulled TDY for a spell with Alaska's old 71st Air Rescue Service, the 210th's precursor. When the 210th was formed, he was recommended for the last available slot. Upon his arrival, something told him he was home. The first time he pulled alert at Eielson Air Station in Fairbanks he practiced climbing the ice sheets draping from the sides of the base's buildings and hangars. It was the start of a beautiful relationship. Dave was a natural, and he soon graduated to mountains. Even the recent birth of his baby daughter hasn't kept him off the Alaskan peaks. He likes to come home at night after a good climb and sit at the piano after dinner, lulling Victoria to sleep with Beethoven. "Für Elise" is her favorite.

Skip Kula walks into the day room. "Just saw Murphy back in the scuba room," he tells Wayt. "He's cleaning tanks. Says to head on back."

"What's up with the lost hiker?"

"Pretty sure they already got her."

The hallway between the day room and the PJ offices leads to the back of the warehouse, which opens up into a hangar-like space sectioned off with wire-mesh lockers the size of walk-in closets where the PJs stow their gear. Stepping into one is like standing in a miniature sporting goods store stocked with state-of-the-art warrior toys of every description: wet suits, dry suits, Mustang survival suits, flight suits, jumpsuits, scuba gear, camouflage uniforms, all-weather tents, sleeping rolls, skis and ski poles, flight and climbing helmets, carabiners and pitons, pile vests and jackets, camp stoves, hunting knives, wind pants, ice axes, toolboxes, shotguns, and an assortment of running, hiking, climbing, and cross-training shoes and boots. Surrounding the lockers are warehouse-like shelves climbing twenty feet high, nearly to the roof. These are laden with chainsaws, coils of climbing rope, boxes of chemical drop zone lights, Stokes litters and Miller boards, smoke canisters of various colors, binocular kits, portable searchlights, rock climbing racks, and mud-rescue aerators the size of bazookas.

The components of two military amphibious reconnaissance systems, or RAMZ packages, are spread out in one corner of the room, disassembled for their monthly cleaning. The packages, which can be dropped by parachute from the hold of a cargo jet, consist mainly of an engine-mounted, twelve-foot Zodiac speedboat that inflates upon contact with water. Above the RAMZ, resting on pallets, is a portable, all-terrain hospital tent called a MARTOK. The acronym stands for nothing; the PJ who invented the MARTOK was a Star Trek fan, and liked the guttural sound of the Klingon language.

In the corridor leading to the hot tub and "saltwater washdown" shower area the wall has been cleared and turned into a rock-climbing station, complete with a rappel rope hanging from an I beam. Most of the squad's heavy equipment—two more Zodiac speedboats, four snowmobiles—is stored behind The Section, in unattached blockhouse garages out near the basketball hoop. But a space has been made near the double garage doors to house two of the team's four blue Ford "sixpacks"—half-ton Workmasters with extra load room in the covered bed. Running along the back and west side of the building is a variety of storage rooms, each dedicated to specific tools of the trade. All that's missing is a tack room.

There is a map room containing nautical charts and topo maps of the entire state, and a medical room the envy of a small hospital. Filling its shelves and open cabinets are cervical collars, emergency surgery tools, IV bags and warmers, and Life Pac 10 kits capable of performing battlefield defibrillations, inflatable mast pants that enhance the blood circulation of hypothermic patients, and portable Pro Pac heart monitors with electrodes attached. A combination safe holds morphine and Valium as well as vials of cardiac drugs: epinephrine, lidocaine, atropine. The room is awash in randomly piled forceps, bandages, syringes, aspirin bottles, nylon suturing material, and saline drips. Sitting on a bench in the center is a life-sized plastic mannequin sporting a tourniquet, several splints, and a C-collar around its neck. The PJs practice on the dummy when there are no officers to be had.

Most parajumpers admit that the triage facet of their profession is the most underrated. Ask a PJ what he does for a living, and the last thing he'll mention is his paramedic qualifications. "But to be realistic," Mike Wayt admits, "guys who can jump out of an airplane or fast-rope from a helicopter are a dime a dozen. What separates us from any other part of an aircrew, from anybody else in Special Forces, is our medical background."

Interestingly, a squad of Green Berets or Navy SEALs will usually include one heavy weapons expert, one communications operator, one medical corpsman, one tracker—in other words, the sum of the unit's parts constitutes its whole. The pararescue career field turns that equation inside out. Like ancient Japanese samurai, who were not only expected to gain a mastery of martial skills but also of tea ceremonies, sumi painting, and the composition of poetry, parajumpers are jacks-of-all-trades, with the heaviest emphasis on medical training. Whereas Army Special Forces medics are for the most part taught to diagnose and treat long-term medical symptoms, setting up clinics in, say, Port-au-

Prince or Mogadishu, to minister to malaria or other tropical diseases, PJs are more attuned to immediate trauma: shock, bleeding, broken bones. To this end the Anchorage PJs are systematically farmed out to patrol with emergency medical crews in urban centers up and down the West Coast, the better, they feel, to learn to treat patients on the fly. Their training with gunshot wounds and knifings comes in handy—Steve Daigle once famously performed open-air emergency chest surgery at 12,000 feet on a Japanese climber who'd crushed his larynx attempting to snowboard Denali's Messner Couloir.

Nearly as often PJs find themselves serving as a sort of on-site translator between civilian rescue parties ministering to a wounded or injured victim and a physician on the other end of a radio or telephone line. "Try telling some state trooper over a scratchy radio band that he has to apply different pressure points to a victim bleeding to death from a femoral artery, as opposed to a brachial artery," says a veteran parajumper. "Hell, just try explaining the *difference* between a femoral and brachial artery. But that's not the sexy part of the job, so nobody makes a big deal out of it."

Around a corner from the medical room are the parachute and scuba rooms. Maintenance and upkeep of these facilities is rotated among the squad. The thirty-three-year-old Greg Hopkins, who despite his commendation for the Mount Torbert rescue nonetheless resembles a grown-up Jimmy Olsen, is currently in charge of the parachute room. Hopkins is one of the few parajumpers attached to the 210th who was never an active-duty airman. Seven years ago, acting on a whim—"I got a bug up my ass after reading a story about some PJs in Vietnam"—he joined the Alaska Air Guard and entered The Pipeline at the relatively old age of twenty-six. Upon earning his maroon beret he was assigned to "augment" the PJ team stationed permanently in Incirlik, Turkey. One of his first assignments was a "body drag" following the accidental downing of two U.S. Blackhawk helicopters by an American F-16 fighter jet over northern Iraq's no-fly zone. The mistaken attack killed all twenty-six passengers, members of the United States–European Command.

Hopkins tells the story with wide eyes and an eerie smile. "It was the only time on this job I ever really feared for my life. We flew into Kurdistan on a couple of Blackhawks to bag these horribly burned bodies. But that wasn't what goosed me. It was the trip in-country that did it. See, at the time the Turks were also flying Blackhawks, they bought them from us, and they used to roar into Kurdistan and blow the shit out of the Kurd rebels. So here I am, manning the 50-cal[iber] machine gun out the left gunner's door, parading into Kurd territory just waiting to get my ass blown off. I mean, we had these huge American flags painted on the aircraft, and we flew high enough to expose ourselves—the Turks would always fly low on their raids. Still, I was shaking."

After Hopkins and his detail spent fifteen straight hours tagging and bagging the bodies of the American, British, and French officers, his Blackhawk *was* fired upon on the return flight to Incirlik. A surface-to-air missile, discharged from somewhere in the Kurd-held mountains, barely missed the tiny fleet of American helicopters, and several of the aircraft took AK-47 hits. No one was injured, and an exhausted Hopkins dozed through the entire engagement. "I suppose, in a way, it's kind of nice to say I faced enemy fire and wasn't afraid. Of course, I don't usually tell people I slept through the whole thing."

Now Hopkins is carefully sorting the various types of parachutes stocked by the squad. The most commonly used for both training and SAR are the static-line "rounds" with a canopy diameter of 35 feet—the mushroom caps familiar to anyone who's ever seen a World War II movie. Rounds are sturdy and reliable, and can be employed from the standard jump altitude of 1,500 feet to as low as 400 feet. A parachutist cannot maneuver a round as effortlessly as a "square," a rectangular chute that can be steered by yanking on the nylon risers that attach the jumper to the canopy. But the rounds are the unit's workhorses—safe, slow, and familiar.

Squares come in two varieties, static-line and free-fall, and tolerate higher winds better than rounds. A parajumper will drop swiftly in a square—as opposed to the more pokey descent beneath a round canopy—but he can "brake" his fall by pulling on both risers simultaneously, which allows him to "flare out" his square. Squares are called lo-pos for their low porosity. The canopy's nylon material is woven tighter, which allows less air to pass through and in turn permits a softer landing. But there is a price to pay for the cushy touchdown. When a lo-po snaps open in midair, the sensation is of being drawn and quartered. Stick your hand out the window of a car traveling at 60 miles per hour. Cup your hand, and it jerks back. That is low porosity. Spread your fingers, and the air flows through. That is high porosity.

PJs also jump with a smaller reserve parachute, or "lollipop," fastened to their chest with a triple fail-safe rip cord. These are piled neatly in one corner of the parachute room next to heaps of instruction chutes (with canopies too tiny to bear the 60-pound rucksack a PJ will usually drop with), two-man tandem chutes, nonpersonnel parachutes (for delivering bulky objects like the MARTOK kits and Zodiac boats), and even a couple of experimental zero-porosity parachutes, should the urge to commit suicide suddenly strike a member of the team.

The metal cabinets and shelves are stacked high with multicolored rolls of crepe paper streamers, infrared Chem Lites, jump helmets, self-inflatable miniature life rafts, magnesium flares, neon-painted fiberglass "disco balls," portable altimeters, and handheld wind drift indicators, indispensable when executing water jumps. There is almost always wind near the surface of any large body of water, and a PJ's first task upon splashing down is to collapse his parachute as fast as possible to avoid skipping across the surface like a flat stone. Knowing which direction the wind is coming from is essential to not only landing, but also to collapsing your chute. Of course, as Hopkins is quick to point out, jumping out of a perfectly good airplane is not the surest sign of intelligent life, no matter the composition of the landing zone. He knows from experience.

A little over a year ago Hopkins was on a free-fall training exercise called a hop-and-pop. On a hop-and-pop, the parajumper is dropped from 3,000 feet, and all he has time to do is face the wind and pull his rip cord. "Don't even bother wearing a reserve on a hop-and-pop," Hopkins jokes, although all U.S. military jumpers are of course required to wear a reserve on every drop. "There's not time to pull it." On this jump Hopkins was barely out the bombay door when a rogue wind shear sent him tumbling end over end in midair. He yanked his rip cord, but his chute became tangled in his rucksack and sprang open between his legs. The unfolding risers slashed his right leg and tore a calf muscle. Once the canopy flared he was fine—if a tad shaken and embarrassed. Later, he had to be helped up the stairs of his home by Garth Lenz and Steve Daigle. His wife, Helen, standing at her kitchen window, at first saw only Lenz and Daigle approaching her door. "The last thing the wife of a PJ wants to spot is two of his teammates coming to her house without him," he says.

The veteran Hopkins' maintenance of the parachute room notwithstanding, one of the more recent arrivals is usually assigned to oversee

The Section's equipment rooms, at least until they have the gear's nuances down cold. Since he transferred to Alaska, Mike Murphy has been in charge of the squad's scuba room. The twenty-six-year-old Murphy has a Black Irish mug and the reputation as someone who knows how to handle himself in a bar fight—a practical attribute for an airman with a strong preference for "handmade" margaritas. Every week Murphy must check off on his maintenance sheet the working order of The Section's state-of-the-art Bauer air compressors, as well as the dozens of twin, 80-cylinder air tanks. From there he will inventory The Section's aluminum cabinets and shelves, which bulge with fins, masks, booties, buoy markers, whistles, tow straps, and waterproof tape. Each PJ also maintains his own, smaller scuba locker, containing dive consuls, air regulators, and depth gauges. Despite Murphy's nominal supervision, every PJ fills his own air tanks before going out on a mission.

Although Murphy is relatively new to the 210th, his combat reputation places him in an unlikely sort of limbo. He is one of the few PJs in the world who has actually fired a gun in anger at an enemy, and all his Alaskan teammates know the story. Three years earlier Murphy was still active duty and ordered overseas to augment the PJ unit based permanently in a secret U.S. Special Forces base in the port city of Brindisi, in the heel of Italy's boot. Not long after his arrival, a two-seater French Mirage fighter jet on a reconnaissance mission over Bosnia was shot down by Serbian artillery. The pilot and co-pilot bailed out. At the time Murphy was pulling alert with the aptly nicknamed James "Black Cloud" Talcott, one of the veterans of the 210th. If there is a hostile mission anywhere in the world involving U.S. aircraft, Talcott inevitably volunteers for combat TDY. Murphy and Talcott were ordered to scramble, unaware that their mission was to locate and recover the stranded French airmen. Both figured it was another of the near-daily training runs.

As they rushed to board the two HH-53 Pavelow helicopters powering up on the tarmac, Murphy pulled Talcott aside. Earlier in the day he had picked up some "personal intel" that the Brindisi parajumpers were scheduled to run on a mock search-and-rescue exercise that was supposed to simulate the real thing, right down to the flight crew not being told of their destination. "This is probably it now," Murphy told Talcott. "So stay cool, and let's have some fun."

The first hint that this was no simulation came when two French commandos and a squad of Green Berets joined them in the Pavelows. They also thought it odd when a file of solemn-faced U.S. soldiers and airmen gathered around the helicopters earnestly wishing everyone good luck.

"What the fuck are they talking about?" Murphy asked.

Talcott shrugged.

Somewhere over the Adriatic the helo's loadmaster began passing out live ammunition for Murphy's modified M-16 rifle equipped with a 203 Grenade Launcher and Talcott's .50-caliber machine gun. Live ammunition is rarely issued during a training exercise.

"James," Murphy whispered, "these are real fuckin' bullets!"

Talcott nodded eagerly. "I guess we're in the shit."

Meanwhile, the downed French flight crew's PRC-112 Survival Radio had been bouncing intermittent signals, or "beacon hits," off an orbiting U.S. satellite over UHF frequency 243.0—the international rescue frequency. But, as Murphy recalls, "the goddamn beacon hits were all over the place." Unbeknownst to the UN High Command, the Serbs had already captured the fliers. Their emergency beacons were in Serbian possession, and a Serb platoon was running them through the hill country of Bosnia in order to confuse—and draw in—any blue helmet UN search-and-rescue parties.

By the time the Pavelow crews were told that the Frenchmen had been captured they had already encountered the Serb platoon. For Murphy, it was a moment outside of time. "I don't remember much about the fight," he says cryptically. "Just keeping my head down and firing like a motherfucker out the gunner's door. Wasn't even looking where I was shooting. Later, on the way home, Talcott told me we blew the shit out of a Serb gun emplacement. By then I wasn't listening too good. I was sort of just staring at all the fuckin' bullet holes in the floor of the helo."

That Murphy has moved from blowing up Serb pillboxes to humping the Alaskan bush in search of lost tourists is a juxtaposition that sometimes leaves his new teammates flummoxed. On the one hand he is still a pup not only to civilian rescue but to the Anchorage team as well, and thereby subject to the same initiation rituals as any other new arrival. On the other hand, his participation in an honest-to-God firefight makes it difficult for any veteran to ride him too hard about, say, a lack of beer in the day room's soda machine. As a result, he performs his newcomer chores with a minimum of complaint and the more experienced Alaskan PJs seem to have accepted him more quickly than most.

Now Mike Wayt pokes his head into the scuba room and spots Murphy sorting through a pile of Spuds Bottles, miniature air tanks that parajumpers attach to their legs before "dropping" into water.

"So what's up with the lost hiker up north?" Mike asks.

"Go on home," Murphy replies. "I just got the call. Brent and Eric Taylor found her. Out by The Tors." The Tors, east of Fairbanks, is a giant, prehistoric rock formation dumped amid the tundra's mossy tussocks by ancient glaciers. From a distance, they appear to be a herd of slow-moving dinosaurs. "Evac-ed her out. You and I were supposed to be pulling backup. I called you at home a minute ago to tell you to stand down, but Lara said you were already on your way in. Sorry I didn't beep you, but I figured I'd see you here in a minute, anyway."

Mike turns to leave, but stops momentarily.

"And a dog? There was supposed to be a dog."

Murphy shrugs his shoulders. "Don't know nothin' about no dog."

The words "bear bait" cross Mike's mind for the second time that day.

TEN
Junkyard Dogs

When the legend becomes fact, print the legend.

—THE MAN WHO SHOT LIBERTY VALANCE

O n his way out of The Section, Mike Wayt passes the day room at about the same time as, one hundred miles to the northwest, Paul Roderick is touching down his skis to recover the frantic Jim Donini. Mike spots Steve Daigle cracking a beer. It is Friday evening, May 21, and, like a drumroll, the sna-pussssh of Daigle's pop-top announces the start of the weekend.

The day room is swarming with PJs in a frisky mood following Ball's rescue, as evidenced by the sodium chloride IV attached to Daigle's arm. One of his teammates needed to maintain his injection proficiency, plus, Daigle swears, the drip pre-empts hangovers. Some of the parajumpers are clad in sweats and shorts, but most sport "The Bag," the ubiquitous pea green, one-piece Nomex flight suit that pararescuemen live in the year round. The Bag is washed once a year whether it needs it or not (though never ironed, which could ruin the uniform's fireproof material).

Daigle and Karl Grugel, off in a corner completing his after action report on the British climber's recovery, are joined shortly by a four-man training unit just back from a free-fall jump at the Malamute drop zone on Fort Richardson, as well as by another group who have completed a "remote bundle drop" across Cook Inlet, near the thick stands of cottonwood that picket Mount Susitna. In the remote bundle drop a Pavehawk drops a simulated "airman" into a tangle of tree branches, PJs parachute from a C-130 with tree-climbing gear to retrieve "him," and the Pavehawk crew recovers the PJs and their "package" with a hoist. Then the Herc A-Rs, or air refuels, the helo. Each component of the 210th is thus engaged.

As beer cans and insults are hurled someone digs out a week-old copy of the *New York Times,* and pandemonium forms around the page-one story recounting the discovery of the body of legendary climber George Leigh Mallory on Mount Everest. The British explorer, who first uttered the phrase "because it is there," was thirty-eight when he and his climbing partner, a Cambridge University student named Andrew "Sandy" Irvine, disappeared in 1924, and a month ago an international expedition searching for their remains stumbled across Mallory's mummified corpse on a windswept ledge at 27,000 feet. Some of Mallory's gear was also recovered, although the camera he was known to have carried remained missing. One theory has it that Mallory entrusted it to his young partner to snap photographs of his triumphant summit. Scientists at Kodak suggest that the seventy-five-year-old film may not have deteriorated at altitude, and there is a minuscule possibility that Mallory may have beaten Sir Edmund Hillary and Tenzing Norgay to Everest's summit by almost thirty years. The whereabouts of Irvine's body and the camera remain a mystery.

For a bunch that does not astonish easily, the PJs are agog over the Mallory implications. They debate not only whether Mallory could have outraced Hillary to the top of the world in an alpine era symbolized by Tyrolean hats and tins of bully beef but also—in a direct connection to their own experience—whether the climbers will risk hauling Mallory's frozen corpse back to their base camp at 17,000 feet.

The conversation drifts to the possibility of the 210th mounting a training exercise into the Himalayas. None of the PJs have ever climbed in Central Asia, and their eyes blaze at the prospect, although their enthusiasm is muted by the knowledge that the Air Force would never pony up the expense for such a dream assignment. Still, they read about anything remotely connected to the area, and most recently have been closely monitoring the artillery skirmishes between Pakistani and Indian troops on the Siachen Glacier in Kashmir. They are staggered by the two armies' ability to make war at 23,000 feet.

"They ain't fighting each other," Daigle says. "They're fighting biology." This leads to an earnest discussion of how much the competing artillerymen must compensate when calculating the arc of a mortar shell sailing through the thin air four miles high, as opposed to the trajectory of artillery fire at sea level. The mechanical engineer Chris Keen is summoned from the scuba room to do the math.

Karl Grugel has finished his report on Steve Ball, and as he grabs a beer, he asks Dave Thompson if he's heard the latest intel from Iceland. It seems the Air Force wants to pull its search-and-rescue unit from the American-built Keflavik Naval Station outside Reykjavik. Only two U.S. fighter planes have ditched in the North Atlantic over the last decade, and should another plane go down, the high command feels the pararescue units from New York or Great Britain can handle the SAR. At the notion of losing the American parajumpers, however, Iceland's legislative body, the Althing, issued an ultimatum that said, in effect, "Pull the PJs, shut the base." The Air Force scrapped its plan.

"Yeah, the Icelanders got no use for that fighter squadron up there," Thompson tells Grugel. "But they sure do appreciate that rescue team pullin' their fishermen out of the drink."

Now Skip Kula bounds into the room and inserts a videocassette into the VCR. "Grugel's revenge," he announces. A crowd settles about the television like Eskimos around the hearth. The first images, shot this morning, reveal Karl Grugel exiting The Section's bathroom soaking wet. Someone jimmied the toilet to explode when he flushed it. Grugel and his fiancée are getting married next week in Connecticut, and he has been the victim of a string of practical jokes. But messing with the groom-to-be today turned out to be a tactical error of colossal proportions. Prior to running on the Steve Ball mission, Grugel had been drop zone manager during this morning's jump at Malamute. One of his jobs was to gauge ground wind speed and act as a "com," or communications, conduit between Fort Richardson's air traffic controllers and the C-130 ferrying the "stick" of PJs. In addition, a drop zone manager is responsible for selecting a site to lay out the two 10-foot-long, bright orange arrows that designate a jumper's landing area. The PJs pride themselves on hitting these arrows on the button. In retaliation for the toilet trick, Grugel draped both arrows over mud holes.

Now, on the screen, several PJs, including Staff Sergeant Mario

Romero, are plopping knee-deep into the mud. Romero misjudged the wind direction, and when the footage shows him being dragged by his parachute face-first through the frigid muck the boys in the day room bark like red-throated loons. Even the normally staid Mike Wayt is howling, taunting Romero, "Hey, Burrito Boy, the Mexican Air Force teach you to jump like that?"

Romero, a quiet twenty-six-year-old from McAllen, Texas, has the hard, sinewy physique of a professional bull rider. He does a slow burn as his awkward landing is replayed over and over. Mario came to the unit two years ago, and he has become the team's whipping boy. He is a small, wiry man, and his feelings are easily hurt, a terminal flaw among PJs who will pick any scab bloody. It is not the ideal work environment for the thin-skinned or politically correct. Mike Wayt, for instance, arrives at work each December 7—Pearl Harbor Day—prepared for his team- mates' taunts. And each time he steps onto an aircraft someone is bound to comment about "the little nip in the air today." Mike doesn't let it bother him. He gives as good as he gets. He'll flash that quixotic grin that spreads up his cheekbones. Damn right, he'll agree. "That little nip in the air means some civilian's got a damn sight better chance of getting his ass pulled from the wringer than with one of you lazy, round-eyed bozos." Sooner or later, his teammates all agree, Mario will learn to let the insults roll off his back. "His wet back," interjects Thompson. It is not as if Romero hasn't demonstrated the *cojones* to handle pararescue. Last August he and Technical Sergeant John Paff ran on an alert out to Mount Eldridge. The two PJs arrived at the scene to find that a single-engine Cherokee had plowed into the mountain at 8,000 feet.

Romero and Paff fast-roped from the helicopter to a ridge a half mile above the crash site and began downclimbing a near-vertical flank. Hammering pickets into the soft, sugar snow to anchor their belay lines, they downclimbed for several hours to traverse to the impaled bush plane protruding from Mount Eldridge's headwall like a winged javelin. The Cherokee's pilot had been killed on impact, his face implanted into the control panel. His body rested beneath a load of gear that had flown forward on impact, and Paff was forced to pry open the passenger-side door with his ice axe. In the pile were: A sleeping bag. A disassembled ten-speed bike. A Gore-Tex parka. A box of Fig Newtons. And, sitting atop it all, a book entitled *How to Fly Your Way Out of Danger.*

Guess the guy never got to the chapter on mountain flying, Mario remembers thinking. As he tenuously propped the tail of the plane up with his back, Paff got a hacksaw out of his ruck and began shaving away at the fuselage to cut out the ELT (emergency locator transmitter). One misstep could have sent the plane and the two men hurtling down the mountain. At one point he lost his footing and the tail boom tottered precariously over Paff.

"You want to see somebody sweating bullets in below-freezing weather, that was me," Mario says. "See, we left the pilot there—he's still up there—but we had to get the ELT out. It'd be pinging and fouling up the RCC for weeks. Funny thing is, once the location of the crash got out over the radio, every bush pilot within a hundred miles flew by to rubberneck."

Now it is the PJs who are rubbernecking, watching Mario fly nose down into the mud. At one point the videotape shudders to a halt. Daigle slams a wrench into the side of the television. The picture returns. For all their training, parajumpers are not often burdened with what Twain called "too elaborate a conjunction of ideas." Or, as Chief Master Sergeant Scotty Denton now says, "Ain't nothing ever broke that a wrench won't fix."

"Or an acetylene torch," cackles Daigle with a screech that would shatter Baccarat.

Grugel jabs Mario in the side as on the screen the young Tex-Mex nosedives yet again into the mud.

(Grugel may have won today's round of pranks, but in a few days the team will throw him a bachelor party during which he will be de-pantsed, bound with masking tape, tied to a Stokes litter, and have his pubic hair shaved. Sexual instructions addressed to his fiancée will be scrawled across his stomach and thighs in indelible green sea dye. He will then be carried, à la Cleopatra on her divan, through the doors of perhaps the town's sleaziest strip joint. There he will be placed supine, a towel covering his privates, on the small stage and "entertained" by a harem of broad-beamed nude dancers of whom the kindest that can be said is that not every one looks as if she's suffered a stroke. The night will not end here. A dozen PJs will pull a hat trick, being ejected—or rejected at the door—by three separate clubs and bars, including the subtly named Great Alaskan Bush Company. Such was the anticipation for this fete that it was difficult finding three PJs to serve as designated drivers. As it turned out, it was a good thing someone was sober enough to break up the fistfight that broke out between Romero and Greg Hopkins.)

Grugel's home movie stimulates a cinematic exchange. The team calculates the number of Hollywood movies that have featured parajumpers. Someone remembers the parachute scene in Goldie Hawn's *Private Benjamin.*

"And those Russian paratroops in *Red Dawn,*" says Daigle, "they were PJs."

Thompson comes up with the PJs who rescued Harrison Ford from insane Russian terrorists at the conclusion of *Air Force One.*

"Naw, those were actors," Mike Wayt says.

"Yeah, but they were playing PJs. I didn't know you meant the real thing."

"Those were real PJs in *Firefox,*" Scotty Denton says. "The helo crew that rousted Clint Eastwood in the beginning of the movie. The producers hired them out from the reserve unit at Moffett."

"And *Goldfinger,* don't forget *Goldfinger.*" Dave Thompson is showing his age. "The guys in the scuba scene."

Mike Wayt is nonplussed. Once past the *Star Wars* series and the *Top Gun* genre, a blank look settles on his face as Thompson and Daigle throw out the titles of an eclectic stream of films—*The Longest Day, It Takes a Thief, The Full Monty,* and John Ford's *The Informer.* When they toss him a softball and ask him what he thought of the television mini-series *Lonesome Dove,* everyone is incredulous that Mike has never heard of it.

Now Daigle flashes a toothy grin. "I'll give you a great movie, my all-time favorite. *Papillon.* It had everything. Survival. Adventure. Violence. And man-sex."

Mike Murphy has just bought a new Glock .9 mm sidearm. He is off in a corner swanning it around, comparing it to an older model Technical Sergeant Eric Taylor has produced. Marty Kimble is just down from Denali relay camp, where the sun has tanned his face like a Kabuki warrior's and he has lost twenty pounds. He announces that he spotted Captain Joseph Hazelwood, sentenced to 1,000 hours of community service for running the *Exxon Valdez* aground, serving meals to the homeless in an Anchorage soup kitchen. Several of the PJs hoot and growl at the mention of Hazelwood's name.

Daigle breaks the tension by telling a story about rushing to adminis-
ter medical treatment to a recently released mental patient who'd
stabbed herself several times in a remote cabin up in the Mat-Su. The
woman was black and a midget. When Daigle asked her why she'd tried
to kill herself, she'd turned on him and snarled, "You have to ask? Jesus!
I'm small. I'm black. And I live in Alaska."

Master Sergeant Paul Reddington, a red-haired baby bull of a man
who recently went part time after fourteen years of full-time service,
wanders into the day room carrying his two toddlers, Peter John and
Holly. Redd is pulling weekend helo alert with Mike Wayt. Some of the
guys ride Redd about his son inheriting his father's large head.

"Babysitting, how sweet," Thompson taunts.

"Don't start with me," Reddington warns. Thompson backs off. One
of the reasons Reddington went part-time is because he is thinking about
opening up a motel near Fairbanks. Guesthouses on the rolling steppes
of the interior are rare. But Redd has heard that the few that do exist do
hellacious tourist business in summer, and are kept afloat in the off-
season by a steady stream of Japanese newlyweds who believe that any
child conceived under the pale green and rose auroras that play among
the wintertide constellations will be born with mystical powers. It is no
coincidence that the Inuit people call them the Spirit Lights.

"That true, Hop Sing?" Daigle inquires. Mike Wayt gives him the
finger.

Now the rookie Steve Wolf wanders in and someone drops him.
Since Wolf is still in The Pipeline, he remains, technically, a pararescue
candidate, subject to the whim and caprice of the team. If this seems an
indignity to the veteran Navy SEAL, Wolf's stony face does not reveal it.
He dutifully gives the group fifty push-ups, counting off each at the top of
his baritone voice while being showered with beer bottle caps.

The 210th is fast becoming an unofficial stop along pararescue's eighteen-month Pipeline even for PJs who, unlike Wolf, are not slated to join
the Alaskan team. Because of his SEAL experience, Wolf is not required
to attend the scuba course in Key West, and has been splitting time
between Anchorage and The Schoolhouse in New Mexico while he
waits for a slot to open at the three-week Special Ops Combat Medic
Course at Fort Bragg.

The ex-SEAL's appearance at this Friday afternoon soiree soon engenders a can-you-top-this argument over the relative harshness of the Indoc, or Classification, Course. Every graduate from Lackland ardently believes that the Indoc Course becomes immeasurably easier to get through once he has graduated. To hear some of the older PJs tell it, Steve Wolf—Navy SEAL or no Navy SEAL—was lucky not to be hit over the head with a ball peen hammer several times before being dumped from a cargo jet without a parachute into the South Pacific and told to swim home.

"How about HALOs, man, HALOs were the bitch," says Daigle, referring to high-altitude, low-opening paradrops. He describes the "pleasures" of dropping from a Herc at 17,000 feet with 120 pounds of commando gear packed into his ruck, screaming toward the earth at 110 miles per hour before pulling his rip cord seconds from the ground. "It's not like dropping," he explains. "It's more like pushing a pile of shit out the door."

"Forget about that, I'll take HALO over The Crossovers any day," Mike Wayt shoots back. "My class lost ninety percent doing Crossovers." The Crossover drill entails sitting at the bottom of the deep end of a swimming pool with twin eighty-pound scuba tanks strapped to your back, no air regulator, and a training instructor attempting to prevent you from surfacing.

"Nuh-uh, you're both wrong." Dave Thompson has joined the fray. "Surfing the Cones. Surfing the Cones was *the* bitch." The room echoes with murmurs of assent. Surfing the Cones also takes place in a swimming pool. It involves swimming fifteen underwater laps while a training instructor rides a recruit's back using any means within his power to keep the swimmer from finishing the course in the allotted time.

Says Thompson, "They'll push you back under when you reach the pool wall, pound on you upside the head, try to rip your mask off. They're basically trying to drown you. I remember they hit me so hard my mask cracked."

"Ah, they don't allow that shit anymore," Skip Kula says. He shoots a pointed glance toward Steve Wolf, in the manner of an older relative trying to impress upon some young whippersnapper the harshness of his upbringing. "The Pentagon calls it harassment now. But if you can't handle that, how do you expect to operate out in the dark, in the cold, floating alone somewhere out on the Bering Sea?"

Mark Glatt's Herc had landed earlier and he'd headed directly to The Section to work out in the gym. Now, taking a break, he ambles into the day room and drops seamlessly into the conversation, describing one particularly fiendish drill he endured at Indoc. A training instructor would throw a coin, a penny, into the pool. The trainee scramble that ensued was no-holds barred. Whoever came to the surface with the penny passed the drill, the rest remained in the pool, and the exercise was repeated. "The last guy left is washed out." Glatt's eyes twinkle. "Until the recruits figured out that if we all snuck a penny into our Speedos beforehand, and all surfaced with the penny, we'd all pass." His point is that the drill instructors were trying to compel the recruits to think like a team.

Glatt spots Wolf and points with his chin. "Man, this guy is proof positive that The Pipeline is a process where some of the junkyard dogs get through while a lot of the purebreds get weeded out." Everyone laughs except Karl Grugel, who appears lost in thought. Glatt senses there is something bothering Grugel, and he thinks he knows what it is. The kid never comes out and mentions his frustration over the Steve Ball rescue, how it in no way stacks up against something like the Torbert mission or the Kim save, how it turned out to be so . . . so anticlimactic (except, of course, to Steve Ball). But Glatt can sense the young PJ's disappointment.

He thinks about saying something to Grugel; instead, he turns back for the gym. On his way to the treadmill he passes Grugel outside the day room and flashes a weary smile. Shaking his head slowly, he calls out over his shoulder. "Hey, Karl, don't sweat it. There's always tomorrow. We're in Alaska, for chrissake."

On the corkboard wall near the gym there are sign-up sheets for various upcoming classes: a dive medic's course, a swift-water rescue course, a wilderness emergency medical training course. Mark Glatt affixes his name to each one. While he signs the pages he hears someone ask who's pulling weekend alert. Mike Wayt and Paul Reddington answer, but Steve Daigle's voice drowns them out.

"No worries for the next couple of days," Daigle is saying. "We got all the Brits, and everybody on Denali's accounted for. I just talked to Daryl, invited him down for cocktails. But he's battening down up at base camp. Everybody enjoy, with that front moving in nothing's happening this weekend."

The last thing Mark Glatt hears before the gym doors close behind him is the sna-pussssh of another pop-top.

Daryl Miller had indeed considered driving down to Anchorage for the evening before receiving word of the oncoming storm. He hadn't tied one on with the PJs for quite a while, and the thought of bouncing through town with Daigle and the boys held a pleasant allure. But he also had a social obligation to fulfill, and as much as Daryl disliked the idea, he was a man of his word. Tonight is the inauguration of the Alaska Mountain Climbers Hall of Fame exhibit, the first of its kind in the state, and as Denali Park and Preserve's lead high-altitude ranger, Daryl was asked to be a member of the judges' panel that selected the original nine inductees. So upon returning to Talkeetna after supervising the airlift of Steve Ball he'd made his way directly to the lobby of the spanking new, $8.5-million Talkeetna Alaskan Lodge. Though determined to make a graceful exit as soon as possible, the main room of the lodge now closes around him and he realizes what he needs more than anything in this life is a bed.

Daryl has managed to snatch but a few hours of sleep over the last week as he supervised the medevac of, first, the Spaniards, then the Italian photographer, and finally the two-day SAR mission for the three Brits. From the moment the Spaniards flew off The Autobahn he feels as if his life has been a chaotic vortex of snow, wind, and ice, and now he finds himself straddling a gaggle of raven-eyed real estate developers clucking about commercial zoning rights, environmental impact statements, and property setback laws. The snatches of conversation he overhears only heighten Daryl's pet fear that America's last true wilderness will soon morph into a sort of outback theme park.

He picks up a sterling silver spoon and stares at his reflection, first convex, then concave. Either way, he decides, he looks like shit. He turns to his partner, Judy Alderson, a pert blonde Park Service's natural resources manager who's driven up from Anchorage for a weekend visit.

Which way's the bar, hon?

Still dressed in his forest greens—National Park Service–issue denims and buttoned-down shirt—he makes his way across the room with a rolling limp, heading for the nearest bottle of gin, skip the tonic. He moves as if his joints were installed backward. It is painful to watch him walk. He threads his way through the climbing crowd and the polyester set, across the lobby, and into the lounge. He's thought better of straight hooch, a word that entered the vernacular via the Auk tribe, who distilled a drink they called hoochinoo down on the island-starred Alaskan archipelago. The bartender pours him a tall gin and tonic. No fruit.

The rustic Talkeetna Lodge is set on a high knoll just east of town, and on this crystalline evening the floor-to-ceiling windows set amid stone columns and polished Sitka spruce girders offer majestic panoramas of cloud-shrouded Denali and the misty cordillera beyond. Though Mounts Foraker and Hunter pierce the pinkening sky, the view will not last for long. The Park Service has gotten word from meteorologist Gary Hufford down in Anchorage. Daryl looks forward to hunkering down for the big blow.

He slugs his drink, orders another, and spots the soiree's eighty-eight-year-old guest of honor, the legendary explorer Bradford Washburn, sitting in a corner of the lounge. Washburn's leathery face, as tough as an old boot, bobs amid a sea of well-wishers and autograph seekers. Brad Washburn is America's foremost living exploratory cartographer, a climber and photographer whose three summits of Denali in 1942, 1947, and 1951 unlocked much of the mountain's mystery. As the Alaskan alpinist Colby Coombs writes with a certain poetry in his *Denali Climber's Guide,* "The name *Washburn* is synonymous with the West Buttress, so well does this pioneering mountaineer know the terrain. His photographs are so detailed and revealing that they transcend any language barrier or lack of proficiency in reading topographical maps."

Washburn's early bush plane reconnaissance of the massif and the range beyond enabled the National Geographic Society to produce the first accurate topo maps of the preserve and its environs, and Daryl reflects with irony that Steve Ball nearly met his maker on the descent route named after the Boston octogenarian. He also notes that the old patrician looks fit enough today to tackle the West Butt. Seated next to his eighty-four-year-old wife, Barbara—the first woman to summit Denali—Washburn has aged into a lithe, sinewy, balding man with the countenance of a hungry eagle. Among the exhibits and photos of the Hall of Famers surrounding Daryl stands a glass case holding Washburn's leather boots, elk-skin snowshoes, and unwieldy Kodak box camera. Above the case hangs a lithograph of the members of the 1910 Sourdough Expedition—Peter Anderson, Tom Lloyd, Charlie McGonagall, and Billy Taylor—whose startlingly swift ascent of Denali's north summit was fueled solely by sourdough doughnuts, beer, and thermoses of hot chocolate. Daryl has often wondered what it was like exploring Denali before all the routes had been charted, before the climbers knew there was a rescue helicopter powering up in Talkeetna, hell, before Gore-Tex or polymers or neoprene were invented.

In true outback fashion, the Sourdough Expedition had formed partly as a result of whiskey-induced outrage. In 1906, when the arctic explorer and con man Frederick Cook grandiosely announced that he and a companion had reached McKinley's summit, most serious mountaineers were dubious. The East Coast press, however, conferred celebrity status on Cook. It was years before Cook's assertion was conclusively proved a hoax, but even at the time this shady cheechako's boasts festered with a group of miners who congregated in Fairbanks' bawdy taverns. In late 1909, after a night of serious drinking, the gold miner Tom Lloyd decided to pull together his own climbing party to tackle Denali.

The Sourdough Expedition set off from Fairbanks by dogsled in March 1910 with seven members, none of whom had ever seriously climbed before. Along the thirty-five-mile trek to Wonder Lake by way of the Muldrow Glacier a drunken brawl erupted, and three of the miners turned back, leaving Anderson, Lloyd, McGonagall, and Taylor. Hefting a fourteen-foot spruce flagpole, the remaining four sourdoughs completed a remarkable eighteen-hour ascent with a minimum of basic climbing equipment. Perfect weather helped, and Anderson and Taylor negotiated the final 9,000 feet and planted their flagpole on McKinley's 19,470-foot north peak—unaware that the south peak is 850 feet higher. When they returned to Fairbanks their claims were doubted—until the first cloud-free morning dawned, and their six-by-eight-foot American flag could be seen flying from the summit 120 miles away. The Sourdough Expedition remains one of the most remarkable climbs in the history of mountaineering.

Hanging catty-corner to the picture of the scruffy, heroic gold miners is a photo of Belmore Browne. Browne and his partner, Herschel Parker, came within a few hundred vertical feet of Denali's south summit two years after the sourdoughs reached the north peak. A year later the Archdeacon Hudson Stuck's party made it. Staring out at the room across from Browne peers the unmistakable visage of Terrance "Muggs" Stump, the respected guide who climbed the Cassin Ridge in an astounding fifteen hours and who was killed in a crevasse fall on the mountain in 1992. Next to Muggs smiles Ray Genet, the pioneer guide whose twenty-seven summits are believed to be a Denali record. Genet led Susan Butcher and her Iditarod-winning dogsled team's ascent to the summit in 1979 before perishing the same year in a small ice cave after reaching the top of Everest.

Daryl sees Washburn in deep conversation with Ray's son, Taras Genet, and Dave Johnson, a local Talkeetnan and the only other living inductee into the Hall of Fame. Johnson, Ray Genet, and Art Davidson completed the mountain's first winter ascent in 1967. Daryl decides it is time to pay his respects to the icon of McKinley mountaineering, and begins rolling across the room. He makes it halfway to Washburn when he feels a tap on his shoulder. Without thinking, he glances at his watch. It is a little past 8 P.M, and he feels the back of his scalp contract. Punky Moore, one of the administrative rangers from Park Service headquarters, is standing with her hands crossed behind her back to keep them from fidgeting. She is biting her lower lip nervously and shifting her weight from one foot to the other. Daryl, in his exhaustion, does not wait for her to speak.

"You gotta be kidding me!"

Punky lowers her head and the words pour out in a sort of gibberish. "I'm sorry, Daryl. We've got something developing. Near Hunter. They kind of need you now."

Daryl knows it is Malcolm. He kisses Judy goodbye, finds his jacket, and follows Punky out. He is suddenly more tired than he's felt since he humped a ruck in Vietnam. He throws his mountain bike into the flatbed of Punky's truck and pumps her for details as he hops into the cab.

All she can tell him is that Paul Roderick has radioed for Daryl and a doctor to meet him at the airstrip. He's coming in with Jim Donini, who's hurt, but Punky doesn't know how badly.

"Just Donini?"

"Just the one. Paul said something about the other climber—a friend of yours, right?—still stuck up on Thunder Mountain."

Daryl pictures the backdoor low moving in, and his stomach hurts. He thinks about Mike Vanderbeek and the two dead Koreans and ordering a halt to the rescue of the four doomed Canadians all those years ago. Such was the fine line he now walked with his friend Malcolm Daly. It has been some time since he was afraid.

Jim Donini refuses a doctor, insisting his wounds can wait until after he's been debriefed. He is as morose as ever, but the moment Daryl and Punky meet him at the airport he begins a minute-by-minute account of Malcolm's fall. He describes the terrain where he's left his friend bivouacked, the amount of food and clothing Malcolm still has, the details of fall lines and ice overhangs, and what he reckons to be the shortest rescue route up the headwall. As Jim Donini gives the details of the disaster, Daryl feels as if he is tracking footprints that slowly disappear into snow.

After three hours Daryl asks Punky to take Donini to a doctor. Outside, the outriders of the storm front Gary Hufford predicted have boomeranged around Alaska's coastal mountains and blown through Talkeetna. At first they were merely torn shreds of cloud surfing down the massif's hanging glaciers, but by ten o'clock the entire Alaska Range is weathered in. Occasionally Jim Hood pops his head into the ranger station to brief Daryl on what he already suspects: there is no way the helicopter is flying tonight. In a way it doesn't matter. Daryl wonders if the Lama could get to Malcolm even if conditions were perfect.

ELEVEN

Notification

All mankind is but a flickering flame in a strong wind.

—MICHEL DE MONTAIGNE

J im Donini had not wanted to make the call. He'd have preferred to wait a bit, see how things played out. That's what he'd suggested to Daryl's boss, J. D. Swed, the chief administrative ranger for the Park Service's South District, while the doc from the local clinic patched up his injured shoulder and punctured thigh. But Swed insisted Karen Daly be contacted immediately. He's probably right, Jim thinks now. There are still plenty of reporters hanging around Talkeetna in the aftermath of the Steve Ball rescue. A bunch stayed in town to attend the Hall of Fame's opening ceremony at the Talkeetna Lodge. Swed didn't want the media getting hold of the story before Karen was informed.

Swed offered, but Jim said, no, he'd do it.

So at 1 A.M. in Boulder, Colorado, Karen Daly is jolted out of a deep sleep by the ringing phone.

"Karen? Jim Donini."

Karen stares at the receiver uncomprehendingly. Jim Donini? What is he doing calling me? He doesn't even carry a cell phone. The cobwebs clear from her mind as if washed away by an ocean wave. Something is terribly wrong.

"Karen, Malcolm took a fall. Uh, a bad fall."

She feels a clammy dread at the base of her spine. The nerves at the back of her skull tingle.

"He's alive," Jim says quickly.

"Jim, where is he?" Why is Jim calling? Karen wonders. Why not Malcolm?

"He fell on a mountain, Thunder Mountain."

Karen is confused. What happened to the Hunter ascent? Thunder Mountain? The Disneyland ride mountain?

Jim lays it out. They hadn't yet gotten to Hunter. Malcolm took a long tumble. He's got multiple fractures of his legs. Jim mentions something about "still bleeding."

"What does that mean, still bleeding?"

"He's still up there, Karen. On a ledge. I left him there and climbed down to get help."

What? Still up there? "Is anyone with him? Where the hell is Thunder Mountain?"

Jim assures her that the rangers are pulling together a rescue team. Details are still sketchy. Karen will have to talk to the head ranger. Jim gives her J. D. Swed's phone number.

Karen hangs up, her mind crowded with a million thoughts. Would she be overreacting if she flew up there? Malcolm always gets so angry when she overreacts. Should she call someone to take care of the kids? Should she call anybody at this hour? No. First, calm down. Malcolm knows what he's doing in the mountains. He's going to be fine.

Karen walks downstairs and turns on her kitchen light. She needs time to think. She paces the floor, and finally lifts the phone and dials Swed's number.

The ranger picks up on the first ring. Karen has the impression he's been waiting for her call. Swed can't add much to what Jim Donini has already told her except to say they've been trying to get in near Malcolm's location with both fixed wing and helicopter, but the weather's keeping them out. Malcolm's trapped in a sort of vertical gash in the mountain. They can overfly it, but they can't see in. The Alaska High Mountain Rescue Team has already been contacted. The Air Force's 210th Pararescue Squad, too. They're all on their way.

Then Swed mentions something about a harrowing rescue of some Englishmen on Denali, and how all the rangers have just come off a long, arduous couple of days. "The pilots, the rangers, everybody up here is exhausted."

Karen doesn't like the sound of that. She checks the kitchen clock. It's only eleven-thirty in Talkeetna. Probably still light in the mountains. Still light for Malcolm. Maybe the weather will break. The thought of him stranded in the dark scares her.

Then J. D. Swed drops the bomb. "Malcolm will be spending the night alone up on that ridge."

Karen is almost afraid to say the word. "Alone? For how long?"

The ranger says something about the situation being difficult to assess and advises her to ring him back first thing in the morning.

Karen cradles the receiver in a daze. Malcolm is alone on a mountain. With two broken legs. Bleeding. Jesus!

Karen puts up a pot of coffee and debates whether or not to call Malcolm's mom, Sally. No, let her sleep. If she has to fly to Alaska she'll need Sally fresh for tomorrow, to mind the kids. She picks up the receiver again.

In Connecticut, Malcolm's father, Jerry, groggily answers his phone.

"Hello, Jerry, it's Karen. I'm sorry to wake you, but there's an emergency." Her options become clear. "I have to go to Alaska."

Daryl telephones Karen Daly at 4:30 A.M. He's spoken to Swed, and knows she'll be up. He paints a bleak, disturbing picture and the words catch in his throat. He can sense that his unease is registering with Karen. Finally, he says, "Karen, it's not going to be good. This rescue is going to be one of the hardest things we're ever going to do." He does not add what he is thinking—if, in fact, we can do it at all. He promises to call later, and clicks off

Daryl wonders if he is going to have to be the one who must ultimately break the news to Karen that her husband is dead. No, he tells himself, get that option out of your brain. You keep a thought like that and, man, it just wracks you. Wracks you frozen.

Nine-year-old Kitt Daly is up at 7 A.M., and Karen sends him into the basement to watch Saturday morning cartoons. Mason, twelve, is still asleep. Three hours earlier, in the lonely recesses of an eternal night, she'd booked a seat on an afternoon flight from Denver to Anchorage. Now, with the audio of Kitt's cartoons discernible in the background, she checks her watch and dials Swed's number.

Not much has changed. Despite the weather a team of Air Force parajumpers is already up on the Tokositna organizing a makeshift base camp below Malcolm's perch. Daryl's up there with them, he adds, overseeing the setup. Swed also expects a contingent from the civilian-staffed Alaska Mountain Rescue Squad in Talkeetna at any moment.

Karen hangs up as a friend, Sari Nichol, arrives with plates of food. Malcolm's mom, Sally, pulls into the driveway behind her. Less than twelve hours earlier Karen, Sally, and Sally's friend Max had celebrated Sally's birthday. Afterward they'd sat in Chautauqua Park overlooking Boulder, watching the city's lights sparkle as they'd jokingly wondered what Malcolm and Jim Donini were up to. Little did they know, Karen thinks.

Sari has spoken to Daryl, too, and she tells Karen that his end of the conversation was monosyllabic, almost nonverbal. In fact, Sari thought his voice was tinged with a pale gray dread, but she tells Karen only, "He didn't sound like the Daryl Miller I knew from before."

Karen begins to weep softly. "What aren't they telling me?" She whispers it to Sari, but dries her eyes hurriedly when her mother-in-law walks into the kitchen.

For the first time since speaking to Jim Donini, Karen confronts the possibility that her husband may die up in those mountains.

To witness a storm on Denali is to feel humility and terror in the presence of unlimited rage. To cower pathetically with two broken legs as one crashes around you is mental cruelty. Ten minutes after Malcolm watches Paul Roderick's bush plane take off from the Tokositna with Jim Donini aboard, he finishes packing his legs in snow. He wracks his brain but has no recollection of how to treat two simultaneously broken ankles. None of his first-aid manuals or self-rescue books cover that contingency. He's never known anyone trapped on a snowy ledge with two broken legs, either. What he does know is that he has to stanch his bleeding.

Unwittingly, Malcolm is doing just the right thing packing his feet with snow. Three problems concern him. The first is, simply enough, to keep from falling off his narrow ledge. His feet are so unstable that he cannot control their movement, and it could be fatal to get turned the wrong way and need his lower limbs to gain some purchase. In essence, he is using Jim's snowpacked rucksack as a counterweight to his upper body. Malcolm also intuitively reasons that if he intends to save his feet, he has to keep them warm somehow. He guesses that the temperature of the snow is actually a few degrees warmer than the mountain's ambient temperature. Finally, he needs to make a kind of cast to stabilize and restrict any movement that might cause further blood loss. Malcolm can't tell if blood is still weeping into his climbing boot with each raw throb. He is sure, however, that despite the Vicodins he has never been in more pain in his life. The word "pain" derives from the Latin *poena*, or penalty, and Malcolm is paying in full.

Thirty minutes after the last, hushed drone of Roderick's bush plane falls away, the weather turns from clear to misty and foggy. Tendrils of pearl gray clouds shroud Malcolm's vertical defile, and the flakes lashing his face turn from sodden to tiny and angry. Malcolm shivers, his muscles involuntarily contracting to produce body heat, and he can hear what Jack London called "white silence." Malcolm knows it is going to blow tonight, and prepares for the storm with the patience of a python.

He takes an inventory of his scant stores and calculates his rations for a three-day period. A couple of Power Bars. Two big, dense oatmeal cookies sweetened with apple juice. One packet of sucrose-laden Mountain Goo. Two and one-half quarts of water. He decides to concoct some sort of brain game to stay alert, but his mind drifts. He tries to count to one thousand, but his thoughts turn to a buddy back in Boulder who lost a foot in a tractor accident. The guy's still fit as hell, still out on his mountain bike every weekend. No, I can't worry about losing my feet or even any toes. I just have to worry about getting out of here alive. Malcolm has read enough survival stories to accept on faith the ancient Buddhist sutra that thoughts are things, and to differentiate between good thoughts and bad thoughts. Getting off this damn mountain alive is a decidedly good thought. He resolves to contrive some kind of physical activity to keep his blood circulating, but before he's come up with an exercise nature inadvertently solves his problem.

Malcolm is situated directly in the confluence of three shallow gullies that act as natural fall lines. As the snowstorm increases he is bombarded by a succession of small spindrift avalanches. The snow packs in behind him, between his buttocks and the cliff face, and though he is tied onto his pitiful ledge by his climbing harness, each small movement edges him a little farther off his perch. After every mini-avalanche, which seems to come by the minute, he maneuvers into a half turn and uses his ice axe to scrape the ledge clean. He spends most of the night digging out, which provides enough exercise to keep his circulation going. When the storm abates somewhat he begins doing windmill exercises with his arms. He spins them so much they feel as if they will fall off. Between the avalanches and the windmills, the night passes surprisingly quickly.

At the height of the storm he recognizes the low whine of a light plane. He has no way of knowing that it is Paul Roderick overflying his position. Then, at dawn, he hears another engine, a different pitch, but he can't see more than ten feet in front of him. From the direction of the hum, it is obvious someone is flying a grid search pattern over the mountain, and the plane passes over his position nearly fifty times. Then, as if on cue, the plane again approaches just as a mighty wind gust momentarily clears the ravine of clouds. He sees the black granite gunsight notch, the glacier below, and, off in the distance, what looks like a toy airplane heading straight for him at eye level.

Malcolm waves frantically and nearly knocks himself off his ledge. His ankles throb.

The bush pilot waggles his wings in acknowledgment.

Then the ravine again fills with storm clouds.

He's waving, Karen. He's waving. He's waving. You can see him." J. D. Swed is practically yelping over the telephone line.

It is Saturday morning, and the sun has been up for two hours over Boulder when the ranger informs Karen that her husband has not only made it through the storm-lashed night, but bush pilot Jay Hudson reports he is actually doing exercises while pinned to the headwall of Thunder Mountain. By now Karen has told her boys of their father's plight and assured them that Daddy will be all right. Yet even as the words left her mouth she worried that she was telling them a lie. No matter, she didn't feel as if she could leave home without them thinking that everything would be okay.

Karen's older son, Mason, took the news hard. Like his mother, he wears his heart on his sleeve, and Karen could hear him sniffling out in the kitchen. Kitt, who takes after his father, was more stoic. He curled up quietly on the couch in the living room and said nothing to anyone.

Karen had arranged to meet Malcolm's brother, Jed, in Anchorage this evening. In the meantime, Grandma Sally would watch the kids, and Grandpa Jerry was already on a flight to Denver from the East Coast. Her departure isn't for another ten hours, and as the day crawls by she becomes more and more depressed. Friends and neighbors drop by with food and good wishes, and Swed checks in every few hours. But Daryl doesn't call again. It is obvious that the weather is not letting up and there will be no rescue attempt today. Karen dreads the thought of Malcolm spending another night up there alone.

The flight to Anchorage is an unnerving ordeal, made worse by her lack of contact with the mountain rangers. During her forty-minute layover in Seattle, she calls home. Her father-in-law tells her no one has heard from anyone in Alaska. She jams her fist so hard into the phone booth, she is afraid she has broken a knuckle.

"Jerry, you find out what's going on." Karen's voice is tinged with steel. "I don't care how you do it, but you find out what's going on up there. By the time I land in Anchorage, I want to know if my husband is dead or alive."

TWELVE
"Exfil"

Matter will always proceed toward
disorganization or entropy.

—The Second Law of Thermodynamics

The MH-60G Pavehawk lifts off from Kulis Air Base a few moments past noon on Saturday, May 22. The pilot, Colonel Ron Parkhouse, sets a course for the Tokositna Glacier. The helo carries a flight crew of six: pilot, co-pilot, flight engineer, and, squatting against the auxiliary fuel tanks in the aircraft's sixty-five-foot fuselage, Mike Wayt, Paul Redding-ton, and Mario Romero.

Mike and Redd, pulling weekend alert, have been in contact with the RCC throughout the night. Earlier this morning, just before six, they'd signed off as another helo had ferried Dave Thompson, Brent Widen-house, and Scotty Denton up to the Tokositna, where they're now dig-ging out a temp base camp just below Malcolm's ledge. They've been briefed and ordered to wait for reinforcements. Mike, Redd, and Mario are it.

Mario got the call at ten this morning. It was his first day off in a while, and he and Mike Murphy were window-shopping at the local Harley-Davidson dealership when their beepers lit up. The bikers all stared at them as if they were cops. Murph was suffering. Tequila flu. Mario took a good look at his partner's bloodshot eyes and told him to go home and sleep it off. He'd take the alert.

Mike calls a huddle, and the three PJs curse as they crawl over a Stokes litter, a small mountain of backpacks, and several duffel bags jammed with alpine gear.

"This is what we got," Mike shouts over the raw palp of the rotors.

Malcolm's location. His probable injuries. Jim Donini's downclimb. Oh brother, Mario thinks. The list reads like a catalogue of everything a parajumper doesn't want to hear. "The guy's been pinned to the mountain about twenty-four hours now, couple of broken legs, maybe still bleeding. He can't be in great shape."

"So what are we thinking?" Mario asks. "Climb? Shorthaul? What's the weather up there?"

"Not good," Mike says. "I just talked to Sardog on the satellite phone. Right now they can't get anything near the victim with fixed wing or rotor. Got a backdoor front bouncing off the Talkeetnas. Should be hitting the Alaska Range in a couple of hours. It's gonna bury us up there. Naturally, Sardog wants to start climbing. They got a couple of potential recovery scenarios on the board. But with the weather, well, they all look sporty."

"It looks like a goat fuck," Redd interjects. The three men laugh.

"Daryl's running things on site," Mike says. "He's incident commander. We'll know more when we get there."

The helo shivers and lurches south, meandering like a big dog marking its territory. Ron Parkhouse's voice barks through the intercom, "Eyes out for birds," and as the Pavehawk banks steeply over Cook Inlet the crew members swivel their heads in unison like a herd of caribou catching scent of a wolf. Six sets of eyes scan the sky for the dense flocks of migrating trumpeter swans and dusky Canada geese that can sometimes bring a metal bird down.

The heading is north-northwest, following the rolling alpine meadows of the Mat-Su valley. Within moments of liftoff the smoking chimneys of Anchorage's sparse suburbs fall away and the earth is transformed into a fluvial riot of rude folds and gashes. Clouds rise on the northeast horizon, and a tin-roofed hunting cabin tucked into the stunted hills gathers the weak midday light and shines like an autumn bonfire.

The brooding, swampy taiga, a Russian word meaning "land of little sticks," glistens with crosshatched ribbons of icy streams that pour into larger channels. These rivers swirl in dark, purling currents, conveying raft-sized shingles of snow and calved ice. Some reflect the cobalt blue of underground springs. Others run a turbid milky gray, murked by mountain silt, what the locals call glacial flour.

The landscape is littered with hundreds of unnamed kettle lakes and ponds, the deepest still ice-capped, others nearly thawed. The shores of the larger lakes are dotted with small ketches moored tight to their jetties, some still tarpaulined for the winter. On several, float-planes are anchored next to cedar log cabins. Far out on one patch of glassy water a lone sailboat with a light at its stern comes about and tacks for shore, racing the weather home. To the west the snowbound Peters Hills swell up from the floodplain like slumbering polar bears. Beyond the Peters the southern outriders of the Kantishna Hills snake south in a scimitar curve toward the uncompromising, inhospitable wilderness of the Aleutians.

To enter the Alaska Range, Ron Parkhouse must first skim boreal pockets of white paper birch, cottonwood, gnomish dwarf willow, and impenetrable alder thickets laced with rivulets of swampy tundra. The difference between tundra, taiga, and boreal forest depends on the depth of the permafrost. The deeper the soil, the richer the nutrients. At this time of year the fields are fecund, lichen-strafed heaths yielding a Bosch-like carpet. Delicate blue-and-yellow forget-me-nots mix with the tiny white petals of Canadian bunchberry. Violet plumes of the poisonous monkshood, the witch's blossom, overlie snarls of defiant pink fireweed, what the Indians call the consolation flower because it blooms in the ashy devastation left by forest fires.

The timberline approaches, and narrow, hardy stands of black hardwood spruce and hemlock, like fingers on a dark glove, inch up the craggy escarpments. Above the firn zone, at 5,000 feet, the sodden floor turns abruptly into an arid benchland of gray bedrock. Golden eagles waft on the thermals in search of small prey. From the kettle pocket of Sunflower Lake an alabaster blanket of snow rises steadily with the earth's contour. The helo soars over protruding eskers and piebald scree littered with glacial moraine. On the horizon loom the piercing ramparts of the section of the range known as Little Switzerland. They guard the mountain chain like huge, portentous punji stakes.

An opaque sheet of cold rain coats the Pavehawk's windshield, but through it the highest mountain in North America looms majestic. A C-130 Hercules descends through the mist and heaves into view. Parkhouse has requested an A-R. The 210th's helo jocks prefer to gas up every hour or so, on the theory that they might not know when, or from where, their next fill-up is coming. The tanker jet comes close enough for the helo crew to count the hairs of the loadmaster's mustache, which hang from his upper lip like the thrums of a mop as he peers out the plane's aft port window.

A feeder hose, called a drogue, releases from the 130's wing while a badminton birdie–shaped parachute, three feet in diameter, encompasses the nozzle to keep it stable in the high winds. Nearly 150 pounds of pressure are needed to trigger the drogue's coupling mechanism. Parkhouse swiftly closes on the line. He hits the drogue with the retractable probe extending from the helo's nose on his first stab. The two aircraft fly in tandem for five minutes, like a mother whale suckling her young. Parkhouse takes on 2,000 pounds of fuel.

By the time the Pavehawk has gorged itself, Wayt, Redd, and Mario are peering down at the toe of the Kahiltna. Stretching several football fields across, the glacier looks like a broad white toboggan run for a race of Titans. Further west it turns lumpy with huge seracs, strewn like broken molars across a white tongue. The seracs mingle with teardrop shapes of aqua-tinged indigo ice where the wind has scoured away the snow. Across the range's southern flank, the May sun has begun to expose jagged tiers of black granite.

To their right the thin, pointed spires of Little Switzerland tear at the skyline like spikes on an electrocardiogram. A rogue williwaw grabs the Pavehawk, and the helo drops like an E-ticket Disneyland ride. Parkhouse yanks back on the throttle and feathers it out.

Ron Parkhouse has been flying through the mountains of Alaska for sixteen years. He was based at both Elmendorf and Fort Richardson, and when the Alaska Air National Guard secured funding for its pararescue squad in 1990, Parkhouse was one of its first hires, as its chief of standards and evaluation. Last year he took over the entire squadron. Parkhouse has four C-130s and six Pavehawks under his pararescue command, and he still flies a regular helo alert rotation. He was trained at the Air Force Academy as a fixed-wing pilot, but time and tides have turned him into a helicopter jock. Today he rides the Pavehawk's right seat as if born to the saddle.

The U.S. Air Force's MH-60G Pavehawk is essentially a U.S. Army UH-60L Blackhawk reconfigured for rescue. The Blackhawk is the workhorse of the U.S. military, and most soldiers who have ever served in a ground-pounding unit have ridden inside one. When the first Blackhawks rolled off the Sikorsky Aircraft Corporation's assembly line in 1978 as replacements for the UH-1 Iroquois, better known in the Vietnam era as the Huey, they were used primarily to ferry troops on "infil," "exfil," or resupply missions. For a layman's benefit, one Pavehawk pilot describes his craft as a Blackhawk that's been sent back to the assembly line to be upgraded, as a Jeep Wrangler might be turned into a Grand Cherokee. In mountainous Alaska, where helo pilots can feel their craft's power draining as they climb high-altitude glacial valleys, this upgrade is a small blessing.

Each of the 210th's twin-turboshaft MH-60G Pavehawks is equipped with automatic flight-control systems to stabilize the aircraft in typical flight conditions. It also contains instrumentation, engine, and rotor blade anti-ice systems that enable it to endure all-weather operations. The aircraft's maximum takeoff weight is 22,000 pounds. External loads of up to 8,000 pounds can be carried, or sling-loaded, on a cargo hook extending from the helo's chassis. A helicopter's flight motion can be thought of as the instantaneous integration of every force acting upon it in a given moment, from gravity to gusts of wind. Every Pavehawk is equipped with three separate navigation systems. The INS, or inertial navigation system, uses a ring-laser gyroscope sensitive enough to detect even the slightest breeze. This data is fed into an on-board computer that calculates the helicopter's position and speed. The INS is backed up by an on-board GPS. Finally, each Pavehawk is also equipped with a Doppler radar system, which sometimes takes a little getting used to when mountain flying. Water and snow, for instance, send different signatures back to the Doppler, and it takes hours of alpine flying time to be able to read the subtle change. In addition, every mountain jock learns quickly that glaciers create their own atmospheres. It is not unusual for a helo pilot overflying a glacier to read his instruments, check the computerized forecast, and reckon the weather to be clear all around him only to be suddenly hoisted or sent plunging by a "ghost gust."

Now Parkhouse's Pavehawk bucks through Kahiltna Pass at 10,000 feet, close to its ceiling. A layer of glacial fog, what pilots call scud, carpets the valley. The mind-numbingly beautiful Kahiltna icefalls, a 5,000-foot frozen crystal cascade, looms to the right. Turning to port, the helo passes through the Hercules Gate of One-Shot Pass and onto the Tokositna. If a pilot misses One-Shot Pass, he can still make the turn up ahead, at Two-Shot Pass. There is no wind to speak of, yet Parkhouse gives the aircraft plenty of room as he overflies the stark granite cleavage. At these elevations, the winds can whip through the midlevel glacial gorges, and there is no telling whether the shear will form invisible tunnels of downdrafts, updrafts, or side drafts.

"They're all bad drafts," Parkhouse remarks dryly. "So you want to clear these passes with some altitude. There've been missions where choppers going through these passes were caught by sudden downdrafts, winds from nowhere, and just slammed into the ground. Even with full power, you can't buck some of these shears."

The scud has lifted and the shimmering snowfield below beckons like an inviting, sandy beach buffeted by flares of light the color of burnished silver. The thermometer reads twenty-two below. The Tokositna's surface is rougher than the Kahiltna's. Meandering slots slice the glacial tongue horizontally like dark veins, or the filigreed cracks in your grandmother's good china. Tiny clumps of hunkered climbers begin to appear on the trail below, their clamshell tents no more than pencil dots spread up and down the glacier. As the Pavehawk passes over they pause, look up, and shade their eyes. They know the only reason an Air Force helicopter is up here is for a rescue.

In the back of the helo, Mike Wayt stares out the window thinking about Bin Hong Kim. He truly wonders what has kept him and Redd and Mario and Ron Parkhouse and Daryl Miller in the rescue business. It's certainly not the money or even the glory. For the pups, for the Marios and the Murphys and Grugels, it has to be the action. That's why he switched careers all those years ago. But why stay in it? Why keep busting his gut for these guys who go up a mountain or out onto a ferocious sea with no idea what they're getting into? Now his thoughts turn to the man in charge of this mission. He and Daryl Miller have become friends over the years, and Mike understands that in the high-altitude ranger's case, helping others must be a way of soothing his restless soul. But Mike has a wife and two beautiful daughters back home. He could earn a decent living doing anything from adventure trail–guiding to working as a paramedic. And probably earn more money to boot. Am I just some fool who happens to know how to climb a mountain or jump out of an airplane? He wonders. He has no answer for the question.

Ron Parkhouse's Pavehawk banks into the cul-de-sac of the Tokositna Glacier at 7,400 feet. The cloud-shrouded snowfield where Malcolm is trapped rises another 2,500 feet above him. Mike thinks of Lara and Stephanie and Emily, and wonders if this is going to be a replay of the Kim rescue, the worst nightmare of his life.

As Parkhouse sets his machine down he scopes out the possibilities. Jesus, he thinks, forget about getting a Pavehawk in there. Even in good weather the little Lama would have only about twenty feet of rotor space on each side if it tried to nose into Malcolm's ravine. And even if it could get close enough to him, the rotor wash would loosen snow and ice, maybe even rocks. The avalanche, Parkhouse figures, would bury Malcolm alive.

As Parkhouse joins Mike Wayt in the crunchy snow, they spot Dave Thompson and Brent Widenhouse digging out a latrine near their tent. Next to them Scotty Denton is unpacking medical gear. The looks on their faces remind Mike of someone waiting outside a hospital's intensive care unit. Daryl Miller emerges from behind a neon blue tent and strides toward them. The mountain ranger removes his hat, runs his hand through his hair, and shakes his head slowly. "Gentlemen, it looks bleak." He waves wearily toward the sheer wall of grade six ice. "It looks really bleak."

THIRTEEN

The Cult of Me

As they skirted a steep rock promontory called the First Step,
twenty-one-year-old Eisuke Shigekawa and thirty-six-year-old
Hiroshi Hanada were taken aback to see one of the Ladakhi
climbers, probably Paljor, lying in the snow, horribly frostbitten but
still alive after a night without shelter or oxygen, moaning unintel-
ligibly. Not wanting to jeopardize their ascent by stopping to assist
him, the Japanese team continued climbing toward the summit.

—JON KRAKAUER, *INTO THIN AIR*

Early in the 1999 Denali climbing season, a Japanese soloist was discovered near death at 19,000 feet. Much like Bin Hong Kim, he had
reached the summit in a foolhardy sprint from Fourteen-Two camp
before collapsing from exhaustion on his descent. Several expeditions,
including an American party with a vacationing doctor among its members, literally stepped over the semiconscious Japanese on their way up
the trail. One group did stop to check if he was still alive, but when they
roused him and he asked for water, they told him they had none to spare
and continued on.

Finally, a veteran Slovakian mountaineer downclimbing the West
Buttress stopped to help. He had to threaten a fistfight with two passing
groups in order to get the ailing man a cupful of water. The Slovak finally
dragged the Japanese climber to Seventeen-Two high camp, nearly
killing himself in the process. The PJs Lynn Grabill and John Loomis,
stationed at 14,200-foot relay camp, watched through binoculars as the
two climbers staggered into high camp, and subsequently treated the
Japanese mountaineer for hypothermia and mountain sickness.

Grabill was still raging about the incident three weeks later. "That's the
one thing that disgusts me about mountain climbers, fucking summit fever

overrides the value of human life. Man, I've really come to wonder what the hell is going on with those people up there. I mean, a doctor—a fucking doctor!—leaving this guy lying in the snow! That Slovakian was the exception to the rule. He was refreshing, considering all the other assholes up there. And he wasn't looking for notoriety. He just wanted to help."

Now, as Saturday drags on and Malcolm Daly clings to Thunder Mountain by a sliver of life, Jim Donini washes down a rare steak and a side of home fries with mugs of cold lager in Talkeetna's Fairview Inn. Donini appears freighted from his experience—his head looks like a withered balloon on a stick—and walks with a slight limp from his puncture wound. His facial expressions range from sullen to angry, but his injuries and his partner's circumstances have not stopped him from hitting the town, and his appetite does not sit well with several of the locals aware of the recovery operation taking place on the Tokositna. Donini's haughty hypermasculinity calls to mind a variation on the screenwriter Herman Mankiewicz's crack about Orson Welles, "There but for the grace of God, goes God." Meanwhile, up on the glacier, more than a few rescuers wonder why Malcolm Daly's partner has yet to make an appearance. Dave Thompson, upon learning that Donini has been spotted in several taverns, is outraged.

"Let me get this straight," the Sardog rails to Mike Wayt as they melt water for coffee. "This guy's feeling good enough to be drinking in the Talkeetna bars, but he can't get his ass up here to help point out the cuts and grooves of our rescue run? Jesus, he's the guy who knows this route the best. He's only been up and down it half a dozen times in the last week. What the fuck is up with that?"

In the close quarters of the makeshift base camp, Daryl Miller cannot help overhearing Thompson's rant, but he holds his tongue. In his heart he agrees that Jim Donini is not the most personable fellow on the block, and is annoyed at what appears to be his matter-of-fact attitude toward his partner's plight. But he's been around long enough to admit that in the extreme environment of high elevation some mountaineers can barely summon the effort to help themselves. He'd attempted to explain this to the outraged Slovakian, to get across how difficult it is to exhort exhausted climbers even to pick up their trash at 17,000 feet, much less extend a helping hand to a fallen stranger. Granted, Denali may not be quite as grueling as being up there at 27,000 feet on Everest, where he'd heard the horror stories about mountaineers climbing over fallen compatriots in order to summit. But, as Daryl says often, the difference between Denali and Everest is the difference between a .44 Magnum and a .45 Magnum. One's more powerful than the other, but they'll both kill you.

Daryl lost his naiveté long ago and knows that a good many mountaineers are callous sons of bitches. But he also feels that, in general, the camaraderie among climbers is closer than that among flatlanders. Mountaineers get a bad rap, he often tells nonclimbing friends. Hell, at altitude a lot of people are barely making it themselves. "And unless you've been to the hall of the mountain king, you don't know what the fuck you're talking about."

The bottom line is Daryl believes Jim Donini has done all he could. After all, if he hadn't made the successful downclimb after Malcolm's fall—a monstrous descent with those wounds—no one would even have known Malcolm was in trouble. Daryl is also fairly certain that had Jim tried to lower Malcolm the entire route he would have ended up killing both of them, most likely by sailing right over one of those ice cliffs they'd skirted on their ascent. Or they would have run out of rope. Or Malcolm would have bled to death. There were a host of variables, most of them fatal. Jim had done more than most men could or would have in similar circumstances. And contrary to the opinions of the PJs milling about base camp, Daryl doesn't really need Jim up here for the rescue—if there's going to be any rescue attempt at all.

Besides, he has another, larger problem. Dave Thompson has made no secret of his desire to climb after Malcolm and has even pointedly told Billy Shott that every second they waste in camp is as good as another nail in Malcolm's coffin. Dave is a good man, and straining to start up the mountain is just his nature. But Daryl is in charge, and no one is climbing anywhere until he gives the word. He smells a larger argument brewing, and knows there is no sense in picking a fight with Dave over Jim Donini's whereabouts.

Meanwhile, the weather is getting worse. A dark pewter ceiling descended over the Tokositna around mid-morning, and the wind is blowing so hard the snow feels like nails fired from a gun. The meteorologist Gary Hufford has sent word that there is another storm following right on its tail. The Alaska Range is in for at least a week of rough weather, and Daryl knows it. Though the Lama and Jay Hudson's Cessna are managing to run supplies and personnel onto the icy cul-de-sac, Malcolm's ravine remains socked in by what looks like great swaths of gray cotton. Jim Hood has twice tried to get close to his position, but, on each occasion, he's reported back to Daryl that there was no way he's getting near that ledge.

This does not surprise Daryl. Even had the weather cooperated, he's harbored furtive doubts about a shorthaul rescue from the moment Jim Donini described where he'd bivouacked Malcolm. Seeing the ravine up close merely confirmed Daryl's suspicions. The gully is just too narrow for the standard shorthaul, even for a machine as maneuverable as the Lama. Official Park Service policy proscribes any shorthaul rescue using over one hundred feet of line, and Daryl knows that's not enough to reach beyond those ice cliffs overhanging Malcolm's position. To further complicate matters, ranger regulations stipulate that any helicopter sortie must have a rotor clearance one and a half times the eighty seven–foot span of the Lama's blades—in other words, about 215 feet of free space on either side. Impossible.

Earlier this morning Daryl put in a call to his old friend Kurt Mauther, a veteran alpinist based in Whistler, British Colombia, known as "the ayatollah of big-wall rescue." He'd e-mailed Mauther digital photographs of Malcolm's position. After studying the pictures, Mauther called back. His advice: "No way you can shorthaul him out of there."

So much for plan A. That leaves two options, Daryl reckons. Unfortunately, neither is really worth a damn. He takes one final look at Thunder Mountain before stepping into Jay Hudson's Cessna for the hop back down to Talkeetna to brief Swed and the Park Service brass.

Eleven hundred feet above the snowfield where Malcolm Daly is pinned down, a tiny plateau of granite, perhaps fifty square feet, projects diagonally from the sheer face of Thunder Mountain. Because this rocky ledge sits upon a jutting promontory, it is not quite as susceptible to the rolling cloud banks that have been packing Malcolm's couloir since the storm hit. Every so often, in fact, the blue-black protrusion can be viewed from the makeshift base camp on the Tokositna. There is general agreement among the men gathered on the glacier that given favorable wind and weather conditions the Lama could indeed hold a hover

over it, maybe even touch down on it. As the day wears on, it becomes the focus of plan B.

It would take several runs, Jim Hood tandem-shorthauling two men at a time with survival gear—sleeping bags, stoves, rock and ice pro, rope; lots of rope. But a small squad might be able to set up an anchoring rope system. Six or seven men securing the anchor would allow two climbers, a barrelman and a belay handler, to descend the vertical quarter mile to Malcolm's position. Conceivably, they could strap him into a Stokes litter, grapple him back up the face, and haul him the hell out. Given the right conditions.

Staring up at the outcrop, Mike Wayt listens as a couple of the Alaska Mountain Rescue volunteers speculate that once anchored in, the entire operation could optimally take no longer than six or seven hours—if they didn't kill Malcolm with a rockslide. Mike thinks that one glitch could turn the strategy into a days-long ordeal. Since Bin Hong Kim's recovery Mike has had a personal rule of thumb regarding mountain rescues: estimate the time and multiply by three. In more than eighteen hours, Malcolm would probably be dead. But the volunteers do have a point: it's better than doing nothing. The PJs, Mike in particular, are just as anxious, their apprehension heightened by the rangers' inability to make a decision. Once during the afternoon Mike approaches Billy Shott, trying to wheedle some information from him about the parajumpers' role in the rescue attempt. Billy shrugs his shoulders and says something about the nasty weather turning the entire ordeal into a waiting game. It's the same answer he and Dave Thompson had gotten from Daryl soon after they'd arrived on the glacier, when Dave had stamped off in frustration. Mike is more understanding, yet knows something big is going to happen, and he doesn't care whether it's humping gear or climbing an ice wall, he just wants to get on with it. On any rescue there are only so many nervous jokes you can crack around the camp stove before the anticipation becomes unbearable.

At one point before Daryl flew off the glacier Mike had run into him near the PJs' cluster of tents. Neither had said a word, but the look that passed between them was all-knowing. The mountain ranger sees a lot of himself in Mike Wayt. Like Mike's drill instructors all those years ago back in basic, Daryl knows—he can just feel—that the PJ is a lifer in the rescue business. What makes us do it? Daryl, too, wonders. What puts guys like Mike Wayt and me up on this mountain? Mike, in turn, feels for Daryl. He can almost see the weight of the decisions he must soon make the ranger's shoulders, making him hunch over. But even this doesn't allay Mike's fretfulness.

It gets worse when Nick Parker's civilian volunteers move in. The volunteers get to work cooking meals, staking tents, stomping out a landing strip. Nick himself has begun digging out a camp kitchen. You wouldn't guess from looking at Parker that he's spent thirty of his fifty years on earth guiding parties through Alaska's backwoods and mountain ranges, nor that he's summited Denali seventeen times. He's the type of Alaskan whose preferred mode of dress is coveralls and a flannel shirt in winter and coveralls and a T-shirt in summer. In truth, Nick looks as if he's been out of work since *Hee Haw* went off the air. But, as any parajumper will attest, there is no better man to have around in a pinch than the gray-haired, buzz-cut outdoorsman with the cherry red cheeks. A childhood bout with polio left Parker, as he puts it, "pretty deformed up all over my left side." It also precluded a career in hockey or football, young Nick's two favorite sports. Instead, he took to exploring the mountains, and his alpine experience has shone from the moment he stepped onto the glacier. Having checked the weather he foresaw that this was going to be a marathon mission, and knew men could only work so hard at altitude running on less than full tanks. A common mistake in the mountain rescue business is, believe it or not, to forget to eat. The adrenaline rush and the altitude both dull a man's appetite, though Nick figures the minimum number amount of calories a climber needs per day in order to maintain body heat at altitude is somewhere around 3,500. He aims to give these guys that, and more. You have to keep people fed, is his mantra.

Around mid-afternoon, with Daryl still down in Talkeetna, Mike notices Billy Shott having an animated conversation with someone on the other end of his CB radio. He guesses he is speaking to Daryl, and given Dave Thompson's relentless, and clearly vocal, compulsion to get up that mountain and bring this guy down, Mike again braces the young ranger.

Should we start packing our gear for a climb?

Are we going to drop men up on that ridgeline?

Billy tells Mike that the official recovery plan right now is a descent from above before throwing him a furtive look. But Billy says that Daryl, despite his earlier misgivings, is also now considering a bang-bang short-haul if they can catch a weather break. "It's against all the regs, and I wouldn't bet on it happening, though." Then Billy assures the para-jumper that if they shoot for the rock pillow to implement a climbing descent, the PJ team will be involved. This gives Mike a "warm fuzzy." He starts to spread the word among the squad that they'll be part of the action come showtime. Maybe that's why I do this, Mike thinks. For that "warm fuzzy" I get every time. But Dave Thompson is not in a warm, fuzzy mood.

"Fuck this whole Lama idea," he tells his teammates. "They're never gonna get a helo in there if they stick to a hundred-foot rope. We should be going up after this guy right now." Dave's brown eyes are vivid with outrage, and he expels his nervous energy by flashing a mirror in the general direction of Malcolm's ledge whenever the sun peeks through. "Throw me on the end of a 500-foot line and I'll haul the guy out myself."

Like all parajumpers, Dave Thompson has had ample opportunity to study the social interaction among small groups of isolated men. His number one rule: "If you circulate a feasible hypothesis among as many people as possible, it eventually gets adopted as strategy." He has thus spent the morning disseminating two notions. One is an extended short-haul, up to five hundred feet if necessary. "One man, one rope, one heli-copter, we'd be done and back in the bar in Talkeetna buying Jim Donini a beer." The second notion is to push for a climb. Team of four. In and out. Two would reach Malcolm with food, water, medical supplies, and shelter. It's better than watching him die.

"I swear to God," he tells Mike Wayt, "if the Park Service keeps dickin' around like this, waiting for every fucking cloud to clear, I'll go get this guy myself. At least bring him some gear. They got no jurisdiction over me. Christ, Mike, come on. You and me. We'll get Mario. Redd, too. I know he says he's no good at altitude, but I think he can definitely do it."

Mike thinks Dave is only half joking. The other PJs laugh, a dry snort that quickly fades into the gathering gloam.

If any PJ carried weight on Thunder Mountain, it was the Sardog. His teammates know that Dave had indeed once shorthauled at the end of a 600-foot line on a mission in Colorado. And two seasons earlier Dave and two friends had climbed one of the more dangerous aspects of Thunder Mountain, a route two ridgelines over from Malcolm's position known as the Northwest Basin Variation. The Northwest Basin, a mixed technical route of snow, ice, and rock, was notorious as avalanche territory. Sardog, on the sharp end of the rope, had led his party up to 10,300 feet before being turned back by crevasses and weather. Dave had hung his ass out over the line on the climb. At one point he'd even plunged through a slot, but had been able to "swim" his way to safety as the fissures around him spread like spiderweb cracks on windshield glass. Dave's near-miss stumble, as well as several avalanches cascading all about them, had been the "karmic signal" for his party to turn around. The downclimb, he remembers, "was really fucking hairy."

"We started rappelling back down until the shit avalanching all around us got too heavy to descend through. So we found this one crevasse—we nicknamed it the Avalanche Café—where we decided to stop and wait it out. We'd put in a long day climbing, maybe seventeen hours. It's about eight at night now, and we figured we'd crawl into a corner of the Avalanche Café, get some sleep at least until midnight. Let the sun go down and firm up that ice and snow."

By the time Dave's party awoke, weather was already moving in, high cirrus clouds just like those which now encased Malcolm Daly. The three climbers had no choice but to move through it. On the descent the group fell several times. On one plunge Dave belayed his partners above a sheer 2,000-foot drop by the strength of his ice axe and a rusty piton he'd absentmindedly clipped into. His buddies returned the favor when he plummeted several hundred feet. He was saved from rolling into a slot by his partners' belay.

"If anybody'd seen us they would have thought we were a bunch of fucking rookies out there," he recalls in disgust. But the fact remains that he feels his Thunder experience has given him the know-how to begin climbing after Malcolm Daly. The rest of the PJs sense his enthusiasm, and an undercurrent of restlessness runs through the squad.

At 3 P.M. Daryl Miller steps back out onto the Tokositna from Jay Hudson's bush plane. He is immediately peened by the relentless hammering of Dave Thompson. Daryl is not unresponsive to the PJ's insistence, for Daryl shares with the Sardog a view from the ranks, not from the saddle. Yet as much as he likes and respects the veteran parajumper, he feels that any attempt to reach Malcolm via an ascent through that couloir is a certain death route. The storm is increasing, and Daryl can envision a climbing team peeling off Thunder Mountain one by one.

"You want to die up there, is that what you're telling me?" he confronts Thompson in a firm, controlled voice. "Let me tell you something, Dave. Sitting down here in base camp that climb looks a lot easier than you know. I know you want to do something. I know you want to do anything. But you just gotta wait. I'm not running the risk of committing to something that's only going to end up getting more people hurt."

In the forefront of Daryl's mind is the fact that it took Malcolm and Jim Donini, two experienced climbers, three attempts to reach the site where the accident occurred. And their ascent took place in much better weather than Malcolm's rescuers were now enduring. Dave Thompson's rash idea meant not only an expeditionary climb over a serrated row of overhanging ice cliffs through loose snow and rock, it also meant fixing more line, for Jim Donini had taken most of his out during his descent. Moreover, Daryl knows, any rescue party could work the ascent for only six hours a day, maximum. A forced, marathon climb would be too risky. The PJs might have balls the size of grapefruits, but with the possible exception of Dave and Mike Wayt, they were no match for the technical scope of that headwall. And Daryl could have only two people climbing at the same level. You start throwing climbers all over that mountain and you guarantee an avalanche. That meant the entire operation would take at least two days, probably three. By that time all their efforts wouldn't have done Malcolm Daly a whit of good.

Daryl hides his growing annoyance as best he can. But, Jesus, didn't these guys learn anything from the Bin Hong Kim ordeal? And this terrain is even steeper. Once you start lowering a victim, you're committed. And no matter what the conditions, during those lowerings you can almost bet you're going to have another victim. The PJs were lucky they had walked away from the Kim rescue with nothing worse than Mike Wayt's perforated ulcer. Daryl sure as hell isn't going to allow any of them to be killed on his watch. He looks Dave Thompson directly in the eye.

"Climbing up means almost certain death for Malcolm, and most likely serious injuries to some of your guys. But say you did get him, Dave. Say everything goes perfect and you reach the guy. He's got two broken legs and God knows what else. You think you can lower a litter down that mountain? You think you can traverse any litter way out there beyond those ice cliffs and over to the west face? That's a lot of climbing, and Malcolm doesn't have that much time."

"You got a better idea?"

"Let me give that rock pillow some thought," Daryl says, his voice conciliatory. "We do that, I guarantee we're gonna need all you guys."

As Daryl turns toward his tent he feels the Sardog's stony glare boring holes in his back.

Hunching over a topo map, the high-altitude ranger chief figures the good news is that the fall line from the rock dome above Malcolm's position isn't a straight drop; in fact, Malcolm is sitting pretty far to the left of the fall line. So if the Lama can manage to deposit a squad up on that promontory, the people above, even the downclimbers, won't have to worry too much about knocking rocks or ice down onto Malcolm's head. Technically there is a reasonable chance of lowering two men and a litter down the couloir on two separate lines, a main and a belay. Aside from the barrelman and the belay handler, they'd need a brakeman, a couple of edgemen, anchor holders, and spotters. Nine men might do it. The more Daryl studies the map the more certain he becomes that the descent strategy is manifestly less dangerous than a climb. There is still some risk to it. He'd need the Lama to land at least two men on the top of the dome—probably Billy Shott and one of the PJs, Dave or Mike—to set up a fixed line with anchors around the perimeter, to secure it for the remainder of the rescue party. Then he might be able to get another six, eight people plus their supplies.

Daryl filters each option through all his climbing experience while absentmindedly drawing concentric circles on the edge of the topo map. Here are the PJs, who have their own ideas. Here are Nick Parker's rescue volunteers, who also have their own ideas. Here is the Park Service brass back at Talkeetna. And here's Jim Hood and his Lama. At the fulcrum of all these turning gears—he punches his pencil into the paper—is me. I know what our resources are inside. The big picture is coming into focus. I know what our resources are outside. I know what that couloir is like—people who haven't been up there have no idea how dangerous that gully is. I know that the PJ plan to climb up there sucks. I know some of Nick Parker's volunteers think that if we drop people on the pillow above we might kill Malcolm with an avalanche. They're wrong.

Anyone can look, but learning to *see* is the key. I work on fall lines. I know it won't kill him. The problem is the weather. The light's flat. Those clouds above that dome are in and out. Can Jim get in there? More than once? He's one of the best chopper pilots in the world, but if he says no he's got my vote. Who am I to argue?

Unknown to Dave Thompson, unknown to the rest of the PJs, unknown to any of the volunteers now swarming the Tokositna, one more determining factor lingers in the back of Daryl's mind. He knows that his bosses back down in the Talkeetna command center are watching him like a hawk, studying his ability to assess the risks. This morning the Park Service had flown in Hunter Sharp, the ranking ranger in southeast Alaska, from his post in the Wrangells–St. Elias Range. Daryl can almost feel Sharp and J. D. Swed looking over his shoulder, ready to jerk him off this detail in a New York minute should he show any inclination to place a rescuer in harm's way just because his friend is clinging to the side of that hill.

The thought wrenches Daryl's mind like a vise. Yes, Malcolm is my friend. You never want to leave anybody up on a mountain, but abandoning Malcolm to die up there would have more of an impact on me that anything. More than the horrors of 'Nam and more than the dead Canadians and more than Mike Vanderbeek. If it were just me on this rescue I'd already be climbing after him. But there are others involved, others whose lives I'm responsible for. Can I sacrifice the life of a rescuer for the life of a friend? Even one of my best friends?

The answer is clear to Daryl. No, never.

In fact, Daryl is not thinking of Malcolm as a climbing victim in need of rescue any longer. He is a hostage to the mountain. And the hardest thing is knowing that if he doesn't get a weather break, Thunder Mountain will kill its hostage.

Ron Parkhouse strides through the throng of climbers crowding the lobby of the Talkeetna Ranger Station. At the peak of climbing season the men and women signing in for their Denali treks are blissfully unaware of the drama unfolding on Thunder Mountain, and their buoyant grins and happy chatter strike him as eerily incongruous. The juxtaposition becomes starker as he enters the briefing room and is greeted by the long, dark faces of the group gathered to try to save Malcolm Daly's life.

Parkhouse studies Hunter Sharp and J. D. Swed, two thin men with no calluses on their hands and no meat on their bones. He compares them to Daryl Miller up on the Tokositna. He wonders if this rescue will come down to a battle of wills between political rangers and action rangers, "with my PJs caught in the middle." That, he vows, is not going to happen.

Hunter Sharp, having been briefed by Swed, is running the meeting. Topo maps and aerial photographs of the mountain are spread about the room. Men and women pace with a solemn urgency. Rescue and survival gear litters the floor. Outside, in the visitors' parking lot, a unit from Elmendorf Air Base's 206th Communications Squad is unloading a gigantic radio pallet. The RCC has requested the Com Squad, asking them to coordinate all UHF and VHF frequencies used by the PJs, the rangers, the volunteers, and the Hercs. Parkhouse knows these soldiers are called out only for the big emergencies, fighter crashes and the like. The com unit's commander, Colonel Rick Smith, passes the time telling stories about setting up radios on the foundering bridge of the *Exxon Valdez*.

Parkhouse is leaning against a wall in the back of the command center as Mark Williams, a veteran member of Nick Parker's Alaskan Mountain Rescue Squad, sums up the situation for several newly arrived volunteers. "The plan, at least the one they're working on up on the glacier, is to maybe try and drop a bunch of people on that plateau above him, and have them downclimb to Malcolm and try and stabilize him." Williams checks the weather through the window. "But now, with the sky going punk, if you ask me, we either got to get him out of there right away on a shorthaul or pat him on the back and say, 'Malcolm, got any last messages for your family?'"

Parkhouse sees no reason to disagree. A surge of adrenaline has twisted his stomach into knots.

Time has become an abstract concept to Malcolm Daly. There are a few "marks" on the mountain—the gunsight notch, a small rock buttress at the lower edge of the snowfield—where yesterday, following the movement of the sun and shadows, he had been able to guess the general time of day. But since the storm entombed him just after dawn he has no idea how swiftly, or slowly, the hours are passing. He wonders if someday a climber struggling up this route will come across his watch. It is an expensive one, a Tag Heuer.

Malcolm is trying to think like a rescuer. He can't see them, but he knows they are down there on the Tokositna. Lots of them, judging from the amount of air traffic he's heard all day. He's even become enough of an expert to distinguish the fixed wings from the Lama, and the Lama from a Pavehawk. On a few occasions the clouds have broken and he's caught glimpses of the flightseers overflying his position. Showing the tourists the guy trapped on the ledge. Once he even hears the Lama nosing its way into his gully. The rotor wash clears some of the clouds and he sees the helicopter. Malcolm is aghast at the pilot's shakiness. He has no idea that Jim Hood has been working nearly round the clock for the past five days. He has no idea who Jim Hood is. All he knows is that, whoever that pilot is, he doesn't appear to be too steady. There is a little bit of an updraft, not much. Still, the helo is all over the place. Too close to the walls. Man, get that thing out of my couloir. The last thing I need here is a crash.

The spindrift avalanches stopped sometime during the night, and Malcolm steps up his warming whirlybird exercises. Every time he shivers or nods off—he'd compelled himself not to sleep at all Friday night— he wakes and drives himself to do one hundred windmills with each arm. Then he forces himself to complete one hundred stomach crunches from his half-sitting position. It is exhausting. But it keeps his blood flowing and his limbs warm. He can only hope that the seepage into his boots has stopped.

He again decides to keep himself awake by counting aloud to one thousand. It takes longer to count to one thousand than he'd ever realized. His count is continually broken by thoughts of his family. He wonders if Karen is down on the glacier. No, he thinks, even if she's here in Alaska, Daryl would never allow her up on the Tokositna. Daryl would never allow her to watch him die. For some reason, the thought comforts him. He begins his count again.

Malcolm is certain both his ankles have compound fractures, but the Vicodins are keeping things in check. He'll have to write to the company after he gets out of here. Tell them they make a pretty damn good product. Like Daryl, Malcolm has given up on a rescue party climbing to him from the glacier. Instead, he turns his attention to the rock dome over-hanging his snowfield. It looks to be about 1,000, 1,200 feet above him. At one point he hears the Lama circling the dome, the echoes crashing off the granite walls like the low rumble of a diesel train. A moment later a large slab of névé smashes down and buries him. He spends an hour digging himself out.

Malcolm wonders if they are thinking of trying to shorthaul a rescue party up there in an attempt to rappel down to him. He doesn't like that idea at all. They put a bunch of guys up there, he thinks, and guaranteed somebody's going to knock something down on my head, something heavier and more deadly than a slab of snow. Christ, he's done it himself, back in Colorado. Gone after a stranded climber while lugging a Stokes litter. And he's never downclimbed a face like this without sending a bunch of shit avalanching.

No, he figures, the only way to get me out of here is by shorthaul. And no helo is getting into this ravine until the weather breaks. Unless— unless they've called in some really ace mountain men. Hell, a couple of good climbers carrying up some splints, they could bind my legs together and haul me down in no time. They might be on their way already. Maybe that's what that flashing mirror I saw meant.

Malcolm is glad he has rationed his food and water. He can't see whether he's still bleeding, although the snow on his ledge is fairly pink. Depending on the loss of blood, he thinks he can probably hold out here another two or three days.

He thinks of Kitt and Mason. Without a father. He forces the idea from his racing mind.

As the light on the glacier fades Mike Wayt and several of Nick Parker's volunteers begin wanding the makeshift landing strip with chem lights and upturned snowshoes. Daryl chats with Mike about the salmon run-ning down in Ship Creek in Anchorage, about the three recovering Brits down in the hospital. Mike tells him about cooking for his daughter's barbecue. Daryl jokes that perhaps Stephanie should meet his son, Chan; the two can breed a race of super-rescuers. They speak of love and life and everything except Malcolm Daly's chances.

Over in camp, people are eating quietly, getting hydrated in case of a sudden order to move. No one relishes the idea of Malcolm spending a second night on Thunder Mountain. As Daryl walks away Redd and Mario approach Mike from one of the PJ tents.

"You believe how we ate this day up doing nothing?" Redd asks.

Mike smiles, and suggests a walk. The three rope up and trudge through the twilight, skirting a large crevasse. Mario hocks a loogie into the slot. They reach the base of Malcolm's couloir and stare upward at the fifty-degree slope. This close it appears almost vertical, a mile-high petrified wave that could break any moment. Certainly more technical than Mike had presumed. No one says what they all feel. Even if the weather suddenly turns, they are fast running out of "functional light" for any sort of helicopter maneuvers. Malcolm, if he's still alive, is in for the evening. Mario wonders how much food and water he has left.

"Yell on up to him," Redd says to Mike. Mike is hesitant. He doesn't want Malcolm to think that help is approaching. But Redd goads him on. "C'mon, Mike, let him know we care."

Mike cups his hands around his mouth. "Malcolm! Malcolm Daly! Hang in there, pal! Help is on the way!"

The three stand in silence for a moment. Then Redd says, "You hear that?"

Mike and Mario shake their heads. "No, what?"

"I thought I heard him yell back. I swear I heard him yell back."

FOURTEEN
The Mission

Now faith is the substance of things hoped for,
the evidence of things not seen.

—HEBREWS 11:1

Late Saturday evening Malcolm hears a man's voice yelling up to him. At least he thinks he hears someone. He cannot see through the cloud cover, but somehow he knows, he just *knows,* there are three men down there at the bottom of that gully. They are coming for him, climbing up to him. He screams back.

I'm here! I'm alive!

No reply. Malcolm hollers again and listens until, unable to keep his eyes open, he finally nods off.

When he wakes his legs are throbbing. He swallows a Vicodin. From the long, low angles of the sunbeams gilding the glacier to the southeast he guesses it's somewhere near four-thirty Sunday morning. He's made it through another night.

He rubs his face with snow and squints into the distance. At the base of his snowfield, 350 feet away, he sees four or five spectral figures approach, as if through a gauzy white drapery. The men are carrying shovels. They begin digging near the ledge.

"What are you doing down there?" Malcolm shouts. "I'm over here. What are you guys digging?"

None of the men say a word. None even look at him. Maybe they're constructing a landing pad for the helicopter.

As the dawn breaks full, the men seem to fade into the diaphanous clouds. Malcolm straightens up in his perch and rubs more snow in his eyes. When he looks again the ghostly figures are gone.

Daryl Miller catches Jay Hudson's last shuttle off the Tokositna Saturday night. His first stop is Jim Hood's rented room near the airstrip. He tells Jim to go get drunk because he is grounded. Not only is the pilot dead tired, but the last week's worth of rescues have put him way over his FCC-mandated flight time. Hood fights the order halfheartedly. In his stead, J. D. Swed has put in an emergency call to the helo jock Karl Cotton, a Californian the Park Service keeps on standby. Cotton caught the red-eye out of Los Angeles this afternoon and is already asleep in the Talkeetna Roadhouse, getting his FCC-required eight hours.

Daryl flops into bed around midnight. Three hours later he is out of the shower and checking the weather forecast on his computer. He rubs his eyes and checks again. Somebody is smiling big-time on Malcolm. The National Weather Service is calling for a window of clearance between successive storm fronts later this morning, with luck perhaps an hour's worth of letup over the Alaska Range. An icy rush squirrels up his spine as he reaches for the telephone.

At 6 A.M. Sunday morning Karen Daly calls Swed's cell phone. She touched down in Anchorage last night with Malcom's brother, Jed, and on Swed's advice booked two hotel rooms in town on the off chance Malcolm was medevac-ed to Anchorage General. Karen and Jed, a feature film producer who'd flown up from Los Angeles, shared a bottle of white wine before drifting off into fitful sleep.

An exhausted Swed cuts right to the chase. "Karen, we're not going to shorthaul him," he says. "We can't get the chopper in there that close. We're going to go from the top." The ranger explains to Karen their lowering strategy.

Karen asks him for a time estimate. He hesitates. Finally he tells her that with luck they could complete the entire operation in twelve to fifteen hours. This slams Karen's heart. *If he's telling me twelve to fifteen hours, well, that's like a contractor saying how long it's going to take to*

redo your kitchen. Like Mike Wayt, she immediately doubles the estimate in her mind.

"I'm coming to Talkeetna," she says, and hangs up.

And then she thinks, He's telling me my husband's not getting out.

At six-thirty Jed Daly and Karen are on the Glenn Highway, three hours
south of Talkeetna. Jed rings Daryl from his rental car. Daryl has never
met Malcolm's brother, but his voice sounds eerily familiar.

"Daryl, I know you guys are doing everything possible, and I don't
want to second-guess you. But I'm willing to hire the best climbers in the
world to get my brother down. Whatever it takes, Daryl. Malcolm has
friends in Boulder. Because of Trango, he's got associates and contacts all
over the climbing world." Jed Daly repeats the phrase "whatever it takes."

Daryl is beyond being insulted. He realizes Jed is grasping at straws.
The guy just wants his brother out of there. He explains that between the
rangers and the PJs and Nick Parker's group, some of the best alpinists in
the world are already working on saving Malcolm. Badass climbers,
unfortunately, are not the problem. The problems are weather, the ice
cliffs bisecting the gully, and the time factor.

It is as if Jed is not listening. He reiterates his offer to round up the
best mountaineers in the world—Alex Lowe, Mark Twight, Scott Bakke,
each a high-altitude superstar. "I can get guys like that," Jed says.

If Daryl had the time he would try to enlighten Jed. The best climbers
don't necessarily make the best rescuers. Instead, he says, "Jed, if we
have to climb to Malcolm we won't reach him alive. We've got a plan.
J. D. Swed will fill you in on it when you get here."

He does not tell Malcolm's brother that his plan differs markedly
from J. D. Swed's.

By 7 A.M. the sky is light gray, the color of a crocodile egg. Daryl cannot
believe his good fortune. Malcolm's good fortune. He calls the RCC from
his office and tells the dispatcher, "Get everyone up on the glacier activated."

He rushes out of the ranger station, jumps in his truck, and speeds
toward the Lama's landing pad on the other side of town.

. . .

Daryl doesn't know the blond, mustachioed forty-two-year-old Karl Cotton except by his reputation as an ace technical flier. But when he introduces himself on Talkeetna's gravel airstrip and feels the firmness of the pilot's handshake, he knows he's met a simpatico. Cotton has twenty years of rescue experience flying helicopters for the Los Angeles County Fire Department, and knows the Lama as well as Jim Hood. When Daryl asks him how long a rope he's ever shorthauled, the helo jock smiles and says he's long-lined up to five hundred feet back in the San Gabriel Mountains.

"I just did one yesterday," Cotton adds. "Those ravines that cut through the San Gabriels are real vertical, and we do pick-offs out there all the time."

"How long was the one yesterday?"

"Hundred feet."

"You might be going a little longer today."

By 7:15 Sunday morning Cotton powers up the Lama. Ironically, Daryl has always considered it a tool for the rescuers, as opposed to the rescuees. Screw the victims. The Lama's presence was first and foremost to prevent the rescuers from putting their lives at risk. Naturally, to the climbers, the Lama was a get-out-of-jail-free card.

Now Daryl explains his plan to Cotton. When he finishes, the pilot says, So we're gonna be breaking a few rules.

Well, we'll have to fudge it a little because of the regulations. But, in essence, well, for sure.

Cotton grins. "I like that."

"I'll take responsibility. I want it understood that this is my decision. But once you get up there it's all your call."

"I could use a spotter, the lightest person you got."

Daryl says that'd be one of our female rangers, Meg Perdue.

Malcolm's couloir is intermittently socked in, but, unlike yesterday, the clouds appear to be racing in and out as opposed to just camping there. For a brief moment on their approach Daryl and Cotton even spot Malcolm. He appears to be waving from his ledge. Cotton waggles his bird.

Whaddya think? Daryl asks.

Hell, with no clouds I can hover my ass in there all day. Who'll be taking the ride?

Daryl tells him Billy Shott. Billy's our wildman, Daryl says. You know, danger, speed, he likes pushing the limits. In Daryl's mind Billy Shott is the Steve Daigle of the mountain rangers. Or maybe Daigle is the Billy Shott of the PJs. Either way, on this rescue Daryl would have no other man dangling from the end of the rope. He reminds himself to break the news personally to Dave Thompson.

The thirty-four-year-old Billy Shott wears a perpetual smile on his mountain-tanned face. He is one of those rare men, like the balladeer Sting, who actually takes on a rugged handsomeness as he turns prematurely bald. What hair Billy has he keeps cropped close to the skull, and he gives the impression of an impish boy who's just stirred up trouble and is waiting to be caught.

Billy grew up in Woodland Park, just west of Colorado Springs. With Pikes Peak and Turkey Rock and the Garden of the Gods in his backyard, Billy was crack-climbing the sandstone canyons by his early teens, teaching himself how to rappel with his mother's old clothesline. He met Daryl at Colorado State University fifteen years ago. The two dated some of the same women, and even roomed together for two years after Billy took a job at the Experiential Learning Center. After graduation Billy roamed the Continental Divide as a mountain guide and instructor for Outward Bound before migrating north to Alaska like Yeats bound for Byzantium. He'd hooked up as a Volunteer-in-Park on the ranger mountain patrols and four years ago was hired as a full-fledged high-altitude ranger. Billy had become shorthaul-qualified as a volunteer in 1992, and since working as a mountain ranger he'd gradually taken over most of Daryl's shorthaul duties. He seemed to have a natural affinity for maneuvering on the end of the line, the way some people take to water or others to music.

"You're just a dope on a rope, mere baggage" is how he liked to describe the experience. In fact, there was much more to a shorthaul rescue than dangling from the bottom of a helicopter. Foremost, it took a certain inborn quality to maintain good communication with the helo pilot while swinging in the wind, in essence acting as his eyes and ears.

And then, of course, you had better be able to judge instantly what kind of conditions you were dealing with when you were finally set down. Given the Park Service regulations, Billy had never done a shorthaul on a rope longer than one hundred feet. Now, as Daryl sketches out his plan in the glacial snow, Billy looks over to Karl Cotton with his Sundance Kid grin. "Hey, a hundred feet, two hundred feet, how hard can it be?" Cotton smiles back.

The ranger huddle breaks up and Billy begins measuring his short-haul line. He is joined by Dave Thompson and Mike Wayt. "You ever gone longer than a hundred?" Dave asks.

"Only in training," Billy says. "And that was a couple years back."

"The trick is, the longer the line, the further away you're gonna land from where you think you're gonna land." The cloud cover is definitely breaking up, and Dave Thompson points to the vertical snowfield below Malcolm's ledge. "Now you got a big platform to land on up there," the Sardog continues. "No problem, okay? You and the pilot aim right for Malcolm. Don't worry about the wall behind him. I guarantee you're gonna come down somewhere near the bottom of that field. So have your ice axes out and ready. Be prepared to climb."

"Got it," Billy says, truly thankful for the advice.

"Now, how much rope you got here?" Dave asks.

"Looks like close to two hundred feet. That's an unofficial count, of course."

Dave smiles. "Of course. And as long as we're counting unofficially, why don't we spool out another forty feet or so. Give that Lama pilot a little extra room to maneuver with."

As the ranger and the two PJs measure out more rope, Daryl is on the phone to Talkeetna. "Yup, looks like we're getting a weather window. I'm sending Billy and Meg up with Karl." There is a pause. "Well, we might be going just a tad over a hundred. But I think we can do this and still try and stay within the service limit."

Daryl Miller cradles the telephone, scans Thunder Mountain, and turns to the pilot and two rangers. "You guys set?"

Karl Cotton loves mountain flying and he loves handling the Lama. He mostly flies a Blackhawk back in Los Angeles, and compared to it, the easy maneuverability of this little machine is like the difference between a tank and a roadster. As they lift off from the Tokositna he tells Meg Perdue that wherever he's worked rescue, in the San Gabriels, the Rockies, even down in Mexico, his technique is the same. "Get in and get out as fast as you can. You don't want to be in the air any longer than you have to. I guess in Alaska you just tighten up your margin a little bit more."

Meg Perdue likes the pilot's confidence. Her nerves are wracked and it's comforting to know he is trying to put her at ease.

In order to ensure that the person at the end of the shorthaul line has the safest and smoothest ride possible, a helicopter pilot looks on to visual landmarks to maintain his stability. But with a white-on-white glacier as a backdrop, even the most experienced pilots can be plagued by vertigo during takeoffs. To avoid this, Cotton picks out a bright red tent as a reference point and keeps his eyes peeled to it as he rises from the ice. But he discovers that even with the tent in sight, lifting off from the vast white expanse of the Tokositna is a dizzying maneuver. Cotton fights the natural tendency to rise too fast and jerk Billy into the air. At about two hundred feet he eases off the throttle. Another thirty feet and Billy Shott levitates like an angel without wings.

Cotton has already directed Meg to plant herself behind him, on his right shoulder, and watch for weather rolling into Malcolm's couloir. When they reach the ravine he will have to focus on one reference point in the rocks to his left in order to maintain a steady hover for Billy. If the helicopter begins wobbling, Billy will certainly be smashed into the mountain, so it is crucial that she let him know how close the Lama is to the escarpment on their right. Finally, if she has time, Cotton would like her to keep an eye on Billy over two hundred feet down at the end of the rope. This is no longer a shorthaul, and longhauls have been known to kill people.

At nine o'clock the sky above the Tokositna is as clear as good gin. Cotton edges the Lama into the gully. They see Malcolm for a moment before a wave of clouds roils over the mountain as if in angry response to a trespasser. It fills the couloir and obscures Malcolm completely.

"Abort! Abort!" Billy Shott hears Cotton's voice shouting through his portable headset. He knows that the pilot's reference points must be obliterated by the haze.

Two hundred forty feet below Billy drifts through the clouds in soft, parabolic arcs. The sudden billows are so thick he can barely make out his cramponed boots beneath him. His fingers unconsciously grip the shorthaul line so tightly he reminds himself to ease off lest they go numb. Through his gloves he can feel that the God ring attached to his chest harness is already freezing up.

Cotton swings the Lama back out over the glacier, jerking Billy backward violently. To his right Billy spots a patch of granite protruding from the headwall like a cannon jutting from a castle's keep. Instinctively he lowers his head into his right shoulder.

Jesus, something like that coming out of nowhere could fucking kill me.

Now, as suddenly as it had fogged up, an updraft sweeps the narrow couloir clean. "Tryin' again," Cotton radios Billy. He turns and heads back in. Billy feels a giddiness rise in his stomach, as if he is a kid on a carnival ride.

"Here's how we play this," Cotton shouts to Meg. "When we get back in there this time I want a weather check every thirty seconds. I want you sitting up and looking for clouds rolling in over us and I want you yelling out the conditions twice a minute. I'm going to be concentrating on that rock wall on my left. So I also need to hear what's happening out to my right. So, clouds are your first priority, and as we get closer, our distance from that headwall. Every thirty seconds. Got it?"

"Got it."

They are back in. The Lama has no more than thirty feet of rotor clearance off both its left side and nose. Meg is bellowing weather reports every thirty seconds. She reports he has a good fifty feet of maneuvering room to his right. She feels as if she could reach out and touch the side of the canyon wall.

Billy swings into the ravine as if on a pendulum. The snowfield looks about as large as a postage stamp. Malcolm is flush to the ice wall and Billy remembers what Dave Thompson told him about the optical illusion. He concentrates on the snowfield and on his second pass puts down about seventy-five feet below and to Malcolm's right. There is no slack to his shorthaul line.

From the Tokositna Glacier the view of the Lama itself is obscured by the gunsight notch, but every pair of eyes is trained on Billy Shott. He looks like a spider clawing his way up and across the sloped snowfield. It takes him no more than ninety seconds.

Malcolm turns his ruddy face to the mountain ranger like a sunflower to the light. As Billy scrambles up the slope he screams to the rescuee to be ready for an airlift. Malcolm begins disengaging his belay lines.

At 9:20, Billy Shott's voice squawks over the radio, "I'm on him."

By the time Billy reaches Malcolm he is held to the ledge by just one rope. He points to the carabiners attached to his chest harness. Billy nods and clips him into the shorthaul line while simultaneously uncoupling Malcolm's last lifeline. But his torso is frozen into the ledge. Billy desperately chops him out with his ice axe. The effort takes three minutes. With each passing second Billy wonders if an updraft will grab the helicopter and yank him and Malcolm into a headwall.

Karl Cotton trains his vision on a granite crack in the gully as if he were trying to hypnotize the stone. Downdrafts buffet the machine, but Cotton, his right hand massaging the throttle, flows with each gust— back here, up there—ensuring his crack never strays from eye level. It is as if his arm has become an extension of the helicopter, as if he is sensing the wind's intentions a split second before they are evident. It is freezing in the helicopter's cockpit, yet when Meg snatches a glance at Cotton she notices tiny beads of sweat forming a ridgeline along his forehead and temple. She is staggered by the pilot's capacity to hold the helo steady.

"We're free, we're out, take us up," Billy Shott screams into his headset. Nothing happens. "We're out, let's get out of here." The Lama continues its hover.

Billy looks at Malcolm, smiles, and shrugs. "I think we lost com," he says. He begins waving his arms above his head.

"Well, Meg, I knew things had been going too perfect. I think we lost com with Billy." Meg wonders if she actually detects a touch of *amusement* in Karl Cotton's voice. "I think he's trying to signal us to get the hell out of here. But why don't you see if you can make some hand signals to him just to double-check. I want to keep my eye on that rock wall."

She leans against the helo's Plexiglas bubble and gives Billy the thumbs-up sign. Billy signals back wildly. "He's ready."

Suddenly the couloir again fills with haze. The watchers below lose sight of Billy and Malcolm. At 9:23.54, Billy Shott and Malcolm Daly rise off Thunder Mountain. No one sees them until they are soaring above the glacier.

"He's got both of them," someone shouts. Pandemonium. The PJs begin prepping their medical station. Near the triage tent, Daryl Miller, down on one knee, takes a deep breath and lets it out slowly. Mike Wayt walks up and pats him gently on the back.

As Cotton feathers the throttle, he purposely offsets the helicopter to allow Billy and Malcolm to sway out from the headwall. They are swung off the ground in a long, lazy arc, gliding only a foot or two over the snowfield.

"Thank you, Billy," Malcolm sputters. "Thanks a million, man."

"Are you kidding me?" Billy replies. "You know how many girls are gonna be falling in love with me when they hear about this rescue?"

As Malcolm and Billy are safely deposited on the glacier Daryl hangs back, allowing the PJs to trundle Malcolm onto a stretcher. But before he is lifted from the snow he strides over and leans in close, his nose nearly rubbing Malcolm's. "You weren't kiddin' about that worst nightmare stuff, were you?"

Malcolm reaches up with his good hand and tousles Daryl's hair.

In the medical tent, Daryl blanches as Mario Romero cuts away Malcolm's boots and blood-encrusted socks. His friend's left ankle looks like ground meat, and the toes on both feet are as gray and moldy as a corpse's. Brent Widenhouse and Mario work on Malcolm's feet, while Mike Wayt palpates his neck and back as well as recording Malcolm's injuries for a rolling tape recorder. "Open left tib-fib. Right broken ankle, doesn't appear compound. Broken left pinkie. Patient is self-medicated with Vicodins. Vitals are pretty good. Core temp 93.8. Administering a saline IV to hydrate. Splinting both legs . . ."

At a long picnic table at the Talkeetna Roadhouse, Jim Donini hunches over a tall stack of blueberry pancakes and a side of reindeer sausage. The ranger Punky Moore enters the restaurant, sidles up behind him, and taps him gently on the shoulder. She asks in a whisper if she can speak to him alone.

Donini's face falls ashen as the two walk off to a corner. Punky speaks for several moments and walks away. Jim takes one step back to his seat, and his knees buckle. The morning crowd has stopped eating and stares at him expectantly. He swivels toward the wall, buries his face in his hands, and begins to sob softly.

Karen and Jed Daly reach the Talkeetna spur of the Glenn Highway, twenty minutes outside of town, at nine-thirty. Karen dials J. D. Swed, who asks her to hold on as he patches her through to Daryl. She is momentarily addled by the feral howls she hears on the other end of the line. Then, "They got him, Karen." Daryl's voice. "He's off. He's safe. Head for the Talkeetna Airport. We'll chopper him into there for a little visit with you before we LifeFlight him to Anchorage."

Karen drops the phone in her lap. She is sweating, dizzy. She thinks she is going to faint. She cannot speak, but Jed intuits from the look on her face that his brother is alive.

Within the hour the parajumpers have triaged and stabilized Malcolm in the medical tent, and he is airlifted off the glacier.

As the Lama approaches the Talkeetna landing pad Karl Cotton notices a brace of cars and four-wheel-drive vehicles encircling the landing zones. When his skids touch down a man and a fetching woman emerge. The woman starts toward the helicopter in a tottering trot and Cotton fears that she is going to fall over. He notices that the three men hang back, allowing the woman to approach his helo alone.

Karen Daly feels like a shark. She is afraid that if she stops moving she will fall over and die. She feels as if she is going to throw up. She ducks low beneath the rotors of the Lama and leans into the backseat. Malcolm lifts his head up off the stretcher and smiles weakly. The first thing Karen notices is his eyes. They are as bright and clear and blue as a mountain cairn.

She wants to say something, but her vocal cords won't work. She throws her arms around her husband's shoulders and fights back the tears.

"Malcolm, I'm so sorry you were alone up there."

"But I wasn't."

. . .

As they break camp on the Tokositna, Mike Wayt motions Dave Thompson over and shakes his hand. He is convinced it was Dave's constant goading that made the longhaul a possibility, that put the idea in Daryl's mind. From near his tent Daryl watches the two PJs embracing.

"You know, Sardog, a couple of years ago I'd have been disappointed that it wasn't us pulling that guy off the hill. I don't know. Maybe as you get older you get more logical or something."

The Sardog wears an odd, smug look. He waits a beat before breaking into a tight grin. "Well, don't get too logical on me just yet, 'cause I just got off the phone with Glatt down at The Section. We got a Fish and Game biologist trapped up in some high cols down in the Aleutians. Fell and broke her leg. Glatt's heading up in the Herc. But somebody's still gotta go get her on the ground.

"Whaddya say, Mike? You up for a climb?"

POSTSCRIPT

Upon Mike Wayt's return from Thunder Mountain, Garth Lenz, who had cut short his fact-finding trip and flown back to Anchorage, ordered him home. Lenz, Marty Kimble, and Dave Thompson recovered the stranded Fish and Game biologist marooned in the Aleutian chain. One of the first things Mike did was sit down with his daughter Stephanie and tell her the whole story of the Bin Hong Kim rescue. Much to Lara Wayt's consternation, this only increased her daughter's desire to become the first pararescuewoman in the history of the U.S. Air Force.

A week later, during the team's Memorial Day barbecue at The Section, Mike, Lara, Stephanie, and Emily Wayt lost a cutthroat volleyball game to Steve, Maria, and Ernie Daigle. Mike spent the rest of the afternoon pleading, unsuccessfully, for a rematch.

Malcolm Daly spent his forty-third birthday in Anchorage General Hospital. Doctors discovered that he had nicked his medial artery with his ice axe during his fall and had been bleeding the entire time he was pinioned to Thunder Mountain. He had suffered a compound fracture of his left tibia and fibula, which required a bone graft, and the tip of his left big toe was later amputated. His right ankle was completely shattered, and after his talus was fused, several tendons in his right foot were severed and deemed unrepairable. Within the next six months Malcolm underwent three operations on his legs and feet, and a year later remained wheelchair-bound.

According to his doctors, the function in Malcolm's left leg should return to near-normal strength, but because of the damage to his right ankle he will walk for the rest of his life with a limp. He says climbing again someday in Alaska "is certainly on my radar screen."

Karen Daly says her relationship with Malcolm has not only mended, it has never been better. "We're doing really good, really good," she says with a coquettish laugh. "It's back to being kind of cozy around here." Of her husband's plans to someday again climb in Alaska, she is dubious. "That's what he's telling me. But I don't know about that."

Malcolm and Karen remain friends with Jim Donini.

Donini spent the turn of the millennium on a climbing expedition in Patagonia. He continues to climb each season in the Alaska Range. He still vows to never make an ascent with radios.

After Steve Ball returned to England, his left leg was amputated below the knee. He also lost the front portion of his right foot and all ten of his fingers. He undergoes daily rehabilitation therapy with Nigel Vardy, whose fingers were also amputated, along with his toes and the backs of both heels. Antony Hollingshead came out of their ordeal the least afflicted, suffering only amputations of the tips of three fingers on his right hand. All three Englishmen incurred permanent circulation damage to their noses and faces. They have planned to return someday to Denali, "not to climb," says Vardy, "but to perhaps make a final flyover."

Despite a thriving powder-coating business, Dave "Sardog" Thompson finds that he puts in exactly the same number of hours as a part-time pararescue as he did when he worked full time.

Mark Glatt passed his annual physical and remains a member of the 210th Pararescue Squadron. He still spends hours each day in The Section's gym. He and his wife, Melanie, continue to discuss the possibility of Mark's taking a paramedic's job with the Anchorage Fire Department.

Bin Hong Kim, who lost both his hands in 1991, returned to the Alaska Range seven years later. He became the first double amputee to summit Denali.

During the 1999 spring climbing season 1,183 climbers from 317 groups attempted to summit Denali. Five hundred nine made it, a 43 percent success rate. What most gratified Daryl Miller was that, for only the second time in the history of the mountain, no climbers died on Denali. Daryl remains Denali's lead high-altitude mountain ranger.

ACKNOWLEDGMENTS

Without the acceptance and trust of the pararescuemen and flight crews of the Alaska Air Guard's 210th Rescue Squadron, this book would not exist. For their gracious tolerance of a reporter in their midst, I therefore extend my most sincere thanks to each member of the squad, particularly Squadron Commander Colonel Ron Parkhouse and PJ Team Leader Chief Master Sergeant Garth Lenz. For their insight, courteousness, and availability I am also grateful to Lackland Air Base's Head Training Instructor Sergeant Rod Alne and his team of TIs. Moreover, writing about the deeds of the 210th required virtually living, flying, and working with the Anchorage PJ team for a period of several months. For extending that permission, I would like to thank the United States Air Force. Specifically, those who smoothed my entry into the parajumping "career field" included Captain Donna Prigmore and Major Mike Haller and his staff in Alaska, Air Force Public Affairs Officer Doug Thar in Washington, D.C., and Public Affairs Officer Rene Witt at Lackland Air Base.

This book began as an exploration of the PJ way of life, but midway through my research I realized it had morphed into a joint account of the bravery of the airmen of the 210th as well as the selflessness of the Park Service's high-mountain rangers and their support staff in Denali National Park and Preserve. I owe a debt of gratitude to each of them for their time and efforts to educate a green flatlander. For his inspiration, hospitality, and sage advice I must expressly cite Daryl Miller. He is one of a kind.

The survivors of Denali's 1999 rescue season—Malcolm Daly, Jim

Donini, Steve Ball, Nigel Vardy, Antony Hollingshead—were all kind enough to speak to me despite the delicate and painful issues surrounding their plight. For this I thank them. For her grace under pressure, I must also thank Karen Daly.

The genesis of this book began as an article in *Men's Journal* magazine, and I must thank the editors there for their help, as well as Art Cooper and Martin Beiser of *GQ* magazine, who assisted me greatly with their insight. My stay in Alaska was made so much easier through the efforts of Angela Blomberg and the Long House's Kate Harlow. And I benefited tremendously from the friends and family who reread draft after draft of this manuscript—particularly David Hughes, John Pierse, and Bobby Kelly.

Finally, my agent, Nat Sobel, and his staff virtually kicked me up to Alaska to go get this story, and the matchless editorial team at Simon & Schuster—particularly David Rosenthal and Ruth Fecych—shaped the thousands of pages of material I returned with into a coherent narrative. I am forever in their debt.

INDEX

About the Author

Bob Drury, a contributing editor at *GQ*, has written for *Men's Journal, Vanity Fair,* and *Details.* For years he was a foreign correspondent, crime reporter, and sports columnist for the New York *Daily News,* the *New York Post,* and New York *Newsday.* He lives in East Hampton, New York.